Trauma and Resilience
in Holocaust Memoir

Trauma and Resilience in Holocaust Memoir

Strategies of Self-Preservation and Inter-Generational Encounter with Narrative

Shira Birnbaum

LEXINGTON BOOKS
Lanham • Boulder • New York • London

Published by Lexington Books
An imprint of The Rowman & Littlefield Publishing Group, Inc.
4501 Forbes Boulevard, Suite 200, Lanham, Maryland 20706
www.rowman.com

6 Tinworth Street, London SE11 5AL, United Kingdom

Copyright © 2021 Shira Birnbaum

All rights reserved. No part of this book may be reproduced in any form or by any electronic or mechanical means, including information storage and retrieval systems, without written permission from the publisher, except by a reviewer who may quote passages in a review.

British Library Cataloguing in Publication Information Available

Library of Congress Cataloging-in-Publication Data Available

ISBN 978-1-7936-2303-4 (cloth)
ISBN 978-1-7936-2305-8 (pbk)
ISBN 978-1-7936-2304-1 (electronic)

For Daniel, Helen, Sarit, Zev, Koby, Nellie, Rachel, Zoe, David, Owen, Amelia, Nathaniel, Harry, Agnieszka, Martina, Pascale, Ori, Gal, Tamara, Dan, Zachary, Jordan, Adam, Jessica, Erica, Ari, Jennifer, Jon, Nathan, Eitan, Jed, Cal, Noah, Jace, and Eli

Contents

Acknowledgments and Permissions ... ix

Introduction: What We Learn about Child Development and the Refugee Experience by Reading the Memoirs of Holocaust Survivors ... 1

1 1939 ... 21

2 1940 ... 47

3 1941 ... 63

4 1942 ... 81

5 1942 in the Warsaw Ghetto ... 91

6 1943 ... 113

7 1944–1945 ... 131

8 Young People in the Confrontation with Disaster ... 137

9 Resonances of War ... 149

Epilogue: Conversations across the Generations: Finding a Vocabulary of Remembrance ... 163

Bibliography ... 175

Index ... 189

About the Author ... 193

Acknowledgments and Permissions

I am thankful to Nina Admoni and Irene Birnbaum for permission to use excerpts from their memoirs, to Zahava Gutman for permission to use stories and excerpts from the essays of Nathan Gutman, and to the children of Marysia Rubinstein and Wanda Birnbaum for permission to use material excerpted from their mothers' memoirs. I am very grateful to Yad Vashem, the International Institute for Holocaust Research, for permission to use material included in "From the Testimony of Nina Admoni—The Righteous among the Nations Featured Stories: Chiune Sempo Sugihara." I am also grateful to Irene Birnbaum for her generous permission to use her memoirs and story material that appeared in her books *Non Omnis Moriar: Pametnik z Getta Warsawakiego* (Warsaw: Czytelnik, 1982); *Non Omnis Moriar. No Moriré del Todo. Memorias de una Adolescente en el Gueto de Varsovia* (Buenos Aires: Milá, 1991); and *Non Omnis Moriar. No Moriré del Todo. Memorias de una Adolescente en el Gueto de Varsovia* (Santiago: Self-published, 1997). Several members of the family recorded oral testimonies of their war experiences, and some elements of the stories presented here can also be found, in different form, in those testimonies. I am grateful to the USC Shoah Foundation Institute for Visual History and Education for access to the Archive recordings of Nathan Gutman, Interview Code 45548, 2012, and Irena Birnbaum, Interview Code 17960, 2012. I am also deeply indebted to many individuals for their support and encouragement of this project. Dr. Anna Ornstein contributed deeply to my thinking. I am grateful to her for observations and insights offered over many hours of lively and inspiring conversation. I thank Drs. Bennett Simon, Roberta Apfel, Marcia Zuckerman, Richard Gomberg, Franny Sullivan, and Eva Fogelman, who read drafts or portions of the manuscript in various stages and provided helpful comments.

Jonathan Kolb, Elisa Cheng, and my seminar colleagues in psychoanalytic training at the Boston Psychoanalytic Society and Institute offered many useful and interesting ideas. Dr. Susan Duty, my department chair at Simmons University, and Meg McCabe, my program director at Children's Hospital of Philadelphia, were supportive of my work. I thank Lucy Davis for her astute manuscript assistance and Olga Umansky, librarian at the Hanns Sachs Memorial Library, for her invaluable research support. Courtney Morales, at Lexington Books, believed in the value of this project and offered helpful guidance. I am thankful to Stanley Gonczanski for his collaboration and friendship over the years and to Barbara Grannis for her always thoughtful and sharp-eyed editorial insights. Tania Gutman Gray's warmth and welcome and her many Shabbat dinner invitations were more enriching to me than she realizes. Rona Birnbaum accompanied me on this journey of discovery, and I continue to be deeply moved every day by her remarkable kindness, sensitivity, and boundless generosity. Daniel and Helen bring me joy beyond measure, and I am grateful to them and to Ruth Birnbaum for the wisdom and luminous beauty they bring to the world.

Introduction
What We Learn about Child Development and the Refugee Experience by Reading the Memoirs of Holocaust Survivors

This is the note we received from my father:

> I was born in Warsaw, Poland, on February 10, 1932. My birth certificate says "Dawid," but as a child, I was known mostly by my Polish first name, Stanislaw, and by my nickname, Stasio. My parents and I escaped from Poland during the Second World War. Ninety percent of Polish Jews died in that war, in a period of just six years, but my parents had all those things a person needed in order to escape and survive: money, political connections, timely information, a willingness to abandon property, and children who were old enough to walk, crawl, run, climb, and not cry when told to stay quiet. My mother was one of nine siblings and my father one of eight. Among all these, any who were the parents of young children perished, together with their children. Of my very many cousins, only a few survived. The youngest to survive was six when the war broke out. I was seven.

My father's papers, for which this note served as a kind of cover letter, sat for years in a box in the attic. But as happens sometimes to people in middle age—for a variety of sometimes inexplicable reasons—certain questions from childhood seemed to force their way to the surface of my consciousness. Long after my father's death, I felt a compulsion to unearth his papers and reengage with the voice in them. This psychological moment is what led to the book you are reading here.

The book is organized around excerpts from the memoirs, essays, and personal stories told by my father and five other members of a large extended Jewish family living in Poland in September 1939, the time of the German invasion that started World War II. Ranging in age from six to nineteen when the war began, they lived, with one exception, within blocks of one another in a wealthy section of the city of Warsaw, Poland's capital. Six years later, they were dispersed across five continents—beleaguered survivors of a genocide in which 90 percent of Poland's Jews were annihilated and most of the rest of their family members lost. The physical survival of these six young people, following startlingly different and uneven pathways, reflected circumstances over which they had, individually, very little control—the power of money, the benefit of social connections, the good will of neighbors or strangers, and, perhaps above all, many accidents of luck and random chance. But their emotional survival speaks to something more complex—something inside each of them—that stands as evidence of the resources that young people bring to the experience of a cataclysmic rupture of the social order. Those resources are the focus of this book. This book is about the strategies of psychological self-preservation of six young people who became objects of violent persecution and wrenching social dislocation. It traces the pathways of their internal development through the course of World War II, using their personal memoirs as a lens for exploring the diversity of coping and resilience trajectories of young people who experience profound adversity at different life stages.

Even after suffering significant deprivations, a great many young people grow up to be well-functioning adults; traumatic exposure in the early years does not foreclose prospects for achieving stability and vitality later in life. The stories collected here provide insight into some of the processes that enable that to happen. For many decades, research on traumatic experience tended to focus on the connections between adversity and psychopathology—on associations between extreme situations and symptoms of dysfunction and distress. In recent years, however, across disciplines as diverse as medicine, neuroscience, sociology, anthropology, psychology, education, and public health, a rich and nuanced body of work has emerged that calls attention also to matters of capacity building, patterns of self-organization, and processes that protect and promote coping and affect regulation both within individuals and at family, community, and systems levels.[1] At the core of this emerging science of resilience is a concern for multidisciplinary and longitudinal research—for studies that link social-ecological and neurodevelopmental frameworks, highlighting the dynamic unfolding of resilience processes in evolving and reciprocal interactions between individuals, situations, and broader community and societal contexts.[2] This book attempts to contribute to that research by exploring what might be learned about development and resilience when these are viewed retrospectively through the lens of a single family's collected memoirs of holocaust-era separation, uprooting, diaspora, and near-destruction.

Many tens of thousands of memoirs and scholarly texts have been written in English and other languages addressing the places and time periods that appear in this book.[3] The stories collected here add relatively little new information to this remarkable and extensive record. Rather, they reassert particularity and specificity—illuminating a variety of experiences of personal dislocation during the war and the diversity of response strategies and pathways, even within a family. There are many ways to tell the story of war and its consequences, we see here. Historical events get folded unpredictably into personal biography. Superimposed onto complex configurations of individual and family capacities, intersecting with a wide range of material, psychological, social, and institutional resources, they generate an unnerving and disturbing unevenness of outcomes. Popular social-science and mental-health concepts of "trauma" and "identity" help organize people into broad demographic cohorts, facilitating clinical generalization by emphasizing commonalities of presentation and shared sensibilities about self and historical experience. In the material collected here, however, we see that the language of generalization can erase as much as it preserves. Stark differences even within a family belie reductive characterizations of loss and social disruption and indicate how much can be hidden by the concepts of "identity" or "trauma" and their attendant simplifications. A more nuanced understanding of past traumatic exposures can inform our understanding in the present and enhance efforts to improve the situation of young people who today are affected by persecution and violence.

In the summer of 2018, during a federal government crackdown on Central American migrants crossing the southern border into the United States, a six-year-old Salvadoran girl was forcibly separated from her parents and taken to an immigration detention center in the state of Texas.[4] Her voice was captured on tape by news organizations during coverage of the roundup. Over national radio that afternoon, the girl could be heard in the background, calling out a phone number and repeatedly asking the detention center staff to contact its owner. My sister phoned me. She was sobbing. We had grown up in the 1960s in the safety and comfort of a middle-class New York City suburb. But during the years of our childhood, we, too, memorized phone numbers. It was "just in case," our father used to say. We wrote distant family members' names and addresses on little slips of paper, hiding them in our bedside dressers where they could be close at hand, "just in case." We drew maps of neighborhood escape routes, "just in case," and we sat around the dinner table sometimes plotting strategies for finding one another "after." After what? It didn't matter. We invented code words and chose the fake names we'd use if captured. We knew the "good" hiding places in the bushes in the backyard. More than once, we climbed into the crawlspace under the basement stairs to practice sitting very, very still, "just in case." Dad had taught us about stillness and silence—and how those mattered.

Many immigrants lived in our community, and plenty of other children had refugee parents like ours, so we saw nothing particularly unusual or disturbing in these household ritual reenactments of terror. Some of our neighbors played out similar scenes in their own backyards. Privately, we often joked among ourselves about our parents' neurotic obsessions about the war, their embarrassing European accents, and the social events where adults talked about nothing but "the Germans" and argued heatedly over seemingly inane details of long-past events. But here we were in 2018, two American women in late middle age, educated professionals with grown children of our own, haunted by the voice of a child caught in transit and forcibly separated from her family. That evening, I made some phone calls to cousins and old neighbors. All of them had heard the voice of the little Salvadoran girl and reacted similarly. A child from long ago still lives within each of us, it appears, and finds herself concerned anew when observing the struggles of other children.

Acts of holocaust remembrance, as the literary theorist Susan Rubin Suleiman has written,[5] are not simply statements about history. They are statements, as well, about what concerns us in the present day. Analogies can be misleading or, worse, a form of erasure, as the industrial mass murder of the Jews of mid-twentieth-century Europe is unparalleled in its magnitude and technological efficiency. But analogies speak to the natural propensity for emotional and intellectual exploration, neuroscience tells us; they are the cognitive basis for ethical reasoning. They emerge in the mind, moreover, from deep recesses of the self, and for reasons often beyond awareness and control, as my sister and I discovered on the evening of her call. When my generation encounters the stories of today's young refugees, certain narratives from the past awaken and assert themselves in our consciousness. The lines we draw are not straightforward equations of past and present; nor do we weigh on a balance the crimes of yesterday and today. Rather, something deeper resonates—something uncanny that calls up a still-reverberating note of the straining of young people to sustain themselves against darkness.

The upheavals sending migrants across the globe today have complex roots—in social inequality, ecological degradation, rampant crime, corruption, and the residues of colonialism, among other factors.[6] But the pitched cultural debates emerging in response—the resurgence on all continents of far-right ethno-nationalism, the imposition of draconian border controls, the seething racism and anti-Semitism animating populist social movements in our own country and abroad—have awakened a multitude of tensions in the sons and daughters of holocaust refugees and survivors, as the stories of our parents' pasts are the framework from which we make sense of the world today, even as we see clearly the differences in context and circumstance. While this book is about the past, then, its real purpose, as with many discussions about the past, is to comment on what is happening in the present. The last generation of holocaust survivors is coming to an end, its living memories soon to be extinguished, and yet much of the world today is again spiraling toward chaos, and many millions of children again find themselves navigating landscapes of pain and loss, much as our parents once did. In this context, this book attempts to find a vocabulary of remembrance that explores what it means to pay tribute to the past—while also challenging a new generation to recognize what the past might demand of it in the present day.

The number of nations experiencing armed conflict is at its highest point now since the establishment, in 1989, of the UN Convention on the Rights of the Child, and estimates in 2019 placed at 31 million the number of children forcibly displaced by violence—a consequence of contemporary strategies of war-making that increasingly emphasize attacks on civilian infrastructure.[7] Not since the end of World War II has the global population of displaced people been as large as it is now,[8] with numbers estimated to be almost tenfold today compared with just a decade ago.[9] Most among today's displaced populations are internally uprooted, but many have crossed international boundaries in their quests for safety, and a small but significant minority are objects of state-sanctioned ethnic or religious hatred; like the Jews of mid-century Europe, they have been intentionally targeted for persecution and death.[10] What unites such young people today with the survivors of Nazi terror—despite the many differences among them—is that children do not choose the chaos of war. They do not choose to be the objects of hatred and persecution. Nor do they choose the circumstances under which these forces meet them. A world beyond their understanding foists on them its titanic impacts, in a great multiplicity of ways.

Literature about children in war and civil strife is rich in accounts of the outwardly visible aspects of the experience—the symptomatic presentations familiar to medical and mental-health agencies; the diagnoses tallied by aid organizations of malnutrition, disease, or repeated physical abuse; the great migrations across landscapes. Far less is known, however, about the internal experiences of such children, their trajectories of emotional and developmental change during the course of their struggles.[11] Writing about refugees and other trauma survivors, particularly in popular media, has tended to portray young people in sweeping, generalized terms, as Peter Gatrell has observed—in language that can promote static, undifferentiated images of suffering, as if all child victims of collective violence are essentially the same.[12] Portrayals of this type can serve diverse agendas—those of governments promoting important policy goals, aid agencies requesting resource support for interventions of a particular type, social or religious activists or, on the other side, anti-immigration nationalists concerned with swaying public opinion regarding the opening or closing of borders.[13] There are good reasons to understand traumatic experience in broad terms, of course, since there is no doubt, from a clinical point of view, that victims of collective violence and social dislocation often share certain well-known symptomatic presentations. But the textures of individual life become flattened when highly varied historical and psychological experiences are packaged too tidily under singular labels made for exchange in the market of political opinion, as the psychoanalyst Anna Ornstein has written.[14] Simplified or overgeneralized images erase not only the facts of history and the uniqueness and agency of each child but also the developmental dynamism that is an inherent element of childhood.[15] They distance us from individual-level understanding and can obscure the varied effects of physical, institutional, and social environments on health processes and outcomes.

Children are not static objects; nor are they passive recipients of history imposed from outside. Rather, they bring vastly different elements to the confrontation with traumatic events and are affected in diverse ways. Under conditions of grave threat, as Bennett Simon and Roberta Apfel and others have written,[16] even quite young children endeavor to impose order and meaning on the circumstances they are given, to make some kind of sense in situations that make no sense, and to seek what they need developmentally, each in his or her own way, from what is accessible in the environment. They deploy combinations of internal and external resources as best they can, in whatever form these become available, and often in ways that are creative and ingenious. Time, place, age, gender, personality, developmental stage, cognitive style, family, community, and previous life experiences intersect dynamically, research increasingly demonstrates, with evolving on-the-ground circumstances and changing patterns of opportunity, threat, and access to resources.[17] The stories collected here, in this context, have much to offer. They linger as details belonging to a specific family, time, and place. But they have also been given new life—as retrospective "data" that illustrate, albeit indirectly, the ways young people at different ages and life stages confronted the challenge of cascading and sometimes devastating losses sustained over periods of weeks, months, and years. The power in these stories is not only in the outward personal facts they preserve or the global diaspora they recount. Equally important is their status as documentary evidence of internal processes. At a time of great global change and suffering, they speak with salience and renewed urgency, illustrating the sensemaking pathways of children in grotesque situations—revealing insights not only about specific young people but also about the flexibility and capacity of childhood and youth more generally.

Excerpts from six narratives are compiled here, three of them written originally in English, the others in Spanish, Hebrew, and Polish, respectively. Several were quite lengthy when first set to paper, mostly in the 1990s, and have been translated, edited, and excerpted for this book. Others are compilations of letters, essays, and oral testimonies transcribed by family members over a period of years. Together they represent the mid-life reflections and recollections of a particularly elite variant of early-twentieth-century Jewish life and multiple branches of an extended family tree consisting at one time of many hundreds of members with roots in Poland dating back perhaps a thousand years. On the eve of the war, in September of 1939, David Birnbaum, my father, was seven years old, about to start second grade. He had been attended throughout early childhood by German- and French-speaking governesses. His father, president of one of Europe's larger specialty-food import-export firms, owned race horses and art collections and had been vice president of the Warsaw Chamber of Commerce. Wanda Birnbaum, David's sister, was nineteen and newly married, against her parents' wishes. She and her husband, a chemist, had just moved to an apartment of their own. Nina Wertans, their closest maternal cousin, was living downstairs from David in the same apartment building. She was six, preparing to start first grade. Marysia Rubinstein, eighteen, another maternal cousin, was newly graduated from Warsaw's top high school, where she had been one of only two Jewish girls admitted to a class of 600 students. Irene Birnbaum, thirteen, was a paternal cousin whose family sometimes vacationed together with David's in the summer villa they owned. Nathan Gutman, a cousin on my mother's side, was born in Katowice, where his father ran a scrap metal yard. Nathan's parents spoke Yiddish, observed the Sabbath, and went to the synagogue for Jewish holidays. He was twelve, just finishing summer camp, when the first bombs fell.

When the war began, each small family unit was in its own unique stage in the life cycle of families, and each young person positioned in his or her own way in relation to the others in his immediate circle. But each came to see that he is despised by society, that his existence is under threat, and that the world he knows can be quickly obliterated. The stories here illustrate how, in each of these young people's encounters with this reality, diverse resources came to be accessed and activated. We see something unique and internal to each young person; we also see the differential framing effects of family, community, ideology, and social status. In a way that is at times quite startling, each of the entries conveys a different sense about the war, a unique self-image of the person at the story's center, and in a language unique to the teller. David, Wanda, and Nina, the luckiest, wealthiest, and most privileged of the group, avoided the war's worst brutalities. We follow their chaotic refugee odysseys across a global diasporic arc of three continents—David's very brief but tumultuous journey to Haifa as the rest of his extended family is left behind, Nina's many-years-long sojourn in the Jewish temporary ghetto in Japanese-occupied Shanghai, and Wanda's long trek to a remote jungle outpost in what, at the time, was Northern Rhodesia (later Zambia), where the British colonial government briefly attempted a little-known refugee resettlement project.

Told in lucid and sometimes dizzying chronological detail, with charm and verve, even frivolity, their stories reveal the bizarre interplay of great wealth and intense desperation that characterized the experience of a certain class of refugees of that period. Nathan, by contrast, relates his experiences in a very different kind of vocabulary. Slave labor, internment in a series of concentration camps, and years of grotesque brutality are relayed primarily as images, episodes suspended in time, in a stark language that circles back to sights, sounds, and smells, to inchoate and basic bodily experience. Nathan's stories are mostly not accompanied by specific dates or geographic detail, as memories of a certain kind defy such containment and reduction. Rather, one receives a glimpse, in reading them, of what it means to struggle to preserve oneself against erasure and annihilation under circumstances that do not lend themselves readily to verbal description. We follow Nathan's journey from a family vacation outside Katowice, Poland, to the liberation of Mauthausen concentration camp by Allied troops in Austria in 1945.

The stories of Marysia and Irene are haunting in yet a different way—as chronicles of a distorted passage into adulthood. Blonde and blue eyed, Marysia "passed" as a gentile and joined the Polish underground as the Warsaw ghetto gates closed around her family and friends. We follow her work with the Polish resistance movement, her subsequent capture and imprisonment at the notorious Pawiak Prison, and her love affair and eventual marriage to a fellow resistance fighter. Irene, by contrast, labored as a slave in a Warsaw ghetto factory supplying materials to Nazi military forces. Hiding in a bombed-out cellar bunker and dodging repeated roundups and deportations that wiped out almost everyone in her social circle, she escaped only days before the ghetto's final destruction. We follow her journey from the ghetto to a house in the Polish countryside, through a series of postwar refugee camps, and ultimately to Buenos Aires. In their telling, we see narratives imbued initially with adolescent hope, optimism, and the desire for independence—transfigured, over time, to a dark vocabulary of enduring loss.

Born into families, children bring to those families their own styles, preferences, and personal dispositions. Each child contributes to the family's unique reality, even as each family has its own way of shaping reality for the child. A child learns from his family the expectations and obligations of role, status, gender, relationship, and chronological age. The family is influenced, in turn, by its wider field of class, culture, ideologies, traditions, and religious affiliations; by regional and national contexts; and by the quality and quantity of economic, institutional, and social resources within its reach. Childhood and youth do not determine the rest of life. But in childhood and youth, deep aspects of our selves are made. Raw materials are established from which young people later in life cultivate relationships with others and with the world. It is difficult to measure the impact of losing one's fundamental safety in childhood. But young people bring to such losses their own physical, imaginative, and emotional capacities as well as the cognitive and developmental capabilities associated with a particular chronological age and previous range of experiences and exposures. Connecting us with the unique voices and personalities of six people who were lucky enough to live through a cataclysm, the stories collected in this book also reveal clues about the interplay among these multiple life layers—the intersections of internal and external worlds in the development of identity and understanding of self and others.

Memoir is a complex and fraught source of evidence, and a book organized around personal testimonies is built on foundations that need to be considered carefully.[18] This is partly because of what memoirs contain, partly because of what they do *not* contain, and partly because of the nature of writing as a form of meaning-making. If we regard a testimony as a historical document, we miss its emotional content and find ourselves inevitably disappointed by misremembered details, personal biases, or incomplete information. If we regard a testimony as a literary or artistic creation, on the other hand, we miss what it contributes to historical understanding and perspective. A middle path is called for, and my father's own writing illustrates this paradox. In the years I was in high school, my grandfather came to live with us. His short-term memory flagged, he had bouts of confusion, and, toward the end of his life, he started experiencing rather shocking nightmares. Returning home from school, my sister and I would find him sometimes on the reclining chair in the living room, half delirious, obviously in the throes of what seemed to be a war memory. He'd call out for his long-dead brother, Jakub, or for his brother-in law, Julius—warning them, in urgent tones, about impending Nazi troop movements and aerial bombardments. At the time, my father explained these strange outbursts as the stuff that "happens sometimes" when people get old (my grandfather was in his mid-nineties). But Dad's memoir, written some years later, revealed something considerably more complicated, and in my adult reading of it, I came to appreciate the gravity of my grandfather's torments. Family members had piled into a get-away car during the first days of the German invasion. Space in the vehicle was limited; many family members had to be excluded. Dad's memoir describes the scene of his Uncle Jakub holding up a young daughter, knocking and knocking at the window of the car, pleading for her to be let in. In his last days, I came to see, my grandfather had faced again the agonizing decisions he'd been forced to make in that final hour of his life in Warsaw.

Just as it can reveal certain elements of historical and emotional truth, however, so, too, does a memoir have the capacity to conceal them, as the writer Lawrence Langer observed.[19] My father had written almost nonchalantly about an encounter with his nanny at the family's summer villa. There had been a Nazi bombing raid; an orphanage had been leveled. Dad recorded this event as merely one among many—a passing episode in a much longer chronology containing dozens of such grim scenes. But years later, the story returned—not as a narrative, but as a physical sensation. In late-life dementia, Dad ruminated about those incinerated orphans. He felt them in his nostrils as a nagging, lingering presence of ash and acrid smoke. Charlotte Delbo,[20] the French memoirist, noted that memory has a dual nature. There is, she observed, a normalizing kind of memory—the kind that organizes catastrophes into chronologies. It creates stories that serve as antidotes for the disasters they convey, insinuating the consolation of triumph and redemption by the mere fact of someone having survived them. But there exists as well, she said, a deeper "sense" memory—the kind that remains locked in the body, in the physical imprint of an experience, and refuses to submit to narrative ordering. Caring for our father during that excruciating period of his reawakened body recollections, my sister and I came to realize what the psychoanalyst Roy Schafer famously noted:[21] that stories are never mere retellings. Testimony and memory bear a complicated relationship with one another—the former an attempt, perhaps inevitably limited, to tame and order what is not readily tamed and ordered in the latter.

The psychoanalyst Dori Laub[22] wrote movingly three decades ago about the fundamentally relational nature of holocaust testimony. In every telling of a story, Laub noted, a witness changes in certain respects the nature of time, as he creates a distinct present and future by the very act of narrating distance between what is now and what was then. What's more, as Thomas Trezise has observed, every act of transmission involves both the producer of a story and its receiver. It invokes the presence of an addressable "other," calling into being a new dialogic community where the former victim can be a participant once more.[23] Petra Schweitzer has gone so far as to link holocaust testimony to the metaphor of birth. Against the backdrop of erasure, she reasons, writers of testimony call into the world a renewed, *living* self, and they create, in the process, a memorial life for those they have lost.[24]

But scholars of holocaust writing have emphasized not only the performative and self-creative aspects of testimony but also its "polyphony"—the degree to which it reflects something other than the exclusive voice of the teller. A story is determined not only by its content, these writers note, but also by cultural norms of style, conventions of narrative structure and form, expectations about the interests and concerns of specific audiences, and, in some contexts, as is the case here, by the demands and interventions of interviewers and family translators and editors. Fluid, stylized, genre-bound, and often heavily processed by others with a variety of interests in their outcomes, testimonies change in response to the circumstances of their telling, as Tony Kushner and others have shown.[25] The "same" story can be told in different ways, as each time it is told, and with each person who tells it, it is inflected with ideas and themes emanating from the teller's unique relationship with more contemporary political events and struggles.[26] Sons and daughters of survivors readily attest to this, as so many of us heard our parents and their friends arguing heatedly among themselves about the accuracy or precision of various "remembered" details. There is no single version of a person's holocaust story, as Nanette Auerhahn and Dori Laub have written.[27] Liberating affect and facilitating mourning, any episode of narration connects to an ongoing project of personal construction and is mediated through prisms of family, culture, politics, and motivations for self-definition and self-presentation in a particular time and place. Representing past events within the frame of current sensibilities, Marianne Hirsch and Leo Spitzer and others have written,[28] memoir records and reveals, preserves and persuades, analyzes and interrogates—shaping and promoting particular versions of self and history over others.

The stories here indeed have been chronologized, as will be seen— "packaged" and sequenced with purpose and intent. My father and the other family members wrote them and told them, in some cases again and again, in part to create what the historian James Young has called "narrative tombstones,"[29] memorials that acknowledge and commemorate lost loves and lost lives. They were produced, as well, with an audience in mind—so that children and grandchildren might know something our parents and grandparents believed we needed to know, some version of themselves they felt was important to convey. The choice of people and figures to include or exclude, what to call out in detail and what to gloss under broader generalizations, and so on, reflects the writers' postwar and later-life affiliations and identifications— each family member's own evolving construction of himself or herself as a Jewish parent or grandparent with something worth "saying" to the world and to subsequent generations. In ways that can't be distilled out, moreover, the framing of these stories reflects encounters—and perhaps even some measure of uptake—of the multiple disparate images and representations of the holocaust that have circulated in general public life and culture since the end of the war. To read the material excerpted here is inevitably to witness these multiple processes simultaneously.

I honor and cherish the gifts of text and the people they present, but acknowledge, as well, that while much is revealed in them, much also is deeply hidden. The truth of this generation's memories lies not simply in what its members deliberately selected to share and present of themselves, emphasizing endurance, defiance, persistence, heroism, or loss, and so on. Rather, the truth traverses a space between what they tell us—what we can try to engage and understand—and what they don't tell us—what is private and inaccessible and is now rapidly disappearing as that generation comes to a close.

PLAN OF THE BOOK

Excerpts from six narratives are organized chronologically here, arranged into seven subsequent chapters beginning in 1939 with chapter 1 and ending in 1944–1945 with chapter 7. Each chapter contains material from multiple authors. The material varies in length and tone, as will be seen, reflecting the styles of different narrators. Some entries have dates; others do not. Some are in the present tense, written in the form of diary entries; others mix present and past tense. Chapter 5 contains only one person's story of a single year; it was separated out because of its length and distinctively intimate character. The stories can be disturbing when they are encountered side by side, as they reflect sometimes shocking differences in circumstances and experience. But chronological organization facilitates a developmental view, enabling us to discern in each evolving story the evidence of key developmental transitions and to observe changes in affect, self-management, and strategies of self-regulation. Within dynamic configurations of obstacles and opportunities and many accidents of luck and chance, each young person found ways to engage in fundamental sensemaking, as will be seen, and carry out the core developmental tasks of childhood and young adulthood. Each did so, moreover, according to his or her starting age and developmental level.

I am a professor of education and development and also a mental-health nurse with a psychodynamic orientation, but the analysis here draws from diverse methodological and conceptual frameworks. First is a narrative method of inquiry. The manner in which a story is told reveals important aspects of the young people that storytellers once were, as psychologists tell us, just as it reveals aspects of the adults they later became.[30] Over decades of interviewing holocaust survivors and their families from within a psychoanalytic frame, Judith Kestenberg and her colleagues[31] observed that multiple meanings are embedded in silences and absences, repetitions and hesitations, turns in rhythm and in the perspectival positioning of a narrator vis-à-vis people and events. Trajectories of affect and transitions in feelings of proximity and personal coherence reflect the multiple "tracks" that the writer Salman Akhtar identified as "domains" in the journey of identity.[32] Few survivors remain with whom a direct narrative interview might still be conducted, but narrative analysis of holocaust testimony continues today in studies of published memoirs, videotaped oral histories, and interviews with children and grandchildren of survivors, particularly in the recent work of Sharon Kangisser-Cohen, Eva Fogelman, and Dalia Ofer.[33] Informed by that body of work, this book takes up a modified version of its general approach to textual analysis of the material.

Second is a social-ecological systems and developmental framework. Urie Bronfenbrenner's[34] classic ecological model of child development posits the individual within reciprocally influencing systems of family, community, society, and chronology and provides a broad conceptual lens for considering the interconnections among processes operating over time at multiple life levels. Risk accumulates and opportunity ameliorates, as James Garbarino and others have written from within an ecological framework.[35] Resilience seen through this lens is viewed not as an internal or fixed personal trait, but rather as a dynamic process of evolving interactions among mutually impacting systems, including the quality and security of attachment relationships, family organization, access to social capital, status, institutional and community supports, and cultural and ideological influences. I also adopt elements of an Eriksonian developmental framework.[36] Erik Erikson proposed that identity development is culturally mediated and that personality integration is achieved in stages across the lifespan, not only in early childhood. Each stage of life presents a particular constellation of psychosocial problems that need to be solved in order for growth to proceed in a healthy way. A stage framework, loosely construed, calls attention to the specificity of the developmental challenges that confronted each young person at different points during the war years. Scholars working in the area of refugee studies have taken up many aspects of social-ecological systems and developmental theorizing in their understanding of child trauma and resilience, across a range of academic and scholarly disciplines and theoretical perspectives.[37] Contemporary theories of resilience, accumulation of risk, and conservation of resources, for example, are attuned to pathways of resource loss and access and to the interplay of different systems levels in structuring opportunity and risk.[38] Writing from within this emerging body of literature, Wai Kai Hou, Brian Hall, and Stevan Hobfoll,[39] for example, have proposed the metaphor of "fabrics" to describe how families and individuals attempt to sustain and repair the everyday rituals, routines, procedures, and practices that bind them in times of disruption and danger. The analysis here draws in a general way from this rich body of work.

The chronological narratives are followed, in chapter 8, by a consideration of what they reveal as a whole about processes of development and strategies of psychological self-preservation under conditions of persecution. It is commonplace in popular media today to hear triumphal accounts of the resilience of almost anyone who has endured profound life challenges. Here, however, we see that the concept of resilience might be better understood not in monolithic terms, but rather as an emergent property, always bound to context, an intersection between people and the evolving variety of situations they are forced to confront. For each young person, depending on his or her previous experiences, family situation, and the challenges associated with his or her particular age and life stage, the quest for safety, security, affirmation, and validation took a distinct form, and "resilience" meant something different.

Chapter 9 outlines what happened to each young person in the postwar years and briefly addresses the question of what is commonly understood to be intergenerational "transmission" of war impacts. The psychologists Hadas Wiseman and Jacques Barber[40] have argued that contemporary definitions of holocaust trauma and its intergenerational effects have tended to be reductive and rigidly dichotomous, treating the effects of the war as if they are a clear-cut and straightforward "package" of pathologies that is handed down over time. A more realistic understanding, as will be seen here, is far more complicated. Across a range of very diverse wartime experiences and exposures, themes from youth come to resonate in later life, but not necessarily as psychopathology, and the past is never a straightforward determinant of the future. Rather, people find their own ways of confronting a tragic history, and traces from the past meander across the life course in an array of subtle habits of mind and body and in styles of relating to new situations. They echo in the lives of families in sometimes uncanny ways.

In the Epilogue, we address the matter of the politics of remembrance. Remembrance is complicated, as will be seen, since it involves a representation of the past but is also irreducibly a creation of the present day. It is malleable and not absolute, and we mold it to our needs. It speaks to us about who we want to be and also, as Michael Rothberg and a growing cadre of contemporary holocaust theorists have suggested, about the political and social alliances, affiliations, and objectives we deem most important for the present and future.[41] This chapter addresses the recent history and social uses of holocaust memory, situating this project in the context of some of the current debates about the politics of holocaust memorialization, and summarizes some of what might be learned from the stories here by those who work with refugees and trauma survivors in the current day.

Studies that focus on young people's resourcefulness and self-regulation must be viewed with caution, because they can be turned easily into a form of denial.[42] Highlighting the experiences of a very small minority of escapees and survivors, they can be taken as an attempt to divert attention from the full extent of atrocity in the world and from the social and political origins of violence. They have the potential to "normalize" extremity and injustice by treating their consequences as mere clinical puzzles—matters requiring post-facto technical expertise or intervention. Holocaust survivor narratives in particular can have the paradoxical effect of seeming to soften or minimize the reality of the crimes committed against the Jews of mid-century Europe, since they tell the stories of the living and cannot speak for the millions dead. Stories that highlight the creativity and vigor of young people, moreover, can be taken to imply that we do not need to be especially concerned about the many millions who today are affected by ongoing persecution, armed conflicts, state oppression, and other factors that erode their safety and life chances. Stories about the children of privilege, children from wealthy families, as mine was, can serve to erase the experiences of the vast majority of less privileged others or obscure the roles that wealth and social capital play in war and disaster trajectories. The collected material in this book serves the purposes neither of diversion nor of denial, neither of minimization nor of overgeneralization and erasure. Rather, as a form of witnessing to the remarkable vitality and ingenuity of six young people, each confronting to a different extent and in his or her own way the most massive of the last century's injustices, the stories here remind us that even as we are outraged by persecution, by racism, and by violence, we can take note of the sometimes stunningly creative capacities of the young people who are its targets. Moved to acknowledge atrocity, we can be moved, as well, to recognize the strategies of young people attempting to sustain themselves in the encounter with it.

NOTES

1. Ann Masten, "Resilience Theory and Research on Children and Families: Past, Present, and Promise," *Journal of Family Theory and Review* 10 (March 2018): 12–31; Steven Southwick, George Bonanno, Ann Masten, Catherine Panter-Brick, and Rachel Yehuda, "Resilience Definitions, Theory and Challenges: Interdisciplinary Perspectives," *Journal of Psychotraumatology* 5 (October 2014): 1–14; Catherine Panter-Brick and James Leckman, "Editorial Commentary: Resilience in Child Development: Interconnected Pathways to Well-Being," *Journal of Child Psychology and Psychiatry* 54 (April 2013): 333–336; Theresa Betancourt and Kashif Khan, "The Mental Health of Children Affected by Armed Conflict: Protective Processes and Pathways to Resilience," *International Review of Psychiatry* 20, no. 3 (June 2008): 317–328; Michael Rutter, "Annual Research Review: Resilience: Clinical Implications," *Journal of Child Psychiatry and Psychology* 54 (April 2013): 474–487.

2. Mina Fazel, Ruth Reed, Catherine Panter-Brick, and Alan Stein, "Mental Health of Displaced and Refugee Children Resettled in High-Income Countries: Risk and Protective Factors," *Lancet* 379 (January 2012): 266–282; Michael Ungar, "Systemic Resilience: Principles and Processes for a Science of Change in Contexts of Adversity," *Ecology and Society* 23, no. 4 (2018): 219–235; Ann Masten and Dante Cicchetti, "Resilience in Development: Progress and Transformation," in *Developmental Psychopathology*, 3rd Edition, Vol. 4, ed. Dante Cicchetti (New York, NY: Wiley, 2016), 271–333; Stevan Hobfoll, Vanessa Tirone, Lucie Holmgreen, and James Gerhart, "Conservation of Resources Theory Applied to Major Stress," in *Stress: Concepts, Cognition, Emotion, and Behavior: Handbook of Stress*, Vol. 1, ed. George Fink (New York, NY: Academic Press, 2016), 271–333; Ann Masten and Angela Narayan, "Child Development in the Context of Disaster, War, and Terrorism: Pathways of Risk and Resilience," *Annual Review of Psychology* 63 (2013): 222–257; Antonious Robben and Marcelo Suarez-Orozco, eds., *Cultures*

Under Siege: Collective Violence and Trauma (Cambridge, UK: Cambridge University Press, 2000).

3. For contemporary reference collections, see, for example, Alan Rosen, ed., *Literature of the Holocaust* (Cambridge, UK: Cambridge University Press, 2013); David Roskies and Naomi Diamant, eds., *Holocaust Literature: A History and Guide* (Waltham, MA: Brandeis University Press, 2012); Michael Bernard-Donals, *An Introduction to Holocaust Studies* (New York, NY: Routledge, 2005); Claudia Moscovici, *Holocaust Memories: A Survey of Holocaust Memoirs, History, Novels, and Films* (New York, NY: Hamilton Books, 2019); Jurgen Matthaus with Emil Kerenji, *Jewish Responses to Persecution, 1933–1946: A Source Reader* (New York, NY: Rowman & Littlefield, 2017); Neil Levi and Michael Rothberg, *The Holocaust: Theoretical Readings* (New Brunswick, NJ: Rutgers University Press, 2003).

4. Ginger Thompson, "Listen to Children Who've Just Been Separated from Their Parents at the Border," *ProPublica* (June 18, 2018).

5. Susan Rubin Suleiman, *Crises of Memory and the Second World War* (Cambridge, MA: Harvard University Press, 2012).

6. Stephen Castles, Hein de Haas, and Mark Miller, *The Age of Migration* (New York, NY: Palgrave Macmillan, 2013).

7. United Nations Children's Fund, *For Every Child, Every Right: The Convention on the Rights of the Child at a Crossroads* (New York, NY: UNICEF, 2019).

8. Roberto Gonzales, Nando Sigona, Martha Franco, and Anna Papoutsi, *Undocumented Migration* (New York, NY: Polity, 2019); Roberto Gonzales and Nando Sigona, eds., *Within and Beyond Citizenship: Borders, Membership, and Belonging* (New York, NY: Routledge, 2018).

9. United Nations High Commission on Refugees, *Population Statistics Database, 2019.* http://www.popstats.unhcr.org/en/overview.

10. Derrick Silove, Peter Bentevogel, and Susan Rees, "The Contemporary Refugee Crisis: An Overview of Mental Health Challenges," *World Psychiatry* 16 (2017): 130–139.

11. Nexhmedin Morina and Angela Nickerson, *Mental Health of Refugee and Conflict-Affected Populations: Theory, Research, and Clinical Practice* (New York, NY: Springer, 2018); Richard Mollica, *Caring for Refugees and Other Highly Traumatized Persons and Communities: The New H5 Model. Harvard Program in Refugee Trauma* (Boston, MA: Massachusetts General Hospital, Harvard Medical School, 2014); Richard Mollica, Robert Brooks, Solvig Ekblad, and Laura McDonald, "The New H5 Model of Refugee Trauma and Recovery," in *Violence and Mental Health: Its Manifold Faces*, eds. Jutta Lindert and Itzhak Levav (New York, NY: Springer, 2015): 341–378.

12. Peter Gatrell, *The Making of the Modern Refugee* (Oxford: Oxford University Press, 2015).

13. Tony Kushner, *Remembering Refugees: Then and Now* (Manchester: Manchester University Press, 2006); Alice Bloch, Nando Sigona, and Roger Zetter, *Sans Papiers: The Social and Economic Lives of Undocumented Migrants* (Chicago, IL: Pluto Press, 2014).

14. Anna Ornstein, "Childhood Losses, Adult Memories," in *The Mother and her Children: Clinical Aspects of Attachment, Separation, and Loss*, ed. Salman Akhtar (Lanham, MA: Jason Aronson, 2012), 107–120; Anna Ornstein, "Trauma, Memory, and Psychic Continuity," *Progress in Self Psychology* 10 (1994): 131–146.

15. Anna Ornstein, "The Holocaust: Reconstruction and the Establishment of Psychic Continuity," in *The Reconstruction of Trauma: Its Significance in Clinical Work: Workshop Series of the American Psychoanalytic Association Monograph 2*, ed. Arnold Rothstein (Madison, CT: International Universities Press, Inc., 1986), 171–194; Anna Ornstein, "Survival and Recovery: Psychoanalytic Reflections," *Harvard Review of Psychiatry* 9, no. 1 (January–February 2001): 13–22.

16. Bennett Simon and Roberta Apfel, eds., *Minefields in Their Hearts: The Mental Health of Children in War and Communal Violence* (New Haven, CT: Yale University Press, 1996); Suzanne Kaplan and Andreas Hamburger, "The Developmental Psychology of Social Trauma and Violence: The Case of the Rwandan Genocide," in *Psychoanalysis and Holocaust Testimony: Unwanted Memories of Social Trauma*, eds. Dori Laub and Andreas Hamburger (New York, NY: Routledge, 2017), 104–124.

17. Kenneth Miller and Lisa Rasco, eds., *The Mental Health of Refugees: Ecological Approaches to Healing and Adaptation* (New York, NY: Routledge, 2004); Ann Masten, Angela Narayan, Wendy Silverman, and Joy Osofsky, "Children in War and Disaster," in *Handbook of Child Psychology and Developmental Science* (Hoboken, NJ: Wiley, 2015), 1–42; Arturo Varchevker and Eileen McGinley, eds., *Enduring Migration through the Life Cycle* (New York, NY: Routledge, 2013); Nathan Durst, "Child-Survivors of the Holocaust: Age-Specific Traumatization and the Consequences for Therapy," *American Journal of Psychotherapy* 57, no. 4 (October 2003): 499–518; Gila Sandler-Saban, Mark Sossin, and Anastasia Yaski, "Age, Circumstance, and Outcome in Child Survivors of the Holocaust: Considerations of the Literature and a Report of a Student Using Narrative Content Analysis," in *Children in the Holocaust and its Aftermath: Historical and Psychological Studies of the Kestenberg Archive*, eds. Sharon Kangisser-Cohen, Eva Fogelman, and Dalia Ofer (New York, NY: Berghahn, 2017), 15–42; Angel Nickerson, "Pathways to Recovery: Psychological Mechanisms Underlying Refugee Mental Health," in *Mental Health of Refugee and Conflict-Affected Populations: Theory, Research, and Clinical Practice*, eds. Nexhmedin Morina and Angela Nickerson (Cham, Switzerland: Springer Nature, 2018), 91–109; Frederick Ahearn, Jr. and Jean Athey, eds., *Refugee Children: Theory, Research, Services* (Baltimore, MD: Johns Hopkins University Press, 1991); Dante Cicchetti, ed., *Developmental Psychopathology*, 3rd Edition (New York, NY: Wiley, 2016).

18. For a cautionary note on the use of holocaust memoir as a source of historical fact, see Raul Hilberg, "Developments in the Historiography of the Holocaust," in *Comprehending the Holocaust: Historical and Literary Research*, eds. Asher Cohen, Yoav Gelber, and Charlotte Wardi (New York, NY: Peter Lang, 1988), 28–29; James Young, *Writing and Rewriting the Holocaust: Narrative and the Consequences of Interpretation* (Bloomington, IN: Indiana University Press, 1988).

19. Lawrence Langer, *Holocaust Testimonies: Ruins of Memory* (New Haven, CT: Yale University Press, 1991).

20. Charlotte Delbo, *Auschwitz and After* (New Haven, CT: Yale University Press, 1995).

21. Roy Schafer, *Retelling a Life: Narration and Dialogue in Psychoanalysis* (New York, NY: Basic Books, 1994).

22. Dori Laub, "Bearing Witness, or the Vicissitudes of Listening," in *Testimony: Crises of Witnessing in Literature, Psychoanalysis, and History*, eds. Shoshana Felman and Dori Laub (New York, NY: Routledge, 1992), 57–74; Dori Laub, "An Event Without a Witness: Truth, Testimony, and Survival," in *Testimony: Crises of Witnessing in Literature, Psychoanalysis, and History*, eds. Shoshana Felman and Dori Laub (New York, NY: Routledge, 1992), 75–92.

23. Thomas Trezise, *Witnessing Witnessing: On the Reception of Holocaust Survivor Testimony* (New York, NY: Fordham University Press, 2013).

24. Petra Schweitzer, *Gendered Testimonies of the Holocaust: Writing Life* (New York, NY: Lexington Books, 2016).

25. Beate Muller, "Trauma, Historiography, and Polyphony: Adult Voices in the CJHC's Early Postwar Child Holocaust Testimonies," *History and Memory Studies* 24, no. 2 (2012): 157–195; Noah Shenker, *Reframing Holocaust Testimony* (Bloomington, IN: Indiana University Press, 2015); Tony Kushner, "Finding Refugee Voices," *Yearbook of the Research Center for German and Austrian Exile Studies* 12 (2011): 121–139.

26. Michael Rothberg, *Multidirectional Memory: Remembering the Holocaust in the Age of Decolonization* (Stanford, CA: Stanford University Press, 2009).

27. Nanette Auerhahn and Dori Laub, "Discussion," in *Cinematic Reflections on the Legacy of the Holocaust: Psychoanalytic Perspectives*, eds. Diana Diamond and Bruce Sklarew (New York, NY: Routledge, 2019), 226–246.

28. Marianne Hirsch and Leo Spitzer, "The Witness in the Archive," *Holocaust Studies/Memory Studies* 2, no. 2 (2009): 151–170; Cathy Caruth, ed., *Trauma: Explorations in Memory* (Baltimore, MD: Johns Hopkins University Press, 1995); Shoshana Felman and Dori Laub, *Testimony: Crises of Witnessing in Literature, Psychoanalysis, and History* (New York, NY: Routledge, 1992).

29. James Young, *The Texture of Memory: Holocaust Memorials and Meaning* (New Haven, CT: Yale University Press, 1994); Young, *Writing and Rewriting the Holocaust*.

30. Dan McAdams, Ruthellen Josselson, and Amia Lieblich, eds., *Turns in the Road: Narrative Studies of Lives in Transition* (Washington, DC: American Psychological Association, 2001); Ruthellen Josselson, Amia Lieblich, and Dan McAdams, eds., *The Meaning of Others: Narrative Studies of Relationships* (Washington, DC: American Psychological Association, 2007); Suzanne Kaplan, *Children in Genocide: Extreme Trauma and Affect Regulation* (New York, NY: Routledge, 2018); Gadi BenEzer, "Trauma Signals in Life Stories," in *Trauma – Life Stories of Survivors*, eds. Kim Lacy Rogers and Selma Leyedesdorff (New Brunswick, NJ: Transaction Publishers, 2004), 29–44.

31. Judith Kestenberg and Ira Brenner, *The Last Witness: The Child Survivor of the Holocaust* (Washington, DC: American Psychiatric Publishing, 1996); Judith Kestenberg and Charlotte Kahn, *Children Surviving Persecution: An International*

Study of Trauma and Healing (London: Praeger, 1998); Judith Kestenberg and Eva Fogelman, eds., *Children During the Nazi Reign: Psychological Perspectives on the Interview Process* (Westport, CT: Praeger, 1994); Martin Bergman and Milton Jucovy, *Generations of the Holocaust* (New York, NY: Basic Books, 1982); Ira Brenner, *The Handbook of Psychoanalytic Holocaust Studies: International Perspectives* (New York, NY: Routledge, 2019); Milton Jucovy, "The Holocaust," in *The Reconstruction of Trauma*, ed. Arnold Rothstein (Madison, CT: International Universities Press, 1986), 153–170; Charlotte Kahn, "Interviewing: The Crossroad Between Research and Therapy," in *Children During the Nazi Reign*, eds. Judith Kestenberg and Eva Fogelman (Westport, CT: Praeger, 1994), 91–108; Rita Horvath and Katalin Zana, "Both Valuable and Difficult: A Meeting Point between Historical and Psychological Interviews," in *Children in the Holocaust and its Aftermath*, eds. Sharon Kangiser-Cohen, Eva Fogelman, and Dalia Ofer (New York, NY: Berghan, 2017), 81–98.

32. Salman Akhtar, *Immigration and Identity: Turmoil, Treatment, and Transformation* (London: Jason Aronson, 1999).

33. Sharon Kangisser-Cohen, Eva Fogelman, and Dalia Ofer, *Children in the Holocaust and Its Aftermath: Historical and Psychological Studies of the Kestenberg Archive* (New York, NY: Berghahn, 2019).

34. Urie Bronfenbrenner, *The Ecology of Human Development: Experiments by Nature and Design* (Cambridge, MA: Harvard University Press, 1979).

35. James Garbarino, Nancy Dubrow, Kathleen Kostelny, and Carolyn Pardo, eds., *Children in Danger: Coping with the Consequences of Community Violence* (San Francisco, CA: Jossey-Bass, 1992); James Garbarino, "An Ecological Perspective on the Effects of Violence on Children," *Journal of Community Psychology* 29, no. 3 (2001): 361–78; Betancourt and Khan, "The Mental Health," 317–28; Masten and Narayan, "Child Development," 227–57; L. Alan Stroufe, "The Place of Attachment in Development," in *Handbook of Attachment: Theory, Research, and Clinical Applications*, eds. Jude Cassidy and Phillip Shaver (New York, NY: Guilford Press, 2016), 997–1011.

36. Erik Erikson, *Childhood and Society* (New York, NY: Norton, 1950); Erik Erikson, *Identity and the Life Cycle* (New York, NY: Norton, 1980).

37. Ann Masten, "Global Perspectives on Resilience in Children and Youth," *Child Development* 85 (2014): 6–20; Linda Juang, Jeffry Simpson, Richard Lee, Alexander Rothman, Peter Titzmann, Maja Schacner, Lars Korn, Dorothee Heinmeier, and Cornelia Betsch, "Using Attachment and Related Perspectives to Understand Adaptation and Resilience among Immigrant and Refugee Youth," *American Psychologist* 73, no. 6 (2018): 797–811; Ann Masten, "Pathways to Integrated Resilience Science," *Psychological Inquiry* 26 (2015): 187–196; George Bonanno, Sara Romero, and Sarah Klein, "The Temporal Elements of Psychological Resilience: An Integrative Framework for the Study of Individuals, Families, and Communities," *Psychological Inquiry* 26 (2015): 139–169.

38. Stevan Hobfoll and Jeremiah Schumm, "Conservation of Resources Theory: Application to Public Health Promotion," in *Emerging Themes in Health Promotion Practice and Research: Strategies for Improving Public Health*, eds. Ralph

DiClemente, Richard Crosby, and Michele Kegler (San Francisco, CA: Jossey-Bass, Inc., 2002), 285–312; Stevan Hobfoll, "Resource Caravans and Resource Caravan Passageways: A New Paradigm for Trauma Responding," *Intervention: Journal of Mental Health and Psychosocial Support in Conflict-Affected Areas* 12, no. 4 (2014): 21–32; Stevan Hobfoll, Natalie Stevens, and Alyson Zalta, "Expanding the Science of Resilience: Conserving Resources in the Act of Adaptation," *Psychological Inquiry* 26, no. 2 (2015): 174–80; Bonanno, Romero, and Klein, "The Temporal Elements," 139–169.

39. Wai Kai Hou, Brian Hall, and Stevan Hobfoll, "Drive to Thrive: A Theory of Resilience Following Loss," in *Mental Health of Refugee and Conflict-Affected Populations: Theory, Research, and Clinical Practice*, eds. Nexhmedin Morina and Angela Nickerson (New York, NY: Springer Nature, 2018), 111–34.

40. Hadas Wiseman and Jacques Barber, *Echoes of Trauma: Relational Themes and Emotions in Children of Holocaust Survivors* (Cambridge, MA: Cambridge University Press, 2008).

41. Rothberg, *Multidirectional Memory*.

42. Paul Michael Garrett, "Questioning Tales of 'Ordinary Magic': 'Resilience' and Neo-Liberal Reasoning," *British Journal of Social Work* 46 (2015): 1909–1925.

Chapter 1

1939

The oldest family record I can find belongs to Felicja Rabinowitz, my great-great-grandmother, who was born around 1830. Felicja is buried in the historic Jewish cemetery on Okopowa Street, in Warsaw, where her gravestone is weathered but intact. Felicja's son, my great-grandfather Dawid, died in 1926, leaving behind a wife, Ester, and eight children, one of whom was my grandmother Rozia. Rozia is associated in my mind with the smell of oleander, as in childhood I played under a living-room window in her apartment, just outside of which a tree bloomed luxuriantly.

When Ester grew old and infirm, my grandmother took over the work of caring for her. My grandfather, Wladek Birnbaum, built a large and stylish five-story building where they could all live together, on separate floors, and have space, as well, for servants. Jews comprised about 10 percent of the population of Poland before World War II, and about a third of the population of Warsaw. The city at that time was a cosmopolitan center and home to the world's second-largest population of Jews. Jews comprised the majority of Poland's doctors, a large minority of its lawyers and scientists, and a significant proportion of its business leaders.[1] While most among this community were identifiably Jewish, some, like my grandparents Rozia and Wladek, had assimilated into Polish society, minimizing outward signs of their Jewishness. Wladek owned vast commercial properties, having invested wisely in the 1920s in the development of the Polish port city of Gdynia, where tea, coffee, candy, and dried fruits arrived from around the world to be packaged in his firm's warehouses for distribution to the grocers and cafes of Poland and central Europe. By the late 1930s, Wladek was serving as vice president of the Warsaw Chamber of Commerce—the only Jewish member of that group.

Rozia immersed herself in ostentatious displays of high fashion and art collecting, and the new house, designed by a maverick architect, was among the first structures to be erected in Poland in the emerging modernist style. With sleek black marble staircases, honey-colored wood panels, and windows extending from the street level to the roof, it welcomed the light from both the front and the back. The Nazis later used this lovely building as a headquarters office, and consequently it became one of the few structures in Warsaw to survive the war. It stands today, as of this writing, though subdivided now into multiple smaller apartment units. When he was five years old, my father moved to the building penthouse with his parents and two teenage siblings—brother Jerzy and sister Wanda, both in high school at the time. Their cousin Nina, then age four, moved with her parents to the floor just below, and their grandmother Ester was set up with some helpers on the floor below that.

In September 1939, we meet David, now age seven, about to begin second grade, and Nina, age six, soon to start first grade. As news of the war arrives, a decision is made for the two youngest children to flee with their mothers and for the older ones to be left behind to manage on their own—a choice familiar to refugees even today. David and Nina climb into a crowded chauffeur-driven limousine (one of the family's four cars) for which David's father, through business connections, has secured military travel passes. Other family members plead to join them but are turned away, as there is no more room. We also meet the now nineteen-year-old Wanda, who has recently defied her parents by leaving home and marrying. Wanda's new husband, a chemist thirteen years her senior, has arranged for construction permits to begin laying the foundation for a new factory, but his plans, like their marriage, will be subjected to a sudden and abrupt change. We also meet Marysia, their maternal cousin, age eighteen, who has just graduated high school—a year behind her slightly older cousin Wanda. As the war begins, Marysia is raising money for a scholarship fund to support a classmate's ambitions to enroll in university. We will be introduced also to Nathan, age twelve, who has just finished summer camp outside the city of Katowice and is visiting his aunts in Krakow. The sixth family member in this book, thirteen-year-old Irene, will enter the story in 1942, when her memoir begins.

The war meets these young people at different chronological ages and at different life stages. From the first day of the German invasion, these differences create divergent structures of opportunity and risk, which will frame the subsequent experience for each person. The writers James Garbarino and Kathleen Kostelny have suggested that children create "social maps" for negotiating the circumstances around them.[2] These representations of the world's patterns and meanings arise from early life experiences, as developmental theorists have observed,[3] but they come to guide young people's later-life ways of feeling, interpreting, and reacting to what is around them. As the bombs begin to fall and the families mobilize, we find that social maps are under threat. Each young person will quickly come to realize, in his or her own way, that previous taken-for-granted assumptions about society and safety are no longer adequate as explanatory frameworks. Each will need to make new sense out of what suddenly seems to make no sense. This is the challenge we will monitor in the pages that follow.

DAVID

September 1

I wasn't put to bed at sundown, my usual time. Instead, I am up listening to the radio. It is terribly exciting to be in my parents' living room without Nanny. Nanny Gertruda is always with me, except when I am at school. But now it is well past bedtime—and no Nanny! The announcer on the radio says "uwaga, uwaga, nadchodzi"—"attention, attention, approaching." This is about German aircraft, Father says. I have never been allowed to stay up so late! War is good!

September 2

Mother and Father have sent Nanny and me to the resort town of Otwock, near Warsaw. It's "for safety," they said. We are staying at Pensjonat Gurewicza. I know this place well—last summer, I learned to ride my two-wheel bike here. People at dinner said "nie damy guzika" ("we won't give them even a button"). I asked Nanny what this means. She said the Germans are asking for too much, but they'll get nothing. I'm sure I don't understand what Nanny is saying, and she won't explain it. I am getting no good answers from her.

September 3, 1939

Early this morning, bombs fell from an airplane, making an awful noise when they hit the ground. The Germans are here, Nanny says. Windows at Gurewicz are broken, and there is glass all over. At breakfast, people said the orphanage across the main street got hit and is completely leveled. Nanny took me to look. Many people were there. We saw a large pile of rubble, which smelled quite bad. Nanny said "forty orphans are buried here." Some people were standing in the dust and crying, but Nanny would not tell me why. She said "England and France are with us—the war will be over in several days." Nanny is not explaining anything to me.

September 4

Today, Father and Mother sent me to Śródborów, our summer villa. It is near Otwock, but deeper in the woods. Right after we arrived, Nanny said she had to return to Warsaw. Now I am by myself. But anyway, Gertruda is not my original nanny. She is the new one. My nanny before her was Tita. Tita goes back as far as I can remember. She spoke to me only in German, and she taught me to pray on my knees to Jesus every afternoon in my room before bedtime. I liked her very much, and she was never mean to me, except once when I asked her about a word I heard at school: "Jude." "Was is Jude?" ("What is a Jew?"), I said, and she became very angry. She said she will not tolerate my using bad language—and if she ever hears this word again, I will have to kneel in the corner on dried peas, and then I may feed those peas to the pigeons on Mokotowska Street. Other than that one time, Nanny Tita never punished me and was always good, and I was terribly upset when Gertruda came instead. I was already six at that time, and I had completed kindergarten, but still I cried very much.

September 5

The caretaker came this morning. He said a chauffeur, Mr. Chackiewicz, will be arriving later to drive me back to Warsaw. I was surprised. "I'll be alone in the car with only the driver?" I asked. "No nanny?" The caretaker mumbled something but I did not hear. Really, the excitement continues! War is quite interesting.

Chackiewicz arrived in Mother and Father's favorite car, a black 1937 Buick stretch limousine they call "Beek." They made up that name. Strangely, I am allowed to sit in Beek's front seat. There is a glass partition separating us from the passenger section, but it has been left open. Chackiewicz drove without headlights. This is "because of the blackout," he said. It was completely dark outside, no lights at all, and the car veered all over the road, left and right, as we were moving quickly. At one point, Chackiewicz slowed and blinked on the headlights for just a moment, and instantly a soldier emerged from the darkness. "Ja ci dam swiatła!" ("I'll show you lights!"), he screamed. He pointed his rifle at us. Chackiewicz turned off the lights right away and drove very fast through the darkness.

It took a long time to reach our apartment house at Jaworzynska 7. But now I am in my bed in my room—without Nanny! I can hear Father and Mother in the living room. Uncle Kuba is with them, and they are arguing about something. They seem to be talking about Beek. But I can't hear everything and I am not able to follow the conversation.

September 6

Father woke me up very early, when it was still dark. I was still sleepy from the excitement of the previous days. He insisted I move quickly. We are getting in the car, he said, and we are leaving Warsaw. He said something about us being Jewish. I have not heard anything like this before. I have seen that in a war, things are done differently, such as having to get up early. And what is all this about Jews? Nanny is not here, so who will dress me up? Father said I am to dress myself today—and I am to hurry. Last September, I started first grade on Polna Street, at Licee Francais de Varsovie, not far from our home. First grade is not like kindergarten: in first grade, there is Religion class. Of course I joined the other children in the classroom with the priest. But after a while, I reported to Nanny that the priest doesn't like me. I am not a good student in his class, even though I am very good in all my other subjects. A few days after that, I was transferred to the classroom with the rabbi. Only a few other children were there. But it was just as bad! The rabbi didn't like me either, and I could not answer any of the questions he asked! Mother went to the school, and after that I was released from Religion for the whole year. The teachers told Mother: "when second grade comes, you will have to make a decision." I have worried about what this might mean. Mercifully, war has come. No school! I am going in the car with Mother and Father, and I am not at Licee Francais! Our little Pekingese, Harry, will stay in Warsaw while we are on our trip. One of the servants will stay with him.

September 6

Chackiewicz parked the Buick directly in front of the apartment house and began loading many suitcases, including one for me. Everyone was talking about the car being out of gas. "There is no gasoline to be had in Warsaw at any price," Mother said. But Chackiewicz said he found some—paying very much money for it—and mixed it with turpentine, because there is plenty of that. He showed us the two large containers in the basement. Eleven people boarded: me; Father; Mother; Aunt Jula and her daughter, my cousin Nina, who is a year younger than me and lives in the apartment downstairs; also Chackiewicz and his wife and son; plus three others whom we do not know but who appeared in the morning in front of the house. Mother told me I am to address the two older ladies as "Pani Pułkownikowa" ("Madame Colonel"), as they are wives of very important men—Lieutenant Colonels—in the Polish air force. The boy, one of their sons, is about my age. The wives need a ride out of Warsaw, Mother said, and in exchange, we have been given "Rodzina Wojskowa"—"Military Family" papers. Father and Chackiewicz said Beek will need these to pass through military checkpoints, since "ordinary" vehicles are no longer being allowed on the roads. This is all quite exciting. Mother says these arrangements were made by Father's friend, Mr. Lambert, from the Chamber of Commerce. He is Father's very good friend. I have met him many times. He has come to our house for dinner.

Beek has a device on the right side near the rear seat, where Father usually sits, that lets us communicate with the driver through the glass partition. But today we were not in our usual places. Nina and I have complained because the children are being forced to sit on our mothers' laps. We feel we are too old to be treated like babies! The grownups paid no attention to us.

Just as we prepared to leave, Uncle Jakub, Father's brother, arrived. He was carrying his daughter, my cousin. Uncle Jakub held her at the car window and knocked on the glass. An argument broke out, and Mother started yelling. This was unpleasant, as I was on her lap, in the middle of it. Mother said "nie ma miejsca" ("there's no room"). Uncle Jakub pleaded and pleaded for us to take her with us. We did not. Then Chackiewicz announced: "Jedziemy na Siedlce" ("We are going towards the town of Siedlce"). And we set forth. Mother said we will have breakfast there. I checked my map: east.

Outside the city, we encountered many, many roadblocks. Chackiewicz indicated the "Rodzina Wojskowa" tags on the military women's dresses and showed all the documents. Each time, the soldiers at the checkpoints saluted and let us pass. Soon we arrived at a roadblock which seemed larger, with many soldiers. They did not let us pass, even after the military papers were shown. Chackiewicz pulled out a pack of cigarettes and offered it to a solider, who refused it angrily. The soldier called us "uciekinierzy" ("refugees"). I have not heard such a word before. Then another solider came to the side of the car. He was much nicer. He pointed to a group of people, men and women, walking on the road behind us. "Grupa szpiegów na stracenie," he said—a "group of spies on the way to execution." They passed next to my window, and I could see they were all tied together with a long shiny metal chain attached to their hands. There were maybe twenty of them. The windows of our car were partly rolled down, and I picked up a few German words which I know from Nanny Tita. Mother suggested to Father that perhaps he should speak to the nice soldier on behalf of these people. Father got quite annoyed and told her "siedź spokojnie"—"just sit quietly." Soon the group disappeared and we heard a long volley of gunfire, and then it was quiet. The nicer soldier came back to the car and saluted, waving us past. From the mood of the grownups, I knew something special happened. But no one was answering my questions. I feel I am being treated like a child.

Not much later, our car ran over a chicken. I was upset. "Poor chicken," I said. Mother insisted it was not a chicken—just a large dry leaf. But I was sure I did see the chicken! I even heard it under the car! Mother laughed at me in a not nice way and told Chackiewicz to turn back and see what it was, and Chackiewicz swerved the steering wheel slightly, pretending to be turning back. Father did not like this at all. He yelled at everyone: "It was a chicken—we ran over it—now keep going!" Cousin Nina said she didn't see the chicken, but it sure sounded like one when we were running it over. At that point, everyone laughed, even the military wives. The grownups all commented about how smart children are nowadays, for our age, how observant and well spoken. We felt good about this, as we do feel grown up for our age.

Suddenly, there was a loud explosion. The front left windshield splintered into hundreds of tiny honeycomb-shaped pieces, and we saw a small hole, the size of a coin, in front of Chackiewicz's face. Chackiewicz leaned way over so that his head extended outside the window, and we started racing very fast to get away. Mother and one of the colonel's wives yelled "jedziemy do rowu!" ("we're going into the ditch!"), but Chackiewicz paid no attention. Father urged him to speed up! After a while, we stopped. Father told us to "look for the bullet," but we didn't find anything. Chackiewicz brought a wrench from his tool box and dislodged the glass pieces one by one as we waited, leaving an oval hole about 15 × 25 centimeters directly in front of his face. Then everyone returned to the car, and we set off again.

We arrived in Siedlce in the afternoon, parking in front of the house of someone Father called the "client." According to Mother, this is someone connected with Father's business. Nina and I and the other children urgently needed to go to the bathroom, and the client asked his daughter, Sure (pronounced "soo-reh"), to show us. What a wonderful thing she showed! An outhouse! I have never seen such a thing before. It is delightful! Many times before, when I went with Nanny Tita to the park in Warsaw, I asked if I may play with other children. Nanny always told me no, because a good boy does not play with "ulicznicy" ("street children"). But in a war, children may play together. Sure and I and the others went to the field behind the house and played—with no nannies! Sure speaks neither French nor German. She taught me a Yiddish word: "Yo" ("yes"). This was great fun, and I wanted to stay in Siedlce and play some more, even when it was time to go. Mother teased me, saying Sure and I are obviously in love. Father said I will be allowed to play here again on our way back to Warsaw after the war. Chackiewicz announced: we continue toward Brześć. And then we climbed back in the car and headed off again.

The first town we passed was on fire. We drove past flames, smoke, and smoldering rubble everywhere. I followed the road on my map—I think this was Międzyrzec. The next town, Biała Podlaska, was also in flames. It was getting dark, and already nearing our bedtimes, so Father found a large two-story house that was partially still standing. The people there told Father it would be the only available space in town, as most of the other buildings were in ruins. As the grownups unpacked for the night, no one was paying attention to me, so I went out to explore the other part of the house. It was still smoky and there was a strong smell, lots of rubble, and charred wood, and I saw bandaged people crying in some rooms. None of them wanted to explain to me what happened. I am sleeping the same room with Mother and Father tonight.

September 7

In the morning, we continued toward Brześć. Soon, German planes arrived, flying low. They filled the sky above us with loud noise, shooting many bullets at the ground and dropping more bombs. Father said we are very close to the "Twierdza" (the fortress) and that is why the planes have come. Chackiewicz drove Beek under some tall trees and parked there, and everyone got out and ran. We hid under branches in a shallow ravine. Some of the planes flew so near to us, I could even see the pilots. These are Stuka dive bombers, Father said. Nina was crouching next to me. She said she is afraid a bomb will fall on her. A childish fear! "Why should the bombs fall on you?" I said, "And not on this tree, or this car, or me?" No one complimented me on my cleverness and bravery. Mother yelled at me, and Aunt Jula yelled to Nina, and we were both told to stop talking and lay flat on our backs. This is fine by me, because from this position, I have a good view of the planes and the noisy falling bombs.

When the planes left, Chackiewicz resumed driving, and we entered Brześć on the main street. Again, planes! We ran out of the car and raced into the doorway of the nearest house. I wanted very much to see the planes one more time, so I stepped back out into the street, just a few steps. At that very moment, the house to my left burst into a thick cloud of white smoke and collapsed to the ground in a big smoky explosion. Someone grabbed me very hard and yanked me into the doorway, and Father was very angry with me.

We did not stay in Brześć for breakfast, but that is no problem, as the car had been packed with many delicious things, especially chocolates. Now we were headed toward Pińsk. Chackiewicz swerved around many large craters in the road, and we passed many, many burned-down buildings. Some of the buildings were still on fire. We were close enough to see the flames moving. We arrived in Pińsk toward evening. Father knows some people who live in a large wooden house. They are Jews and speak Yiddish, same as Sure and her family in Siedlce. The adults spread maps on the table and were talking excitedly about where the bombs had fallen. I have my own map—and I know where we are exactly. I found some boys my age playing in the field in back of the house, and I joined them. Food in Pińsk is delicious! The hard-boiled eggs were especially good. I was allowed to have as many as I wanted. We also had vegetables, bread, biscuits ("biszkopty"), and chocolates. We will stay overnight.

September 8

German planes appeared again, dropping many small funny-looking bombs. Father said these are incendiaries ("bomby zapalające"). The house behind us was struck and burned to the ground in minutes. One of the boys who played with me yesterday, Mother said, has died. We hurried to leave Pińsk. Father said we are to drive toward Czerniowce, in Romania, and ultimately to Constanta, on the Black Sea. From there, we will board a passenger ship to Haifa. Father says it is safe there for Jews. My grandparents have lived near Haifa since before I was born. Father says we are almost there.

We headed south from Pińsk using side roads, mostly muddy and unpaved, because Chackiewicz said the larger roads are full of holes. After a while, one of the wheels stuck in loose sand. Steam billowed from the engine as Chackiewicz tried to get the car out, and the tire was flat. Father and Aunt Jula set out on foot to find a nearby village, returning soon with peasants ("chłopi") and horses. There were some heated arguments with the "chłopi" involving money, but eventually their horses pulled Beek back onto a paved road. Father paid them. We returned to Pińsk and picked up the road south, toward Równo and Tarnopol, veering around the craters. We have stopped at Sarny for the night.

September 9

At sunrise, German planes filled the sky. Some were small, some large, many dropping bombs, making a deafening noise that hurt our ears. We saw the black crosses and swastikas as they flew over, one after another after another. So many of them! Mother grabbed my hand and we ran from the house, and she pulled me under a small tree in the yard. Many people from neighboring buildings soon joined us. Some of the women cried, "Wojna jest straszna!" ("war is terrible"). Father said the Germans are after Sarny Airport. All of a sudden, the adults started clapping and cheering. They pointed up, toward a small plane that was slowly climbing into the sky from the direction of the airport. It had Polish markings. We watched and cheered for several minutes, but then the women cried out in horror: the little plane spiraled downward, trailing smoke. I tried to see where it landed, but just at that moment a second group of German planes roared into the sky directly above us, and Father yelled that I must lay flat on my belly.

After that, we said goodbye to the people under the tree. Chackiewicz announced that were leaving Sarny. And then we continued south, toward Równo, and I followed on my map. A short distance later, we met a large column of armed Polish soldiers in a long line of trucks and cars. Everyone stopped. Father, Jula, and the Colonels' wives all got out of the car, and at the exact center of the road, they met some officers from the column. I couldn't hear what they said. They stood and talked for a long time. But then one of the soldiers began yelling and pointing toward the sky, and soon several more formations of low-flying German planes appeared. "Do lasu!" ("into the forest!"), someone shouted, and we ran. Mother stumbled over a small fence, and Father and I ran to help her. She was pale and breathing heavily, but by then the planes had already passed. They were not interested in us. The Polish soldiers did not fire any shots.

The Colonels' wives announced they would leave our group and join the soldiers, who were headed to Romania. We had planned to go there, too. But the officer told Father that Romania would be "too dangerous now for you Jews." He said we should aim for Wilno, where "there is strength in numbers." Father said he is not sure we would like to go to Wilno, and we might try someplace else first. We watched as every one of the military vehicles made a big U-turn in the middle of the road and headed back in the direction of Równo and Czerniowce. Chackiewicz turned our car around, too, as Father said we would now head in the direction of Dabrowice. Only eight people are in the car. I was quite confused, but even Father could not explain what was said between the colonel's wives and the Polish officers. I see that in war, even Mother and Father do not always know why things happen.

September 10

Dabrowice has no street lights and no paved roads. Our car seemed to float on mud as we arrived. We parked in front of a large wooden house owned by "Chana, the Biezenka." "Biezenka" means "uciekinierka" ("refugee") in Russian, Father said. Chana had fled to this swampy place from Russia during World War I. Chana is Jewish. Her husband is dead. She has six daughters, all of them with Hebrew names starting with "Ch," same as their mother's name. I needed quite badly to go to the bathroom and was hoping for another outhouse. But no luck. Chana said I must go "do krowy" ("to the cow"). I did not understand this, so Mother took me. We entered a large, dark barn where the floor was covered in thick mud with a very strong bad smell. I slipped and fell backward into it. Mother picked me up and cleaned some of it, and when we returned to the house, she announced that Chana's daughter Chinga was to be my new Nanny. Mother called her "Chinka," which in Polish means "Chinese woman." This was not very nice. Chinga told me later, when Mother was not there, that hers is a beautiful name meaning "uciecha, po żydowsku" ("joy, in Jewish"). Nanny Chinga and I speak in Polish.

September 11

Chinga took me to see the carpenter's workshop. The carpenter said he will "adopt" me, and everyone agreed that I will be a good carpenter someday. I asked to help him drive some nails, but he said "Nails cost money." Father must buy the nails before I am allowed to help the carpenter. Father came and bought the nails and I helped the carpenter. This was wonderful.

September 12

A gang of Ukrainian men entered the town. Father called them "Rzad Tymczasowy" ("temporary government"). He said they came here because the Polish police have left. Father said we are "easy targets" now. "Like fish in a barrel," he said. Chinga took me to the house of the town "shohet"—the kosher ritual slaughterer. She said everyone in the village is talking about "the rich Jews from the Buick." The Ukrainians are hunting for us now. I saw an outhouse in the back at the shohet's and asked to use it, but Chinga hurried me into the cellar and warned I must hide there and I must not come out. Inside, it was dark. Chinga pointed to a trap door in the floor, and I crawled through it to an even lower room which was quite large, but very wet and smelly, with a steeply sloping dirt floor. This is a sub-basement, Chinga said, a room for making meat kosher. I noticed a tiny rectangular window on the far wall. I crawled across the floor in order to reach it, as the ceiling was very low. But at that section, the floor dipped, and I could stand without hitting my head. I found a small table and dragged it over. Standing on my tiptoes on the table, I could just see to the outside. Chinga left a basket for me with loaves of bread and bottles of milk and some hard-boiled eggs. She told me that the other two children, Nina and Chackiewicz' son, might also come to the sub-basement, but that we must be completely quiet and not say anything at all, at any time. Several times, I have whispered to see if the other children have come, but no one answers.

At night, I know I am alone. I am used to the smell. But it is terribly boring here. I have nothing to do but sleep, so this is what I have been doing. I lie on the floor and I stay as quiet as I can. I can tell when daytime arrives, because I see the light shaft seeping through my window. At times, I have heard a muffled sound of voices and knocking and heavy footsteps above me, which tells me there are people in the house.

September 16

Mother and Father came. I was very happy to see them. They brought food and water for me and climbed down to see my hiding place. I showed them how I climb the table to the little window. Just then we heard horses, and through the window where I was standing, I saw a horse-drawn carriage ("bryczka") very close to the side of the house. A man came with a long rifle and shot at it. The carriage driver yelled, and some people came out. One, a boy, looked about my age. Father grabbed my arm very hard and pulled me down to the floor. I heard screaming and gunshots, and then nothing more. Father and Mother stayed with me for a short time after that. They warned me I must stay very, very quiet. They said I am being a very good boy. Then they crawled back up through the trap door, leaving me once again by myself.

September 17

Chinga came and opened the trap door. I am free! "The Red Army is coming!" she said. "Rzad Tymczasowy is gone!" I crawled up to Chinga and she hugged me and kissed me and told me everything will be wonderful from now on. I do not feel everything is wonderful at all. I am quite tired of war. Chinga said the Red Army is in Poland and they will arrive here soon. I do not understand this. But I am very happy to be out of the cellar!

September 25

Father and Mother and I have moved back into the house with Biezenka. Nina and the others went to stay elsewhere. I was quite eager to see this so-called Red Army. Chinga took me to see the village square, where people built an arch with many decorations and a small stage. Finally, after several days, they arrived. But look: they are not red! Chinga took me to see "Połkovnik" ("Colonel") give a speech on the podium. I could not understand even a word. Chinga said this is Russian. We stood close to the podium, but Chinga refused to translate into Polish for me, even though I begged her. "Tovarisch Połkovnik ('Comrade Colonel') might get upset if we are noisy," she said. There was applause, and people threw flowers. Chinga is my best-ever Nanny. She has taken me on long walks all over Dabrowice. We went to the town hall to visit Beek, which is parked there. Beek is the only car in Dabrowice that is not a Russian military vehicle. Chinga allows me to talk to many other children. She taught me all the letters in the Yiddish alphabet and showed me Yiddish books for children. I am learning some Russian words, and I have taught her some French words. The Red Army soldiers wear gray uniforms and pointed hats, and Chinga speaks to them in Russian. A few times, Cousin Nina joined our walks. Nina also has a new "Dabrowice Nanny." Dabrowice is cold at night.

September 27

The Russians made many announcements at the town hall. Many of the townspeople came to listen. The Russians told everyone about the Soviet People's Commissariat. They said "the Jewish bourgeoisie" will be "cleansed" out of Dabrowice. Chinga said the Russians want us because of the Buick—but the Russians are better than Rzad Tymczasowy, Chinga said. Ukrainians kill Jews, but the Russians will just send us to Siberia, where "tam nie jest źle, tylko zimno" ("it is not so bad, just cold"). Father says a train is scheduled to leave for Wilno early tomorrow morning, and he has bought us some tickets. But it is not safe for us to wait at Biezenka's, because the Russians will come hunting for us. Father went to some men in town and hired two horse-drawn carriages to bring us to a hotel near the train station. On the way, Father asked the carriage drivers to stop at the baker's. He bought many, many loaves of bread in two large green sacks. Then we passed Beek for one last time. It is still parked in front of the town hall. Father said we will leave Beek for the Soviets. I waved goodbye. At the hotel, Mother said "pluskwy nas zjedzą" ("bedbugs will eat us up"). I was quite eager to look for some of those bedbugs and catch one as a pet. But the hotel has no lights and now it is already dark.

September 28

To reach the train, we needed to cross railroad tracks. A very long freight train was moving slowly along the tracks, forward a short distance, then back a short distance, pausing for a few minutes each time in between. Aunt Jula and Nina and Chackiewicz and his family all held hands and crawled very quickly under the train, hurrying to the other side. Father had already crossed, and I crawled quickly without any trouble. But Mother stopped and was afraid. Father yelled at her until she finally ran under the train and joined us. When the train arrived, it was very full—much too crowded to board. Most of the passengers seemed to be soldiers, and some were even hanging onto the outside! Mother said the war is over now, because it has already been almost a month since we left Warsaw, and now the soldiers are returning home. Father walked to the side of the train and pulled out the two green sacks from the baker's. "Mamy chleb!" ("we have bread") he shouted, waving a large loaf in the air. A mass of soldiers poured out of the doors and windows. They were cheering. Then they grabbed me and stuffed me through a window. It was terribly crowded inside, and smelly, and I complained to the soldiers about the smell. No one paid attention, as by then everyone from our group was on board and sharing out small pieces of our delicious Dabrowice baker's bread. The soldiers said they had not eaten for several days. I was terribly uncomfortable sitting on a soldier's lap, as I am a big boy now. Finally, I complained so much that the soldiers squeezed me through the crowd to the toilet, where they said I could sit "wygodnie" ("in comfort"). The bathroom was small and very dirty, but I was very tired and I did not mind so much. I lay down on the floor and went to sleep. When I woke up, Mother was cleaning my face. She said we have arrived in Wilno.

Chapter 1

MARYSIA

September 2

The apartment is gone—obliterated in yesterday's bombardment. Mother and I had gone out for an errand, and when we returned, we found a pile of rubble. There was nothing left to save—not even a fragment to pick up. Nobody was home, thankfully. But what to do now? There are ruins everywhere we look. We walked to my older sister Lilka's. She and Zgulon, her husband, were just married this past June and had bought new furniture and household items for their little apartment. We arrived to find her crying at the street-car stop, as Zgulon had just boarded. He's on his way to join the other men being mobilized. This little place is going to be our home for now, and we will have to make it work.

September 7

All week, rescue teams have been excavating the destroyed buildings, and up until yesterday—or maybe the day before—people were still being found alive. Mostly, people are staying in the cellars. Carcasses of carriage horses are rotting in the street, their bodies stinking and covered with large blue flies. They are turning into skeletons, but people have been using kitchen knives to cut out slices of meat from the hind quarters, since the shops have all run out of food. Czesław has brought us fresh bread, though I'm not sure where he's getting it. My love and admiration for him grow deeper, as he has shown his true character. Not every man in his situation would take the risk of having a Jewish girlfriend. We know what the Germans have said about such things. But this is the kind of person he is: fair, moral, just, opposed to discrimination in all forms, wherever he sees it. Those are some of the reasons I respect him so much.

October

The Germans are solidly in control of the entire city, and they started issuing all sorts of outrageous new rules, each harsher than the one before. Any Jew over age twelve must wear the white armband with the star. A Jew must step out of the way when others walk past. A Jew must salute. Some German men stopped my sister on the street and took her to a room in an office building, where they made her remove her panties and forced her to use them to wash the windows. For a week, I stayed on the apartment balcony and considered what to do. How can I go along with all this? I looked down onto the street and watched people rushing in all directions—the Jews with their armbands, the rest of the Poles trying to mind their own business as if it were all perfectly normal. But I made a decision: I refuse! I was terrified at first, walking out to the street. I know I can be beaten at any moment—or worse—if someone recognizes me as a Jew with no armband. But after a few hours, it dawned on me: nobody is paying attention. I am eighteen, I am blonde, I have blue eyes. No one can tell that I am a Jew.

October

People gathered to watch the new ghetto wall going up. We've heard rumors for a long time about the Germans' plan to build something like this, but nobody believed they'd do it. It's basically a brick cage, and we are to be imprisoned in it. Lilka has found an apartment on one of the streets within the ghetto perimeter. She traded for it with a gentile couple. We had to sell most of her furniture, though, because it's small apartment. It was almost impossible to find buyers, since so many of us are in the same situation. We've given away our belongings practically for free.

November

Mother was extremely upset when I told her I will stay on the Aryan side. She doesn't want us to be apart, of course, but mostly she's concerned about my safety. "You have no idea what risks you are taking!" she cried. But I do know the risks: The Germans have made no secret of their policy: any of us found outside will be killed. They've repeated this in frequent announcements and posted signs almost everywhere. But the greatest risk to me, I believe, is not from disobeying an order—it's from being Jewish in the first place. All of us are in danger here whether we live in the ghetto or not. The best chance I have, I think, is quite simply to disguise my origins. Besides, Czesław is here, on the Aryan side, and I will not give up my chance to continue seeing him. Now my family, without me, is settled behind the wall, as ordered. I've rented a room in an apartment belonging to a friend of a friend. It's basically a glorified closet. No heat. I need to pass through the landlord's room in order to reach the toilet. But it'll have to do for now. The ghetto gates have closed, and I am on my own.

December

Winter is always a challenge, but this one has been particularly cold. The temperature in my room drops below freezing at night, so I've been dressing warmly for bed—layers of sweaters, a coat, hat, heavy gloves. It's tolerable if I hide my face under the blankets. Czesław and his family are trying to live more or less normally. He even brought me a flower—a beautiful carnation on a long stem. For the price of that flower, I probably could have eaten for a week! But it's a reminder that I am still a woman, and still worthy of such gestures, and he is still a man, and still thoughtful and self-aware enough to act like one. When the landlord saw my flower, he gave me a vase. It looked beautiful for a few days, but then I made the mistake of drinking a nice hot cup of tea before bed. It was just for a little warmth, of course. In the middle of the night, when I needed badly to pee, I used the vase. I didn't want to wake everyone! No harm done: the flower was completely frozen anyway! This is our life now.

NATHAN

September 1

We heard the first air raid siren very early in the morning. The first bombs fell within a minute or two of the sirens. Mother and I were in Krakow visiting her sisters. It was supposed to be a little last-minute vacation before school started. There is mass confusion in the street. A few people started saying it would be over in a few days, but others packed suitcases and prepared to leave. Father was still in Katowice. He couldn't leave the business unattended. We waited for him to arrive so we could decide what to do.

September 7

Katowice fell quickly. Father arrived with the car and picked us up. We headed east, toward Russia, but the roads were completely jammed with crowds of people. The Germans fired down from the air, bombing everyone. We ran for cover and huddled in a ditch, and then we just left the car parked on the road. There was no point trying to leave any more, because there was no way out. The Germans were all around us. We walked back toward the city. We saw them on their motorcycles with their sidecars, firing their machine guns.

September 15

Father found a place for us in Wieliczka, outside Krakow. The Germans were focusing on urban centers, he said, and weren't paying much attention to Jews in the smaller towns. We all slept together on the floor of a room on a little farm—me, both my parents, my mother's two sisters, and my grandmother. Some others, too. We had an outhouse. As I was the youngest and strongest, I was assigned the job of bringing water from the well.

Late November

We felt safe in Wieliczka. I was learning about farming and helping with the chores. I learned to thresh wheat and to grind flour between large stones. We had eggs fresh from the chickens, and I learned to milk the cow, so we had milk, fresh and warm. Our room was a little more comfortable when we made mattresses out of straw, and the farmer gave us a small stove for cooking. Mother and I hardly had any belongings, since we had only our little suitcases with us at the time of the attack. There were other Jewish families in town—a few are like us, families from the larger cities, waiting for the war to end. It was illegal for Jews to attend school, but our families hired a teacher for us, and we held classes in secret, in a cellar attached to one of the houses. In my class there were five boys and two girls. My parents arranged with a family in town for me to practice my piano. Mother had always planned for me to be a concert pianist, and she didn't want me to lose practice time because of our situation. I walked to that house several times every week, and sometimes I stayed and played on that piano for hours. Beethoven. Liszt. The second rhapsody. I immersed myself in the music.

WANDA

September 26

I told Edek: if he insists on staying, I'm ready to leave without him. He's been planning this factory forever, convinced it will make us our fortune. Warsaw is in ruins, and he has 6 million bricks piled up, ready for the start of construction. But the room we'd been renting from the Frenkels was destroyed by shrapnel in the first week, and then we moved in with the family of my old school mate, Antonina. Now, signs all over Warsaw are saying Jews over age sixteen need to register with the Gestapo. If you ask me, there's no reason for us to stay here.

September 27

We agreed to meet at 5 a.m. in a flat on the eastern side of town. Uncle Kuba and Jerzy will meet us there. We'll head toward Wilno, where my Aunt Jula has influential relations. We've arranged for a taxi to be there to pick us up. The driver doesn't want money, but he's prepared to take us as far as his gasoline will last—in exchange for bags of some of the stockpiled food my father hid in the cellar on Jaworzynska Street. We loaded the provisions into packages. I took the money my father gave me before he left and bought four loose diamonds.

September 28

Early in the morning, before we left, I wrapped the diamonds in cotton wool and inserted them in, well, an unmentionable place. We arrived at the arranged meeting spot and got in the taxi. Everybody's carrying a small rucksack except for Uncle Kuba, who for some reason has decided he needs to be lugging a gigantic brass-bound leather suitcase, the contents of which are rattling. He has stuffed it with shirt collars.

The taxi headed out of town, maneuvering around all the potholes and bomb craters, and we sat cramped in the back, very uncomfortable because there was so much luggage and because, well, of what I was carrying, and where I was carrying them. Gangs of German soldiers were working along the roads. A few times they stopped us to ask if we were Jews, pulling the cap off Jerzy's head to see the color of his hair. They have been told to watch for black-haired refugees. These seem to be children—not high-ranking soldiers. We passed some buses full of naked people who looked as though they had been beaten up. This made the driver very jittery, and he started repeating that the taxi is almost out of gas. We reminded him about the food.

When we stopped for a quick break, I went in the bushes and removed the diamonds, and this time I swallowed them. Back in high school, I never used to be able to swallow medicine of any kind—always sputtering and choking even on the smallest pill. But now: no trouble at all.

Within minutes of getting back on the road, we were stopped. The soldiers instructed us to get out and declare our religious affiliation. Jerzy and Uncle Kuba pretended not to understand, and they were cast aside as a pair of idiots. Edek waved his certificate of apprenticeship at I. G. Farbindustrie, Ludwigshafen, Germany's largest chemical manufacturing company, which resulted in a show of politeness from the men. When they got to me, I had just about had enough of this nonsense. I said that yes, I am indeed a "Jude," and then, quietly to myself, I said I will spit in your eye. They took me into one of the buses and had me undress, and then they ripped a few seams. That was that. Nothing major.

The others in the car watched this scene with utter horror and acted like they didn't know me. Jerzy got out when he saw me exit the bus, but then the driver took off. Jerzy and I ran after the car, and the driver finally stopped and let us back in. He said he would not tolerate any more of such goings-on. We reminded him of the bags of sugar, the cartons of sardines, the coffee, the tea, the cocoa, and so on, and again he grudgingly agreed to go a bit further. We drove until the gas ran out. And, leaving the driver with his car full of food but no gas, we started walking east, toward the Bug River.

We walked through an old forest and stopped when it got dark. We built a fire on a small stove Edek had packed in the car, and we made some tea. There were others also camping in the forest, everyone in transit.

September 29

My diamonds are becoming a nuisance. It is all very well to swallow diamonds when you have a bathroom in which to collect them afterward. But in a forest, however pretty it is, and with German soldiers able to spring at you at any moment, inability to dive for a quick poo turns into a pain in the neck.

A kindly peasant with a boat and readiness to accept Polish money took us across the river. Although it was a border, we were not stopped or shot at. We walked all day, except at one point someone gave us a ride in a hay cart, which was terribly uncomfortable. We walked until we came to a small train station where hundreds of refugees were waiting for a train to Bialystok. Some people, we heard, had been waiting for two days.

When the train finally arrived, people squeezed inside, some clinging to the sides of the train. Edek and I pushed our way in, and Uncle Kuba and Jerzy did the same, squashing themselves into the little box where the train guard usually sits. The tightly wedged bodies turned out to be a good thing, as they prevented me from falling down from exhaustion. There was a uniformed Pole of some kind right next to me in the train; you could clearly see the lice crawling on him.

The train headed toward Bialystok but stopped well before the destination. We all got out and looked around, and then we resumed walking. We walked until we reached a small village where the residents were willing to accept Polish money. We were given straw to make a small bed in the corner of the cottage. There is no plumbing.

October 1

We continued walking and arrived in Bialystok in the late afternoon. Edek had the address of a place we could stay—a normal home with normal furniture and normal food. I made a bee-line for the toilet. All four diamonds came out easily, without lacerating my insides, as Edek had predicted, but which did nothing for my mental anxiety and physical torture. I made a terrible mess in spite of my best efforts to clean it up. There was a small sofa in the corner of the living room, and I fell into a warm and blissful sleep. I could barely wake the next day, and Edek had to drag me to the station.

We boarded another train, but once again we were stopped, and everyone was ordered out and lined up neatly in a nearby field. We were supposed to present our credentials in order to be allowed to continue the trip.

The Lithuanians don't want a pile of refugees crowding the city. Afraid of being sent back to Warsaw, Edek pulled me out of the line, and we hid in some bushes. Then we watched in despair as everyone was allowed back on the train. Uncle Kuba and Jerzy boarded with the rest of the crowd as we watched, and soon the train started again, and the field was empty. Wilno is so near, yet so far away! Our hearts sank.

We walked to a nearby town, Grodno, and were taken in by a friendly baker who gave us loads of fresh warm bread and a tiny cubicle behind the hot boiler. It feels like heaven. Another Wilno train will depart in the morning.

December

When we first arrived in Wilno, Edek and I rented a room in a miserable hotel that has a cafe on the first floor. At first, the only food we could afford was bread. But Edek removed his wedding ring and made all kinds of advances toward the young waitress in the cafe, with hints of marriage, and now we have jars of delicious plum preserves, which she stole and gave to him.

My parents and my little brother David are here, as well as my cousin Nina and her mother, Aunt Jula, now reunited with Uncle Kuba. My parents have a comfortable apartment with two large rooms, and they've got plenty of money for food and everything else a person could need. All of our furs are back in storage in Warsaw, so they bought me a new fur coat from one of the shops here in Wilno. They've offered to take me in and give me all the home comforts I want, provided I leave Edek, whom they despise.

Late December

I'd started running a fever, and I'd been hallucinating at night. I could barely get out of bed. My parents and Aunt Jula used their social connections to find me the best and most expensive doctor in Wilno. His name is Trotski—young, blond, and handsome—and I am certain he is madly in love with me. I am getting daily calcium injections, supposedly to heal a spot on my lung. Trotski shakes like a leaf when it comes time to jab me. He has to get up and compose himself before administering the injection. Frankly, I'd be happier if, instead of all that shaking, he'd just offer a few rashers of bacon. It is hell to see the superb displays of all these plentiful foods in the shops—hams, sausages, pork and veal fillets, a plethora of cheeses and dozens of different breads and rolls, whole geese, chickens and ducks, sides of beef, cakes, tarts, flans. I should have lots of nourishment to help my recovery, but my parents are adamant: leave Edek, or starve. So, we starve.

DAVID

October

My new Wilno nanny tried to register me at the neighborhood school this morning, but the people at the office turned us away. "We live in the Soviet Union now," Nanny said. "It is not Poland any more, where nationalities are all mixed up in school." Here, I must go to the school of my nationality ("narodowsc"). This is a good way, Nanny said, because all the kids will speak the same languages and have the same holidays, and there will not be problems like the one I told her—in Religion class at Licee Francais de Varsovie. Mother was quite displeased when we told her. She sent Nanny to find a French school for me, but Nanny said there isn't such a school in Wilno.

October

Nanny and Mother brought me to the Jewish school. It is called YIVO School. We went to the principal's office ("kancelaria pana dyrektora"). Mother told the principal that I was "the best student in the best school in Warsaw," and, in a school such as YIVO, a boy like me must skip the second grade. I do not want to skip second grade, and I do not want to go to third grade. Mother said I am able to speak perfect German, French, and Polish. I am very embarrassed because this is not true. I am not the best student in my class, and my German is not perfect. An argument broke out, and Nanny and I were asked to wait outside in the corridor. Mother and the principal yelled, and I heard the principal tell Mother that all my German, French and Polish are completely useless ("nic nie warte") to me in Wilno, and here I will have to learn Yiddish and Russian like everyone else. I did not hear what Mother said next. But after a short time, Nanny and I were called back and were told that I will be in third grade. The homeroom teacher ("wychowawczyni") came and took me to class.

November 1

It is very difficult for me at YIVO School. The teachers are mean. The other children speak only Yiddish and Russian. I know a little of the Alef-Beis because Chinga taught me in Dabrowice, and Nanny tries to help me with my homework every night. But every lesson is in Yiddish—even Arithmetic and Religion! It is quite terrible, and I am the worst student in my class in every subject. No one likes me.

November 6

The third-grade teacher became very angry with me this morning. He took me by the hand and, without saying anything, led me out of the room to the second-grade class, and he left me there. It was in the middle of class. Then the bell rang, and I now I am a second grader. This was terribly embarrassing.

November 10

Second grade is much better than third grade! The teachers are not mean! The children don't speak German or French, but some of them speak Polish. I am no longer the worst student in the class. I play with the others at recess and I am learning Yiddish and Russian.

December

Jerzy and Wanda are in Wilno now. Jerzy and Uncle Kuba crossed the German and Soviet lines together. Jerzy says they walked the whole way! Wanda is here with her husband, Edek. My parents do not like Edek, and they will not let him visit our apartment. At first, Wanda refused to come see us unless Edek came with her. Then, after some days, she finally visited, but Edek did not come.

EARLY RESPONSES TO DISRUPTION: RECALIBRATING AND RECONSTITUTING:

Home is where we start from, Donald Winnicott famously wrote.[4] We think of it first as a physical location, but it is also a location in the mind. The origin point from which we measure the distances we have traveled, as Salman Akhtar observed,[5] it becomes the place from which we assess the direction that life has taken us. It is not surprising, then, that the memoirs here all start with reminiscences about home. We see that Marysia's home has exploded, its contents obliterated, and that she has turned around rapidly to find someplace new. We see that Nathan's home can no longer be accessed; he shifts it to the background of a distant tableau. We see the driveway outside the apartment Nina and David called home, a busy place where gasoline and suitcases are hurriedly prepared in the darkness, and we note the scene of a desperate family member knocking and pleading at the car window. We see that a story, even from its beginning, reveals clues about what matters most deeply to its storytellers in the end. From the start, these memoirs ring the first notes of their later themes: the finality of sudden loss, the irreversibility of choices made hastily, the merciless forward motion of time.

Fewer than four months into the war, each branch of the family has already experienced significant separations and losses. Minute differences of geography and timing mattered enormously, it is apparent, as their effects were magnified by luck and chance. A corner turned, a road blocked off, an hour out grocery shopping, a brief visit to neighbors—all these cascaded into significant bifurcations in the trajectory of options. We see that each family drew from the reservoir of its previous resources, and even relatively small initial differences in social capital had bearing on what came next. High-placed personal and professional connections, a big car rather than a small one, accessible pools of cash, and handy stockpiles of packaged food —the products of fungible wealth intersected with vicissitudes of age, gender, physical status, timing, and chance, opening certain doors of opportunity while closing others. We also note that in this early stage of the war, each family succeeded to some extent in recalibrating and reconstituting particular elements of its previous lifestyle. Access to money and social contacts enabled the families to cobble back together certain previous rituals and life routines. Wai Kai Hou and Stevan Hobfoll and others have referred to such routines as the sustaining "fabrics" of everyday life.[6]

Marysia, fresh from high school, faced a difficult choice: to join her parents and sisters behind the ghetto walls or to assume a false identity and remain in her boyfriend's orbit. Her situation epitomizes the unique vulnerability of adolescents, as it illustrates the coincidence of loss and displacement with key developmental transitions—important shifts in responsibility and new exploratory voyages into identity and group affiliation.[7] We can see that Marysia's decision, an eighteen year old's momentous opting for adulthood over childhood, is a choice rendered far more difficult and painful by its enormous cost of separation from her family. We might also note Marysia's description of the flower she has been given. Precisely as Marysia is most unsure what to think of herself, most in doubt about her decisions, the flower enters her narrative as a signal of found clarity—it is an anchoring, comforting message that she has become an attractive and desirable young woman, even after losing so many of her previous personal reference points. We also sense, if still vaguely, a theme that will appear in Marysia's later narrative: describing the flower frozen in a vase of urine, she shows us, indirectly, that good news will be matched with bad, optimism will be matched with an unwavering realism. Marysia thus welcomes us to her story with a cautionary note: it will not be sentimentalized.

Nathan's family hides together in a single room in a small farmhouse far from their home, but his parents do their best to provide continuity and routine, and we see how this is facilitated by the presence of other refugee families. Reconstituting a small community for themselves, the families pool their resources to hire a teacher for a secret school where their children can resume their studies. In hiding, Nathan even returns to piano lessons—and he remembers, decades later, exactly the symphonies he played in that brief period. When Nathan describes the family situation, he uses collective and inclusive terms—"we" instead of "I" or "they"—an indication, we sense, that even under conditions of upheaval, and perhaps because they are now living in such close quarters, the family has managed to retain its prewar role organization and also its emotional cohesiveness. Even in hiding, moreover, Nathan takes pride in learning new skills and in having responsibility for important family survival tasks. While defining in a broad sense the family's status as persecuted and endangered, their new living arrangement nonetheless also fosters in Nathan a sense of competence and agency, a feeling of contributing to the milieu in ways that are valued and uniquely his. In Nathan, we see how children's feelings of purposefulness might come to be nourished in small ways even in otherwise degrading circumstances.

Wanda and her husband, Edek, must flee a life they only barely started. Bricks piled on a Warsaw construction site are all that remains of Edek's long-range career plans, and Wanda's parents and youngest brother have fled. Abruptly cut off from the material comforts of her previous luxurious lifestyle, Wanda swallows a handful of diamonds she has purchased with money from her father. She complains bitterly about the digestive side effects, but we can see that this episode enables her to secure inside herself, quite literally, an object link to her prewar social status. She still has it in her! She finds great satisfaction, moreover, in a caustic and patronizing attitude, doled out liberally in her descriptions of Poles, Lithuanians and Soviets alike. Wanda's narrative shows us sarcasm forged into weaponry when no other weapons are available, as it enables small but delicious acts of symbolic revenge. Wanda's story also illuminates the developmental in-betweenness of the nineteen-year-old bride, her still-fresh sense of wanting to navigate between new allegiances and old ones.

Young children measure the danger and threat to themselves by gauging the reactions of those around them, especially adult caregivers, as much research has shown, and they are buoyed by the provision of consistency in scheduling and daily routines.[8] We see here that Nina and David both have been greatly buffered. Even during car chases, they sit in their mothers' laps and complain of being treated like "children," and during bombing raids they enact between themselves what seems to have been a familiar and perhaps somewhat comforting competition over adult attention and approval. By the time the new year opens, we find them resettled temporarily among many other refugees and enrolled in a new elementary school in a city that has not yet been pulled into the war. Their parents have reconstituted, more or less successfully, some prewar childcare and school arrangements. Able nannies exude confidence and optimism and treat the children as if they have much to say and contribute. Conventional understandings of development have emphasized monotropy as a basic component of attachment, the assumption that development of a secure base depends on a singular attachment created by dyadic relationships between a parent and a child. But researchers who study cultural differences in development have suggested that multiple, sequential, and distributed caregiving configurations can also produce functional bonds, and attachment might follow from more complex relational arrangements.[9] We encounter some indications here that patterns of this type might have been operative in the children's relationships with their nannies.

David can barely dress himself when the war begins, but in the early weeks, he learns he can try new things; he takes initiatives that enhance his emerging independence and build his life skills. With his parents distracted and tense, he investigates burned-out buildings, explores outhouses and carpentry shops and other new cultural artifacts, plays with previously inaccessible children in novel settings, and checks his maps as he tracks the family journey. Memorizing new place-names and picking up new vocabulary words, alert to unusual surroundings, David enjoys the grown-up feelings of industry and independence that learning brings, and he finds a sense of mastery in the activity of acquiring knowledge and detailed information. But we see, as well, that he practices what the Israeli psychoanalyst Shamai Davidson[10] called "awareness control." When a boy his age is shot almost within arm's length, David focuses his narrative not on the boy, but on the actions of his father, who has grabbed him out of the line of sight and flying bullets. We see that he diverts attention, in a sense, from disturbing information about his own risk and the reality of being hunted. Early in the story, when reporting the smell of a burning orphanage, David did not dwell on what was lost there, even though his nanny told him what it was. When he reported that a cousin was turned away from the car window on the morning of the escape from Warsaw, he registered from his mother's lap the tension this aroused in the group. But he did so without further comment on what it might mean. One wonders if it is the adult memoirist who has sanitized the story, expunged its dangerous emotional content, or if the adult writer has merely mirrored what the child in him once suppressed from conscious awareness. Even as he is vigilant and attentive to the milieu, we see, David manages to avoid a direct confrontation with certain kinds of knowledge. This interplay of attention and nonattention, awareness and dissociation, is well known in research on the internal management of traumatic experience. We will see this theme returning in subsequent chapters.

The writer Vamik Volkan used the term "linking objects" to describe how specific images or elements of a situation can be taken up in both healthy and unhealthy ways as focal points of later mourning and mourner self-representation.[11] We might note, along these lines, that each young person describes something in the first months of the war that acquired symbolic significance: a flower, a piano, a limousine, a handful of diamonds. These appear in the memoirs as tokens binding each writer to a severed lifeworld, even many decades later.

NOTES

1. Antony Polonsky, *The Jews in Poland and Russia: A Short History* (London: Littman Library of Jewish Civilization, 2013).

2. James Garbarino and Kathleen Kostelny, "What Do We Need to Know to Understand Children in War and Community Violence," in *Minefields in their Hearts: The Mental Health of Children in War and Community Violence*, eds. Roberta Apfel and Bennett Simon (New Haven, CT: Yale University Press, 1996), 33–51.

3. John Bowlby, *Attachment and Loss, Vol. 1: Attachment* (New York, NY: Basic Books, 1969); John Bowlby, *Attachment and Loss, Vol. 2: Separation: Anxiety and Anger* (New York, NY: Basic Books, 1973); Inge Bretherton and Kristine Mulholland, "Internal Working Models in Attachment Relationships: Elaborating a Central Construct in Attachment Theory," in *Handbook of Attachment Theory, Research, and Clinical Application*, eds. Jude Cassidy and Phillip Shaver (New York, NY: Guilford Press, 2008), 102–27.

4. Donald W. Winnicott, *Home is Where We Start From: Essays by a Psychoanalyst* (New York, NY: Norton & Co., 1990).

5. Akhtar, *Immigration and Identity*.

6. Hou, Hall, and Hobfoll, "Drive to Thrive."

7. Margaret Rustin, "Finding Out Where and Who One Is: The Special Complexity of Migration for Adolescents," in *Enduring Migration Through the Life Cycle*, eds. Arturo Varchevker and Eileen McGinley (London: Karnac, 2013), 39–60; Stevan Weine, Norma Ware, Leonce Hazikimana, Toni Tugenberg, Madeleine Currie, Gonwo Dahnweih, Maureen Wagner, Chloe Polutnik, and Jacqueline Wulu, "Fostering Resilience: Protective Agents, Resources, and Mechanisms for Adolescent Refugees' Psychosocial Well-Being," *Adolescent Psychiatry* 4, no. 4 (2014): 164–76.

8. Masten, "Resilience Theory."

9. Heidi Keller, "Attachment and Culture," *Journal of Cross-Cultural Psychology* 44 (2013): 175–96.

10. Israel Charny, ed., *Holding on to Humanity: The Message of Holocaust Survivors: The Shamai Davidson Papers* (New York, NY: New York University Press, 1992).

11. Vamik Volkan, "The Linking Objects of Pathological Mourners," *Archives of General Psychiatry* 27, no. 2 (1972): 215–21.

Chapter 2

1940

MARYSIA

March

It's too risky to look for a regular job. If I try to look for work as a domestic servant, people will immediately start asking questions. I can't take work in child care, because they'll want references and ask about my family. I've had false papers made, but still, I need to be careful. The hospitals are desperate for blood Type O, which is my blood type, as luck has it. So, every other week now, I visit the Blood Center on Kopernik Street. One transfusion covers my rent. The next covers the cost of food. Basically, I have re-invented myself as a perpetual motion machine: from the blood, I receive money. With the money, I buy food. With the food, I replenish my blood. This is working just fine for now.

June

Hitler's armies are gaining victory after victory. All day long, they broadcast news about their conquests: Belgium, Holland, Luxembourg, Denmark, Norway. Hitler personally reviewed a military parade under the Arc de Triomphe, in Paris. I have tried not to think about what will happen if we lose this war. It would be a death sentence for me, my family, and millions more. I have not seen my parents for more than half a year, and I am yearning deeply for them.

July

The simplest way to enter the ghetto is through the courthouse, which is nestled between two parallel streets—one on the ghetto side, the other on the Aryan side. Through a friend, I managed to get a court summons, which means I am supposed to appear as a witness for a case. It's fake. But it's enough to get me into the building and prove my right to be there in case anybody challenges me. I entered and sat in the waiting room for a while, and then, in the washroom, I put on the armband with the star of David. I waited a little while more, and then, as if it's perfectly normal, I walked out to the Jewish side and made my way to Śliska Street. The streets here are all well known to me, but they are hardly recognizable now—dense crowds of people rushing in all directions, skinny beggars in rags sitting on the sidewalks, leaning against the buildings, their eyes hollow from obvious malnutrition. Everyone seems to be frantically trying to sell something. A person next to me called out she has an iron for sale; another offered a spool of thread. There is an edgy desperation here. But I managed to find my parents. Somehow, in their presence, I feel safe, even in the ghetto. This feeling catches me by surprise. Another surprise: Mother had foods hidden in the cupboard that I haven't eaten for months. Father explained how this is possible: because he speaks perfect German, he was able to get a position with a work group that exits the ghetto every day under German supervision. They do construction jobs outside the walls, which gives them a chance to make contact with people on the Aryan side and smuggle food and other items through the checkpoints. It's a terrible risk, of course, but the men pay dearly: each week, Father said, they collect "gifts" so the German supervisor will "not notice" their activities. Father showed me a beautiful leather briefcase with a silver monogram—this week's soon to be "gift." My grandparents come to the apartment every Friday, and Mother sets aside food for them. At the end of this visit it is difficult for me to go. I cannot be sure if I will see my parents again.

August

Czesław took a job as a construction worker, and his mother has been selling off her valuables, so they're making a small amount of money. Even so, everyone is struggling; we are running out of food. On top of daily needs, I've got a debt hanging over me: after final exams at school last spring, some of the girls in my class convinced our parents to raise money for a scholarship fund. It was to help send one of our classmates to university—a really bright girl, from a working-class family, who otherwise wouldn't be able to afford it. She was simply outstanding—such great promise as a budding mathematician.

The scholarship was supposed to be a surprise—and I was put in charge of collecting and holding the money. But now the money is gone—destroyed in the bombing, along with my home. I really feel obligated to pay back all those people. Little by little, I've been putting away what I can, trying to build back the amount we had collected. I can't, in good conscience, pretend the donations never happened, especially now, when so many in Warsaw are struggling. I know it's the right thing to do, but it leaves me even less for my own expenses.

September

For the first time, I had a problem visiting my parents. A man stopped me on my way through the courthouse. An industry has grown along the edges of the ghetto—men who stop you and demand money by threatening to report Jews trying to live in disguise on the Aryan side. He must have been around thirty years old. He came up and whispered, "You are a Jewess." What a bastard! I pretended I had heard a joke, and I burst into laughter. "This is nothing to laugh at," he said. "It can cost you your life. Where are your documents?" Thankfully, I was carrying a "genuine" birth certificate and church baptism papers. On the basis of these, I had portraits made for my personal identification documents. "Oh sure, very genuine," he said sarcastically. And then he grabbed my arm hard. "Haven't you read Mein Kampf?" I yelled at him. "If you know anything at all, then you must know blood donors get their blood checked for Aryan purity! You saw my blood donor card! Don't you know what that means!?" I had no idea if I convinced him or scared him—or if he realized that a blood donor is not a likely source of any profit. Either way, he let me go. It was a close call.

NATHAN

July

When my parents and the others had to leave Wieliczka and go to Krakow, Father arranged for me to be hidden. The farmer got a shovel. I watched him dig a hole in a corner of the barn, along the edge of the foundation—just big enough for me if I crouched. He covered the hole with a wooden plank and threw straw on the top, leaving me a space for air. He dropped food into the hole for me. Several times, I heard the sound of barking dogs and yelling, but no one came to look inside the barn. The farmer told me Germans were searching the farms, hunting for Jews in hiding.

August

A few weeks passed, and then the farmer said I must go. It was no longer safe for his family, he said. He gave me some bread for my knapsack, and he explained what I must do in order to reach my family. I hid in the woods during the day, as he told me. At night, when it was very dark, I walked along the train tracks, just like he said. As he told me, I pretended to be one of the poor peasant boys collecting coal pieces fallen from the trains. He said I am lucky to be blonde with blue eyes. I can disguise myself. The train tracks lead to Krakow.

DAVID

January

Nanny took me to see a parade. There were cannons and a tank pulled by horses, and soldiers marching. Later that day, some men came and attacked the Jewish homes and storefronts. Nanny took me to the main street to look. I saw broken windows and a few of the store owners being beaten up in the street. Nanny said there was blood on the street in one place, and she showed it to me. I told Nanny I have seen much bigger pogroms than this.

February

Our British certificates for Palestine have arrived. Mother said we will visit Palestine and wait there until the war ends and it is safe for us to return to Warsaw. The certificate has a crown on it, and a lion and another animal with a horn coming out of its forehead. We are lucky to have it, Father said, as such papers are given only to people who own property in Palestine. Our property is a farm. It is called Meshek Fetter. Father said he bought it for me on the day I was born, as a birthday present, in 1932. It cost $350,000 American dollars. That little farm has turned out to be far more valuable to us than we ever expected, Father said. Most of the other Jews are stuck here in Wilno. They want to leave, just like us, Father said, but no one is taking them.

February

Mother and Father and I took the train to Kaunas. We are in a group of twenty-eight people. Father says all of us are going to Palestine together to wait there for the war to end. In Kaunas, we met Aunt Jula and Nina. They were standing in line around the Japanese consulate. Father said they do not have Palestine permits. We said goodbye to them and boarded another train. We are headed for Riga, Latvia.

When we got to the Riga airport, we boarded a plane headed to Stockholm. The plane was very crowded with people like us, who are trying to leave. There was lots of luggage. Mother sat near a window toward the back. I sat next to her at the aisle. "Fasten your seatbelts," everyone said, "because we will pass through a heavy snowstorm." Mother said she will not do it. Seat belts make it hard to run away, she said. Instead of a seat belt, she covered her head with a heavy wool blanket. Father was quite annoyed about this. He has flown on many airplanes. He told me angrily that I am to ignore Mother and fasten my seat belt tightly. I found a way to obey Father and also Mother: I fastened my seat belt but left it very loose. I am not afraid of planes. I have seen many of them quite close up!

The plane started with a big roar in a white cloud of snow and wind, and finally, we could feel it lift. Through the windows we saw nothing except white snow. We could feel the plane shaking and tipping from side to side, and we heard the roar of the engines, first loud, then quieter, then loud again. But then there was a sudden thud, and the plane shook violently. Someone said in Polish "uderzylismy srup telefonicznyf" ("we hit a telephone pole"). The plane climbed upward for a short time, maybe a minute or two, and then fell hard to the left, spiraling down. When it stopped, I was on the floor, but still partly held back by my seat belt. There was a soft hissing sound, and the cabin seemed to be filled with a white fog. I heard someone moaning but couldn't see who it was. Mother was not in her seat. We were on a steep angle, as the plane seemed to have landed nose down. I looked out the window. I saw many broken pieces of wood and part of a wood building, maybe a barn. Many large pigs were standing around among the broken pieces, and there was mud everywhere. Some of the pigs were wandering, some limping, and some bleeding. A wing of the plane was there, too, broken into pieces in the snow and mud. I touched my face and felt that my upper lip had a hole in it, but it did not hurt very much. My clothes have blood everywhere, but I am fine.

Through the fog, Mother screamed from the front of the plane: "Gdzie mohe dzieci?" (where are my children?). No one answered, but then I heard Father's voice, annoyed, telling her to get up. "No juz nice si`nice stato!" he said ("well, then, nothing has happened!"). Someone opened the door near the back of the plane, and I walked up the steep incline to look outside. I was very high in the air, and someone called out to me that I mustn't jump, because below us there are many sharp pieces. Soon Jerzy came, followed by Father, who was leading Mother. Mother's eye was all red and her nose and face were covered in blood. She held tight to the blanket. Soon a pickup truck came, and some men in the truck told us to jump out of the open door. I jumped, and the men from the pickup caught me and sat me in the back of the truck. Several other pickup trucks came. Then I heard Father speaking to one of the drivers in Russian, and an argument broke out. Mother, who does not speak Russian, asked what is this about. Father said he had left a brand new hat on the plane and wanted the pickup truck driver to help him climb back to get it. It was a brand new hat, and a nice hat, and Father had just bought in Kaunas before we left. Mother told him to forget it, and then the pickup driver returned us to Riga airport, where we were bandaged up and put into ambulances.

Mother stayed with me in the back of the ambulance. There were four of us: me, Mother, a rabbi, and the rabbi's wife. The rabbi's wife moaned badly, and she died in the ambulance. The only other person with us was the driver, who turned on the siren as we headed toward the hospital.

They gave us new bandages at the hospital, and then we went back to our hotel. Father said we would not be returning to the airport for the free meals offered to all the passengers. We will stay and not speak to anyone, and then we will board another plane to Stockholm tomorrow. I cried and yelled at Father terribly when I heard this. I do not want to go back "do paszczy lwa" ("into the lion's mouth")! Some cleaning ladies at the hotel saw me crying and were very nice to me. They told me in Polish that planes do not usually crash and everything will be better when we fly tomorrow. I do not want to go on another plane. I have been demanding to be taken back to Wilno. Neither Father nor Mother is paying attention to me.

In the bus to the airport this morning, many people were reading a Russian newspaper with a big picture on the front page of the broken left wing of our plane. Father spoke to a man in Russian and asked to borrow the paper. He looked quickly and whispered to Mother that our names are listed. I was listed as "severely injured"! Mother turned to the man and pointed to the paper. "My pasaghiry" ("we were the passengers"), she said. Everyone on the bus stared at us, and Father was extremely angry with her. I begged Father to buy me a newspaper so I can remember our plane crash. Father said no. I asked many times. If someone sees us with the newspaper, Father said, they might know who we are. No paper!

Late February

We stayed in Stockholm for several days. My face had many bandages, and so did Mother's. The number in our group is down to twenty-six, because the rabbi's wife died. The rabbi will stay behind in Riga. Everyone in our group went sightseeing together. We had a lot of fun. Then we all boarded a train to Malmo. From Malmo, we got on a plane and flew to Amsterdam. Father says Holland is not in the war. We are staying at the American Hotel. It is very nice here. Father says it is safest for Jews to be in the expensive hotels. Everyone in our group has papers to go to Palestine, but first we need to go to a few other places.

March

After four days in Amsterdam, we boarded another train. We traveled through Belgium and France. Now, finally, we have arrived in Trieste, in Italy. From here, we are to board a ship bound for Haifa. We are staying at another very nice hotel, the Embargo Della Cita. The other members of our group left on a small passenger ship. Mother and Father took me to the port to say goodbye to the others, but Mother did not want to go on that small ship. She said it would make her seasick. She told Father she would like a bigger ship. Besides, Mother is in love with Italy! We have taken a trip to Venice, and I saw the Lido. Mother and Father say that Italy is very beautiful and that a large ship, the Italian passenger liner "Marco Polo," is scheduled to sail from Trieste to Haifa in two or three weeks. We will take that one. In the evenings, Father and Jerzy play bridge with the other men at the hotel, and Mother sits in the lobby and talks to the other women. There is no nanny for me, so I am permitted to wander around. There are machines to buy chocolates, which are quite good, and Father has given me money for this. I see other people here like us, from Poland, who are waiting to go to Haifa with the Marco Polo.

March

This evening, many people came to sit in the hotel lobby. Some wore soldiers' uniforms. They saw me wandering around near the candy machines, and they called to me, and I sat with them. They asked me many questions, all in German. They asked my name, my school, my grades, and the languages I speak. They asked about my family. I told them about Nanny Tita, and YIVO School, and how quickly I had learned Yiddish and Russian, since I am a good student, but that I was not a good student at first, when I was in the third grade. They laughed and laughed at my stories, and it was a lot of fun. Mother and Father did not see me. Right after that, another group in the lobby called me. These were the other Jews waiting for the Marco Polo. They spoke to me in Polish. They asked if I know who those men were. I said yes, of course I know! They told me they are Germans and Italians, and we had a nice conversation and laughed a lot. The people told me I had spoken with a man named Count Ciano. They said he is the Italian foreign minister. I do not know what this means at all. I asked Jerzy, who is almost eighteen now. Jerzy said yes, it is Count Ciano. He said I am a good boy and behaved myself very nicely in the lobby, and I should not pay attention to the Jews waiting for the ship.

Late March

The Adriatic Sea was terribly stormy, but the Mediterranean is even worse! Mother and I have been throwing up. There is nothing left in my stomach at all, and we are just staying in our room. Father and Jerzy have gone to play bridge in the club room upstairs. I asked Mother what is going to happen to us. She said the ship is certainly going to sink. I went upstairs to tell Father and Jerzy to go to the lifeboat. They were busy with the bridge game and laughed at me. Father said I will feel better if I take a walk on deck. I did not feel better. But I saw an island. I think it is Crete. Such a long way to go!

April 4

From the ship's deck, we could see people waiting for us at the port of Haifa. Father could see his parents on the dock. They were dressed all in white. They were very happy to see us. Father spoke to them in Yiddish. "Baruch Ha-Shem," my grandmother said. I asked her why they were wearing all white clothes. "It is because you are alive," she said.

WANDA

March

My parents have left—they are on their way to Palestine—and Edek and I moved into the apartment they vacated. But now the Russians have marched back into Wilno. They came during the night; we heard them. The very next morning, all the shops were bare. Not a scrap of food to be had. Not much wood or coal for heating, either, as these are now going to be allocated only to those who are working for the Russian cause. I have an exemption signed by Dr. Trotski, of course, because of my health. Edek got together with about ten other chemists, and they have organized a Cooperative of Chemical Engineers to produce synthetic honey for the Russians. It is quite unpalatable, but good enough for the Russian army. The Engineers Coop makes soap that doesn't lather, but the Russians never had any other kind. And they make face powder from white flour for shipment to the Moscow ladies. One day, Edek came home laughing his head off: they had just gotten a government order for one gross ton of this powder stuff, an order they couldn't fill in a hundred years. They've invented lipstick that doesn't work and pens that don't write. But all this makes them infinitely better off than the numerous unemployed Jewish attorneys here in Wilno who can only offer their services as street cleaners and snow plowers.

April

Edek's younger sister, Nina, married a young Lithuanian, Mukla, whose parents own a farm near Wilno. I have spent the past few months with them, recuperating in the country air, drinking gallons of rich, fresh cream—it's all helped my lungs heal. I have a comfortable room, I take long walks in the forest and pick large quantities of wild mushrooms. The sun filters through deep shade, making patches of light on the fallen ancient tree trunks. I have attended my first Seder.

May 1

The Russians marched through the street, proud under their May Day banners. The soldiers' boots are held together with bits of string, and some have no boots at all—just newspaper tied around their feet. No wonder, we said to ourselves, that such a ragged army would sign a peace treaty with Germany. They'd have no chance against the well-supplied, well-dressed, and disciplined Nazis. Edek and the Coop of Chemical Engineers marched in the parade. I stood on the pavement with the other parasites and cheered when they passed by. We saw some well-known Polish actors, singers, and musicians, noted for their rightist views.

1940

The Russians are worried about subversive elements on their vulnerable borders. They have announced that those of us who are foreigners here in Wilno, including all the Polish refugees, will be allowed to leave if we can find somewhere to go. Our passports have no validity, of course, since Poland doesn't even exist anymore, and, anyway, there's no Polish embassy or consulate where we might apply. But our plan is to apply for certificates from the British consulate in Kaunas.

I have lost count of the number of times I have traveled to Kaunas to apply for British certificates. So far, no luck. The Dutch consul, Jan Zwartendijk, announced that temporary visas for two colonies, Suriname and Curacao, will be granted to everyone who has a Russian exit visa. Thousands of refugees are traveling to Kaunas to try to get these stamps, which will enable us to pass through either or both colonies. But how will we get there? The Japanese consul has started issuing visas so we can pass through Japanese territory. We need all these papers stamped with an exit visa by the Russian authorities.

According to Edek, our most valuable possession is the doctor's note certifying that I have incipient tuberculosis. Armed with this, trembling, I entered the lion's den, headquarters of the NKVD. Edek stayed outside, as he insisted that a young woman on her own would have a better chance, unaccompanied by a burly man. So I gave him my handbag and went in.

The officials in the entry hall directed me to Room 76, on the second floor, and they had stopwatches to time my visit. I knocked at the door, but there was no reply. I knocked again. My heart was pounding. In a panic, I ran along the corridor until I came to a room with an open door. The men inside burst out laughing as I explained in broken Russian that I had tried Room 76. Evidently, it was a trap: they had been sending people to an unattended room in an attempt to catch spies who might try to enter and steal information from the Motherland. Now, I was directed to Room 90, where, to my relief, the official was not Russian, but rather a Lithuanian communist. He stamped my certificate but refused to stamp Edek's. I burst out crying, wiping my nose on my sleeve. Fine, he said, he'd consider the application if Edek applies in person. I had a brainwave: I proudly said that my husband is working his fingers to the bone with the Cooperative of Chemical Engineers, for the benefit of the Soviet Socialist Republics. Not only did I get a second visa, but he actually accompanied me to the correct staircase leading to the correct exit. Of course I was timed and searched, but I emerged over the moon, ready to fall into Edek's waiting arms. I found him sitting in a nearby cafe, reading a book, a small black coffee on the table in front of him.

My father decided to try getting me an entry certificate to Palestine. My mother convinced him that I wouldn't come without Edek, so in spite of his better judgment, he sent us enough, about $1000, through a private transfer. It is an enormous amount of money. I traveled to Kaunas by myself, by two-horse carriage, to get to the Russian Intourist office at the railway station. The Russians need foreign currency. I bought two first-class train tickets from Wilno to Moscow, vouchers for a tourist hotel in Moscow, and additional tickets for a first-class cabin on a Russian ship across the Black Sea from Odessa to Istanbul. Edek was angry, thinking I had wasted the money because I bought first-class tickets. He has no idea that is all we are allowed to purchase.

NINA

January

We have been living in Wilno. Cousin Stasio (David) and his parents are here as well, of course, since they traveled with Mother and me in Uncle Wladek's big car. Father arrived with cousin Jerzy, and Wanda and her husband are here now, too. Everyone has run away from the Germans. Mother and Father and I have a nice three-bedroom apartment. A lot of the Szeskins are here. Mother's mother, my Granny Sofia, is here in Wilno, and so are my Aunt Zenia and Uncle Bronek and their daughters, my cousins Irka and Janka.

April

We receive only bad news from Warsaw. More Warsaw Jews arrive here every day. They bring terrifying stories of what the Germans are doing. Mother and Father say the Germans are advancing. They want to control all of Europe. Here in Wilno, everyone is happy that it is quiet and peaceful. I am attending school. I have many friends. We play in the neighborhood and around the house.

June

The Soviets are here. Uncle Miron was taken to jail. Soviet soldiers have come to our apartment several times. They knock at the door in the middle of the night. Father and Mother are getting very worried. They say the Soviets are trying to catch the "capitalists." We feel we are being watched carefully. We are eager to leave here. Mother and Father keep trying to find a way to leave. At school, we are being asked a lot of questions. A man came to my class and asked if Father and Mother ever say bad things about the Soviet Union. They want me to tell things that Mother and Father discuss. I do not tell them anything! Father has warned me not to tell anyone about what happens in our house, or who lives there. I must not tell any news that I have heard about. Father says we must be very careful around the Russians.

My picture appeared in the newspaper! I look nice, and I am smiling. The headline says: "Warmed by Stalin's smile, our children are happy." Mother and Father were quite upset by this. They say the Russians are using pictures like this to tell untrue things. They want everyone to believe we have welcomed them here. But we have not! We are searching and searching for ways to leave Wilno. Mother and Father have been visiting many embassies.

We keep searching for ways to leave Wilno, but no one is accepting us. Mother and Father have spent many weeks trying to get visas. They are constantly traveling back and forth to the embassies. They tried asking for permits to enter the United States. They also tried some countries in South America. Everyone is turning us away. Father says the Russians have closed some of the embassies. That makes it even harder to try to leave here. We would like to go to the Land of Israel, but the British are not allowing it. I can see that Mother and Father are getting worried, even though they are not telling me. On the train, Mother met a young man—a student from the Mir Yeshiva. He said he was on his way to the Japanese consul. He heard a rumor that it might be possible to get a special "transit" visa through Japan. The only problem is: to get a transit visa, you need to have a permit to enter a final destination.

Good news! Mother and Father went to the Consul of the Netherlands. The man in the office gave them a document that says we can go to Curacao! That's owned by the Netherlands. Curacao does not require any special permits.

THE CRISIS DEEPENS

Just over a year into the war, chasms have formed from what started as relatively small differences among the families. The Germans issue an order for Jews in the Krakow region to be confined inside the ghetto. Now alone, Nathan is buried in a hole in the ground that a farmer has dug for him under a barn in the town of Wieliczka. From his brief description of it, we see that Nathan understands this as a reflection of his father's wishes. He has assigned it meanings connected with love and protection rather than with abandonment or terror. This conceptualization sustains the now thirteen-year-old boy, as it calls to his mind the abiding presence of his loving father, even in the pit of darkness as dogs bark outside. Illustrated in this aspect of Nathan's story is what a great many writers have observed in clinical research on resilience mechanisms in development: that children can take in and hold inside themselves the images of loving protective figures, building from these internal configurations a framework for responding under conditions of adversity.[1] Nathan has been remarkably well equipped, we see, to sense continuity in a secure base of love and care, even when his outward circumstances are descending into bleak irrationality.

As the Germans step up surveillance, conditions change on the farm. The farmer feels unsafe in harboring a Jew. Nathan is removed from the hole and sent to walk along train tracks toward Krakow. We recognize in this shift what historians have noted about the actions of many Poles during the war—ambiguous and sometimes contradictory, reflecting very complex and evolving practical and social circumstances, and reducible ultimately neither to heroism nor complicity.[2] We can only imagine, years later, whether that farmer lived long enough to wonder about his choice.

Nina remains in Wilno, but Soviet occupying troops announce they will rid the city of Jewish capitalists—a statement Nina understands to be related in some way to her own situation. She reports the evidence of her parents' growing unease as they fail in repeated attempts to secure immigration permits to the United States or other havens in the West. Monitoring carefully the shifts in their demeanor, Nina senses the rising desperation. Up to this point, her parents have been able to reconstitute family routines and recreate, in a new setting, a feeling of stability and safety. Now, however, as much of the world has closed its doors to Jews and more bad news arrives in Wilno, Nina senses that their capacity is diminishing. Children of Nina's age, Erik Erikson theorized, develop new awareness of how others regard them; they consider the differences between fair and unfair appraisals, reasonable and unreasonable judgments.[3] The message Nina now receives is a painful one that cannot be easily denied—she and her parents are despised. But she derives comfort, in this context, in realizing that even she, a schoolgirl, can wield some small measure of power: we see that she takes great pride in withholding information from the Russians who intrude into her classroom. Even when they are only six or seven years old, we see here, children seek to exert influence. Assertions of efficacy and capacity bind them to family and community, serving as antidotes to helplessness and anchoring them in positive self-representations against a backdrop of rejection and persecution.

Marysia, now hungry, lonely, and yearning for her family, finds she can sell her blood for money. She imagines herself as kind of a "perpetual motion machine." To be in perpetual motion, of course, is to be undeniably alive, as only the dead are perfectly still. Against what was perhaps a rising awareness of danger and the increasing possibility of annihilation, we can speculate, a very concrete image of perpetuity might have served Marysia as a form of reassurance—a reminder she can just keep herself moving. In Marysia's story, we see that imaginative capacity is itself a powerful resource, as the psychoanalysts Bennett Simon and Roberta Apfel have written.[4] As Marysia finds creative means of meeting her daily practical needs and telling herself a story of survival and perpetuity, her confidence also builds, and this enables her to begin, slowly at first, to cultivate a capacity for subterfuge. She devises a clever way to enter the ghetto to visit her parents, and she finds, even there, that transgression feels gratifying and affirming.

Prospects for Wanda and her husband are bolstered by his training as a chemist. He takes a job working for the Soviet occupying forces in Wilno. For Wanda, the benefit isn't merely financial. She gloats over her husband's plans to cheat the authorities who humiliate and endanger them. We see her gravitating in this, once again, to those well-worn weapons of the weak: acts of sarcasm and petty retaliation. Several writers have suggested that resources in war and disaster tend to function like "caravans"—one form of access attaching itself and enabling the next, and so on, so that important survival tools take an aggregated form.[5] This appears to be the pattern for Wanda. An infusion of money from her father enables the purchase of tickets to Istanbul, which will become a gateway to safer settings. International communications and financial systems continue to function in certain ways despite the war's expanding chaos, providing a channel for this resource transfer—a clear example of how relative stability in higher-level transnational institutional structures can frame local-level experience and prospects.

David learns that a parcel of land in Palestine is the "ticket" that enables his family to purchase its safety in the form of British transit permits denied to other families. The land was a gift for his birthday, which seems to indicate that his very entry into the world is implicated in the family's privileged status among the community of desperate Wilno refugees. School-age children can imagine themselves responsible in some respects when they hear about broader social problems, research suggests,[6] and David's narrative from this period holds clues to a vague emerging awareness of the impacts of privilege on differential life outcomes. When David leaves Nina and her parents to an unknown fate, it is a separation so strange and inexplicable that he glosses it in barely a sentence. Years will pass before he appreciates the magnitude of what is about to happen to the Jews of Wilno and can bring himself to articulate his feelings about it.

After an airplane crash-lands nose down in a pig sty, David watches a fellow passenger die in an ambulance. But we see in his telling the rapid shift in perspective—the familiar quick turn from awareness of the proximity of death. David quickly shifts the story to the excitement of his family's multiweek journey through Sweden and across Holland, Belgium, France, and Italy. With money in his pocket, wandering among candy machines in the lobby of a posh Italian hotel, he meets enemy military leaders who engage him in pleasant conversation. He sees that the enemy turns out to be friendly: it is a brief and unnerving glimpse of the duplicity of the adult world, a signal that appearances are deceiving. By early April, David's family arrives in Palestine. His grandparents, white-clad figures on a crowded dock, do not know yet that of their eight children, only one will survive the war.

NOTES

1. Michael Rutter, "Protective Factors in Children's Response to Stress and Disadvantage," in *Primary Prevention of Psychopathology, Vol. 3, Social Competence in Children*, eds. Martha Whalen Kent and Jon E. Rolf (Hanover, New Hampshire: University Press of New England, 1979), 49–74; Michael Rutter, "Psychosocial Resilience and Protective Mechanisms," *American Journal of Orthopsychiatry* 57 (1987): 316–331; Stroufe, "The Place of Attachment in Development"; Dante Cicchetti, "Resilience Under Conditions of Extreme Stress: A Multimethod Perspective," *World Psychiatry* 9, no. 1 (2010): 145–54; Dan Bar-On, Jeanette

Eland, Rolf Kleber, Robert Krell, Yael Moore, Abraham Sagi, Erin Soriano, Peter Suedfeld, Peter van der Velden, and Marinus van Ijzendoorn, "Multigenerational Perspectives on Coping with the Holocaust Experience: An Attachment Perspective for Understanding the Developmental Sequelae of Trauma Across Generations," *International Journal of Behavioral Development* 22 (1988): 315–38; Garbarino et al., *Children in Danger*.

2. Timothy Snyder, *Black Earth: The Holocaust as History and Warning* (New York, NY: Tim Dugan Books, 2015).

3. Erikson, *Childhood and Society*.

4. Simon and Apfel, *Minefields in their Hearts*.

5. Hobfall, "Resource Caravans," 21–332.

6. Ahearn and Athey, *Refugee Children*.

Chapter 3

1941

MARYSIA

January

The sidewalks of the ghetto are filling with bone-thin children, barely more than skeletons, naked and barefoot. By now, when I visit, I see that most people don't even pay attention to them. Newcomers are still arriving in the ghetto. They stand amid the freezing bodies with their few pitiful possessions in wheelbarrows, trying to figure out what to do next. The Germans have been scouring the city, hunting for Jews in hiding and for resistance activists. They are shooting people on the spot. Survival at this point seems like an accident of luck. I have been lucky.

Czesław and I dreamed of finding a room where we could spend time together privately, and I finally found something. It's a little room attached to an attic, but it has its own entrance. The landlords, an older couple, took an instant liking to me because I am young and cheerful, and it hasn't even occurred to them to associate me with Jews. The little room is easy to heat. It has a window, a stove, a bed, and a shelf, and I can use the attic as a closet. It even seems safe. Czesław and I are discovering each other in a feverish hurry. But we hear more and more every day about executions, deportations, and forced labor camps in Germany. Last week, the father of one of my schoolmates left his apartment just for a moment to buy cigarettes—and didn't come back. The next day, they saw his name posted on the execution list. From my window, I have a view of a section of the ghetto wall. Every once in a while, I see a child clambering over to this side, or maybe being tossed. These poor lost children! They wander into doorways, completely confused. My landlord's heart breaks when they show up here. His wife hands them bits of food and hurries them away. Everyone is terrified, as the Germans have ordered the death penalty for anyone caught helping escapees. We are not the only ones under threat now. I have been reading more and more in the Underground newspapers about the partisans hiding in the forest. Many of my school friends have enlisted in the Home Army and in other branches of the growing resistance movement.

One of my former schoolteachers has been active in the command of the Home Army. Visiting her, I was eager for a first assignment, and I expected to return with orders. But I was wrong: the Home Army is suspicious of Jewish volunteers, as there's a belief that Jewish communists may be collaborating with the Soviets occupying the eastern territories. Even a former teacher's best recommendations, I am warned, might not suffice to prove my loyalty. I was shocked to be turned away. Don't they need all the help that's available? I will join the partisans. Czesław has some university friends in this group; they understand who I am.

I have been worrying about my father—his entire life dependent on the business of bribery to a German overseer. I searched around the city until I finally found the construction site he told me about (the workmen's armbands gave it away), and I crossed past the fencing. I had a back-up plan. If I meet the German supervisor, I would tell him I'm lost, looking for an address, and I'll give the number of the building next door. But the German was not around. Someone called out to my father, and after a few moments, we were together. Father was extremely pleased to see me. I could see in his face that he was proud of me for my courage. I saw the love and pride in his eyes. It is wonderful to be with him. He insists that his situation is safe, under the circumstances. The German supervisor, he said, had been a barber before the war, and he is a decent man. I was skeptical, but Father said "not every German is a criminal." I agreed, but we have learned the hard way this very important lesson: you can lose your life sorting out who is who.

I've been visiting Father regularly at the construction site. We have a signal: I arrive each week at the same time, on the same day. If he is standing at a particular spot in front, I know it is safe to approach. If he is not at that spot, I know the German is near, and I move on without stopping. This arrangement is much less risky for me than trying to enter the ghetto through the courthouse.

1941

NATHAN

November

More people kept coming into the ghetto. The Germans pushed us into a smaller and smaller space. It got so crowded, we could barely move. Finally, we had to separate because there were just too many of us in the room. Mother went with the other women to a different apartment, and Father and I stayed with the men. Father are I were inseparable. He kept me in sight all the time. He was very protective of me.

The Germans organized us into work crews. Father said it is good to get in a work crew, because the Germans won't kill us as long as they need our labor. They want brass and copper. Father and I were assigned to a crew that was collecting scrap metal. We scavenged for pieces around the city. They gathered us in the morning. The guards came with their guns pointed on us and their dogs at their sides. Father made sure I walked close behind him. He pointed out the pieces of metal for me so it would look like I am one of the best workers. Father said this will keep me safe. Mother and Father saw that the Germans were taking away all the younger children, so we added two years when we registered my birth date. It was a lie, and I didn't look old, but it didn't matter, so long as I could work.

Father and I went down into the sewer with our crew. In the dark, we got separated from each other. I walked alone for a while, and then he found me. But when we returned to the ghetto, we saw that most of the women were gone. We looked for Mother, but she was nowhere to be found. One of our neighbors later told us that he saw what happened: the Germans went from apartment to apartment, grabbing the women. Mother hid under a wash basin. She didn't make a sound, our neighbor said. But when she poked her head up just a little—just for a minute, to see if the Germans were gone—one of them saw her and dragged her down into the street.

NINA

January

The Japanese consul in Kaunas is run by a very nice man named Sugihara. Mother and Father say he is a good man, and he is helping us. He gave us a visa. That means we will be able to travel through Japan on our way to Curacao. Mother and Father said Mr. Sugihara is disobeying his own country's rules. But he is acting bravely because he knows we are in danger here.

Now we have all our permits! Thanks to Mr. Sugihara and to Curacao! We are all set to go! Father stopped at the government travel agent's and bought three train tickets. He paid in American dollars. Father says the Soviets want American dollars, even though American money is supposed to be illegal here. Our tickets cost $200 each. Father says we are lucky to have this money.

February

The train is full of people. Goodbye, Wilno! We are on our way to Japan! Moscow will be our first stop.

In Moscow, we stayed in a big hotel. It was very nice. We visited Mother's aunt, Mrs. Epstein, who teaches music in a conservatory. I met my great uncle and my cousins and some others. The youngest cousin, about my age, was sick during our visit. He had a fever and a rash on his face, and he was not very pleasant. I was disappointed because, at the end of our visit, Mrs. Epstein asked Mother not to visit her again. She said we will get the family in trouble with the authorities.

What a very, very long train ride! It takes almost two weeks to go from Moscow to Vladivostok! So far, we have spent more than ten days on this train. We are riding a train called the Trans-Siberian Railway. We still have a long way to go! When I look out the windows, it is all white snow as far as I can see, except for small clusters of trees that appear every once in a while. The train crew treats us like we are tourists, so our meals are good, and we have plenty to eat. At night, I am not very comfortable. We are using our seat benches as beds. We fold our blankets to make little mattresses. Students from the Mir and Chabad Yeshivas are traveling in the train cars ahead of us. The train makes a lot of stops. At every station, Father and Mother and I get off to stretch our legs and look around. All the stations are small, with signs offering "Kipiatok" for sale. That's boiling water—the only item you can buy here! Last night, some ragged men approached the window at a train stop. Mother and Father spoke to them. They told us they are Jews. Father said they are political prisoners. They are in a place called a Siberian labor camp. They were very hungry, and we gave them some of our food.

Finally, we reached Vladivostok. After such a long ride, everyone was very excited to be leaving Russia. The grownups had all their coat pockets and parcels searched by border agents. I was not feeling well at all. Mother said I was beginning to run a fever. From the Vladivostok train station, we crossed to the port area. There were Japanese sailors all around, and they watched us closely when we boarded our ship. Our ship's name is Amakusa Maru. We are on our way to the port of Tsuruga. It was funny to see the grownups look for places to sleep on the ship. The inside of the deck is lined with a giant mat that has large rectangle shapes. Mother and Father said each rectangle marks the space for a person to sleep. But some of the adults—my parents, too—can't fit themselves in the rectangles. I managed myself quite well!

Last night, there was a terrible storm. It was very frightening. The grownups are saying I am seasick. But I know that is not true.

Today we finally arrived. Everyone was exhausted. First the twelve-day train ride. Then the storm at sea! It has been quite a difficult journey! We were taken out for an inspection. Mother and Father worried very much about a quarantine. They feared someone might notice that I have red spots all over my face! Mother says I have measles, but we are not telling anyone.

We arrived in Tsuruga and then went on to Kobe. We registered in a nice hotel. The bed is so soft and luxurious! I am extremely happy to be here. A doctor was called to see me.

Today we moved to a new hotel, and I am feeling much better. The new hotel is in a Japanese style—with a beautiful rock garden. I can look at the rocks. Our rooms are separated by rice paper screens and doors that can slide. I have never seen a rock garden or a sliding door! Mother and Father say there are Jewish organizations working here. They are helping us.

March

I started a new school in Kobe. I am in the first grade. My school is called Saint Marie's. Mother says it is a Catholic school. It is run by nuns who wear long cloth hats. We stand up for prayers every morning, but Mother and Father asked that I be excused from crossing myself. A few of my classmates are also Jewish. They also have been given permission to not cross themselves. We feel a little left out because of not crossing ourselves. We do not want to seem different from the others. My favorite class is Spelling. We sing out the longest words by syllables. Spectacles is a word I especially love—"es pee ee cee (spec) tee aye (ta) cee el ee es (cles)!" We are happy to be here, but Mother and Father continue to try applying for visas to enter the United States. They have gone back and forth several times to the US embassy in Tokyo. Each time, they are sent away. We are being told "the Polish quota is full." I like Kobe very much. The mountains all around us are very beautiful! The mountain tops are all covered with snow, and I can see them on my way to school. The children at school are all friendly. Already I am making new friends! Everyone here speaks English.

August

After almost six months in Kobe, we are moving again. Today, Father and Mother and I boarded another ship. Now we are headed for Shanghai. There are many Jews on the ship with us. I don't know what Shanghai will be like.

September

Mother and Father say there are 2,000 other Poles here in Shanghai—just like us. Everyone is a family running away from the war. We have a nice apartment on 925 Avenue Joffre. It is in a neighborhood called the French Concession. We are happy and comfortable here. Mother and Father have many friends. People come for dinner and parties. Mother takes me to the park, and Father joins us and we all take walks around the city. We are not afraid at all! Father has found a job in a trading and export company. It is owned by Russian immigrants. Father says there are Jews whose parents moved here many years ago, around the time when he was still a boy.

December 9

Everyone is talking about Pearl Harbor. The adults are saying the Japanese attacked. Things feel very different here now—so different from just a few days ago. The adults are tense and worried. Mother and Father explained that Shanghai is occupied by Japan. No one knows what will happen to us now.

WANDA

January

We took a horse-drawn carriage to the Wilno station for the journey to Moscow. Edek's sister Nina and I cried when we parted, and we waved from the window until we could no longer see each other. Who knows when I will see her again? Edek and I are on a first-class coach. We can see that the rest of the train is very crowded, and guards are posted in every car. At the door of the coach is an enormous samovar with boiling water. It appears that all the service workers on this train are women, but some of the passengers look like snowmen—bundled in their babushkas, long skirts, and felt boots.

    We arrived in Kiev in the evening and walked through heavy snow to an enormous waiting hall to wait for the next departure. It was very crowded, children running around everywhere, and people sleeping on the benches and floors. Edek bought some pretzels and beer, the only food available. The corks here are made of rubber. This is the first time I have seen such a thing.

All night, through the parted curtain at the window of my bunk, I watched the snowy plains. The train made many stops, but all the crowds were waiting for second and third class. So much for the communists' idea of egalitarianism—what a farce. The train is absolutely chock-a-block full of people, yet here we are in our beds, and nobody can disturb us.

The Moskievskaja Goscinica is a grand hotel—with fantastic chandeliers, magnificent sprawling carpets, and a superb restaurant on every floor. Lots of top brass here. We had a strange encounter. An eye-opener. Back in Wilno, before we left, people wanted to give us all sorts of gifts and letters and parcels, and so on, to take to their family members in Moscow. We refused most of these. But I took a pair of fur-lined Wellington boots for someone's sister. Once we arrived in the city, we approached the first pedestrian we met and tried to ask him where we could find the address we'd been given. He quickened his steps and walked on as if we didn't exist. The same thing happened with the second pedestrian we tried to stop. And then a third. It didn't seem to us that we were being followed, but in any case we had no idea what to do next, so we hopped on a bus. At least there, we'd have a captive audience. The conductor was a woman, and she and the other passengers gave us directions. It turned out to be a long walk, but it was interesting to be in part of Moscow where there were no tourists. We arrived at an enormous apartment house with perhaps a thousand units, and found the lady's name on a long list. We took the lift and rang the bell, explaining to the frightened face who we were and attempting to thrust the parcel into her hands. She slammed the door shut and shouted, through the door, that it was a mistake—she has no family outside Russia, and we should go away and not bother her. So we brought the boots back to the hotel and had dinner in one of the restaurants.

In the morning we stood in line to see Lenin in his mausoleum in Red Square. His ears are very waxy and the soles of his shoes have holes, but otherwise he looks exactly like the photographs. The line moved along like a conveyor belt, and men and women alike were crying, which I find very odd. Afterward, we looked in shop windows but there was nothing to buy. Nearer our hotel was a tourist shop which offered a large quantity of caviar and locally made perfume in primitive bottles with those same strange rubber corks. We bought perfume: unbelievably vile! Edek says it is definitely NOT the product of his Chemical Engineers Cooperative. But I'm sure it is!

At the hotel, during dinner, we spotted a dance band leader from Warsaw whom Edek recognized from his society days. He came over to our table. The Russians love western dance hall music, he told us, and he's been making a fortune traveling the country here. Later in the evening, we had a disturbing encounter. We had gone for a walk. A few blocks from the hotel, we came across a large brick building with very grimy windows. We got up close, just to have a peek inside: row upon row of manacled men lying side by side on the floor, packed tightly like sardines. Somebody started yelling at us, and we turned and ran as fast as we could, back to the hotel.

    The hotel receptionist booked us tickets to the Bolshoi Theater to see Eugene Onegin this evening. In spite of the cold, I put on silk stockings, high heels, black shoes, and a black dress. In my rucksack when we left Warsaw, I had taken only two dresses, my best ones—the first two that had been made for me by my mother's French dressmaker. Finally, an opportunity to wear one of them! The Bolshoi is superb, grand and elegant, but the audience consisted entirely of scarved women in peasant gear and men in identical brown suits. Everyone wore felt boots like we had seen on the women in the train from Wilno to Moscow. During the intermission, we were mobbed. The women reverently came over to touch my dress and stockings—and they had never seen high heeled shoes. We found out all these people are in the theater for free. The workers in officers and factories receive free tickets to the Bolshoi, on a rotating basis. When it's your factory's turn, you go. There was a large buffet in the foyer, displaying nothing but ice cream, caviar, and vodka. Not surprisingly: no customers.

Father has arranged for our British travel certificates. Stafford Cripps doesn't understand why we'd want to leave here, as this is a "worker's paradise," so he claims. We are on our way to Odessa, and from there, Istanbul. There are quite a few Jews on the train, like us, and we are taking turns sharing the bunk beds. Three compartments of this train are occupied by a heavily bearded rabbi and a large quantity of his children, varying in age from two to twenty-four. There is no Mrs. Rabbi, it seems. As we went to and from the toilet or to fetch water from the samovar, we passed their compartments. What a sight: the rabbi and his entire brood, except for the two littlest ones, all sat with their bare legs soaking in buckets of water. This was extremely puzzling, especially since the train is so cold. It turned out that since religious Jews are not allowed to travel on Saturday, except at sea, the rabbi and his family simply pretended they are on an ocean cruise—all of them with their feet in water.

February

Istanbul is bustling and full of life, crowded with people. At one point, strangely, Edek heard my last name being called above the din. This turned out to be Mr. Brod, a local philanthropist and president of a large company here. He is evidently a business associate of my father. My father must have learned somehow that we would be arriving, and he contacted this man to find us and offer help. I can't figure out how he arranged all this from afar.

Nonetheless, we climbed into Mr. Brod's limousine and checked into a hotel he chose for us. He also gave us money, not only for me and Edek, but enough also for a group of five other Polish refugees, about my age, with whom we established friendships on the train. My father is quite a force. Mr. Brod helped us get through customs at the port. There was a rigorous search. Toothpaste was squeezed, seams opened, jars of face creams prodded—even our suitcases examined for false bottoms. But they haven't found my diamonds, which I hid quite snugly!

In spite of rain the first few days, we went for some walks in the city, by the market and around the docks: crowds are jostling, pushing, pulling, thrusting dirty wads of rubles, offering fur hats, walking sticks, umbrellas, saucepans, gloves. There is traffic, chaos, camels, donkeys, shouting, yelling, men in red fezes, women with large bundles on their heads, minarets with their crescents on high towers, the Bosporus.

After our ten days in Istanbul, Mr. Brod took us to the railway station for the long trip to Aleppo. He gave us more money, as the train journey itself lasts almost a week. Turkey is under water. The country has had record floods this year, and for days and days, there was water as far as the eye could see. I can't guess how this train manages to keep going through all the flooding. If I open the door of the train car, the water laps up in waves, like the sea, reaching all the way up the stairs and almost to the entrance of the cabin. It's like being on a boat, except it's a train.

We have reached high, dry land, with imposing mountains all around. Three steam engines pull and push our train, and we have stopped at a few stations high in the mountains. It seems the journey is endless. I have bought food at the stations: what's available, mostly, are those ghastly little cakes soaked in syrup and fat, and something like a bagel, but quite grubby. So far, our British travel certificates have withstood the scrutiny of all the frontier officials.

We have arrived at Aleppo. There are hundreds of Vichy-French soldiers on the streets here. What a contrast to the vast emptiness and majesty of Turkey. Aleppo is an ancient bustling town, with old stone fountains and cobbled narrow streets. We rented a modest hotel room and visited some mosques and a synagogue—reputed to be the oldest in the world still in use, dating originally from before the time of Christ. It is not so impressive except for its antiquity. The floor is bare earth, and underneath, we are told, people are buried. Stone benches run around three walls, with an altar on the fourth side and some worn stone steps leading up to a tiny women's gallery. The place has that scary and thrilling aura of something very old. Edek long ago discarded his I. G. Farbindustrie papers and, thanks to years of study in France, is now acting like a young Frenchman-about-town. I am not sure of the desirability of becoming so friendly with the Vichy French, since I want to spit in their eyes, but Edek has managed to wrangle an invitation to the Officers' Mess, and I plan to wear my black dress.

Dinner at the Officers' Mess was elegant—good food, good wine, good service, a treat for us. A chap from a Jewish organization came to our hotel and asked if we'd be willing to escort a group of unaccompanied youngsters from Aleppo to Palestine. If we agreed, we'd get train tickets right away. No hassle. On hearing this, Edek instantly changed from being a Frenchman-about-town to a full-fledged Hebrew Scholar, and he agreed to take charge of the youngsters' papers and tickets and so on. In the evening, we moved into the place where they are staying. They speak nothing but Hebrew and Yiddish, they are very noisy, and their behavior is ghastly. Some mischievous spirit fed us all bean soup for dinner, with predictable consequences. Now we are being transported to the train station. It is a few hours' ride to Beirut.

Edek and I left the children in the care of a Jewish Agency official we met on the train, and we went out to do a little exploring in Beirut. What a city! Palm trees, modern hotels, wide boulevards, casinos, movie houses, good shopping and smart apartment houses with views of the sea, all bathed in warm sunshine! Everything is gleaming here, even the policemen's helmets and cuffs—so many signs of wealth and prosperity. The women are in Paris fashions, the men in elegant slacks and shirts. The well-kept avenues are lined with lots of bright flowers. What we'd previously known about Beirut probably could fit on a postage stamp: we hadn't expected anything like this!

It wasn't long after leaving Beirut that we found ourselves in the desert. The train stopped in the middle of nowhere, and we were told to get off and walk. We walked through soft sand, though it was just a short distance to the Palestinian border. British soldiers stood guard all around, and there were British customs officials. The children in our charge were counted and recounted, after which, with a great sighs of relief, we handed them over to an official from the Jewish Agency. Jerzy and my father met us on the other side of customs. I have no idea how they knew we were arriving. It was an emotional reunion. We drove to Tel Aviv in my father's car. Edek has gone to stay with his parents, and for now, I am staying with mine. We will look for an apartment.

My little brother, David, has been in bed, recovering from measles. My parents hadn't told him about my arrival; they wanted to give him a surprise. When I entered the room, he took one look at me and burst into tears. "Why did nobody tell me?" he kept crying and sobbing. He is a poor, lonely soul. My parents treat him like a plaything, utterly disregarding his feelings, poor boy.

June

We have moved twice since arriving in Tel Aviv, not including the first moving in, and now we are in the third of our apartments. Practically, we've been living at a sidewalk cafe nearby, which is frequented by many of the refugees. The place closes at 2:30 a.m., and we often stay until then. There's no use going to bed, only to be woken up by an air raid. The Italians are bombing Tel Aviv. They couldn't hit the back of a barn at three yards. My parents are giving us some money to live, as are Edek's. I feel Edek is very much under the thumb of Regina, his mother. He is terrified of her. She only has to throw him a sharp look of disapproval, and he shuts up and trembles. My mother has bought me two dresses: one a shirtwaister in black and white small check, the other a two piece striped white and blue, and a pair of sandals, too. There is a British army captain here who has fallen in love with me. He is twenty-five. His name is John Steiner. I am tremendously flattered, as it seems, in his eyes, I can do no wrong.

July

Rumors were flying that the Polish Government in Exile, in conjunction with British authorities, is planning to transport a hand-picked group of Polish refugees to Africa, supposedly forming the nucleus of a future Polish government. At first, nobody took notice of this strange project, as it seems such a daft idea and doomed to failure. I have no idea what made Edek apply. Maybe the idea of being far away from war and bombs. Maybe because the Germans are getting nearer and nearer to Cairo, and then Tel Aviv will be in the Luftwaffe sights. The Germans are a different proposition from the easygoing Italians. I am sure we wouldn't have a chance of being selected, anyway. The whole thing is quite unreal, and I'm sure it can't actually happen.

August

Nobody believed in the African affair at first, and when news came that we were accepted, it was a terrible shock. To everyone, really. My parents are in despair. Mother cries all day. John Steiner has been walking around like a zombie, begging me to stay. He has offered to marry me if I leave Edek. I am scared and quite nervous about what will happen. We are told this whole scheme is being financed by the King of England.

Today is the day. We left Tel Aviv in the morning. Mother is in deep despair and did not come to see us off. Father didn't come either, as he stayed with her for comfort. Jerzy came, along with John Steiner and another friend. Our train was a special refugee train, with only our group on board, plus the guards. The train stopped soon after it started, and the original group of guards was replaced by Egyptians. In no time, we were traveling through sandy desert, with camel caravans in view. When it was almost dark, just before we reached Al Kantara, the train was attacked by Italian planes. The Egyptian guards, instead of letting us out to run in the desert, locked the whole train from the outside and ran away. We were like sitting ducks—planes swooping very low and strafing all around. We could see bullets hitting the sand and making little craters in it.

September

Cairo is marvelous. It is an exciting city, and it is packed with Allied troops and quite a few American volunteers. Numerous eating and drinking establishments are open to accommodate them. In my school days, I used to devour any book about ancient Egypt. Now the museum is almost overwhelming me. It is a thrill to see such well stocked rooms, gallery after gallery. Edek and I and a small group went to the old section of the city and sat on the banks of the Nile Delta, watching the busy life. We saw the Pyramids and the Sphinx, took a trip to the Valley of the Kings. We had a good laugh at the carefully scattered "antiquities" that had been supplied by the guide, but they were passable replicas of the real thing. We sat on the terrace of the hotel and watched the crowd and drank English tea with cucumber sandwiches and little cream cakes. Most of these nicer places are "out of bounds" for the troops, which feels very unfair to me. These poor soldiers, who are fighting for us, are barred, when we, who have done nothing to help the war efforts, are able to get in anywhere. On the other hand, it is true that some of them are awfully rough, especially the Australians and New Zealanders. There are four women in our little group, and all are excellent looking, so we are turning heads. Unlike the Turks, the Egyptian men do not pinch bottoms.

After a month, news arrived that our ship was ready. We were taken by buses north to Port Said, and there we saw the most enormous ship, "The New Amsterdam," a cruise ship converted to wartime service. It is to be the flagship for a large convoy. We were treated with incredible deference. The Polish group was allowed to board first, and from the upper deck, we watched 6,000 Italian prisoners of war being loaded. They were in great spirits, singing and laughing, as the war is over for them now, and they are quite grateful for it. The British officers saluted the Italian officer-prisoners as they boarded. After these came the South African troops, some on leave and some wounded. Many stretcher cases, many walking wounded, some without legs or arms, some blind. It was a heartrending sight. There are also some Rhodesian troops on board. The loading took hours. I am quite outraged that we, healthy young spongers, have been allocated separate cabins on the top deck, while these boys, on leave or wounded, have been herded to some communal dormitories down inside the ship bowels. Of course, not one of the Polish yobs here agrees with me.

The big ship barely cleared the sides of the Suez Canal. I ran to the lower deck, stretched out my hand, and touched the wall of the canal. We moved slowly, which posed a danger from air raids. But we have decided that the Italians will not bomb a ship full of their own prisoners of war. The Red Sea is really red, with flying fish and dolphins in it—but it was unbearably hot on the ship. In our cabin, in the top bunk, with the low ceiling over my head, it was stifling. The stupid Poles found great amusement in the pools of sweat we left behind us whenever we sat in one of the leather armchairs. It got even worse as we neared Aden—a heat saturated with moisture, heavy and choking.

Trust the Italians to organize a good performance! The prisoners of war arranged to put on a long and delightful revue show for us—marvelously ingenious and amusing. They sang, danced, dressed as women and performed, in broken English, some very funny sketches. This has been the highlight of our long voyage.

We disembarked in Durban. It was evening, and we couldn't see much. A train was waiting there to take us to Johannesburg—a proper train with good dining car and attentive service. We ate and slept and were pampered and cosseted.

In Johannesburg, we were met by some Polish official representatives and several members of the local Jewish community, including one family who took us home, gave us an enormous feast, and will drive us to the railway station in the morning. We are to catch another train to Lusaka, the capitol of Northern Rhodesia.

October

The ride to Lusaka took five nights. The train raced along the tracks at high speed, barely stopping except on occasion, to get water for the engines. We passed a few isolated settlements, but little else over the 3,000-mile journey. We have been provided with everything we need on the train.

Lusaka, the rail terminus, consists of a single main road, unpaved, surrounded by a few scattered shacks. There is one hotel, basically a small shack, and one official-looking building, from which the local officials are flying the Union Jack. We got off the train and were given a choice: some of us could choose to stay in Lusaka; others could go on to Livingstone, the largest town in

Northern Rhodesia; the young, single men, of which there were about eighty in our group, were encouraged to go on to the Copper Belt towns: N'Dola, Wellington, Monze, Broken Hill, and Kitwe. Edek and I almost considered joining them. But we decided to put our names down for Fort Jameson, a tiny settlement about 400 miles east-northeast of Lusaka. One does not come this far, we reasoned, just to settle for some shabby town or copper mine. We were seeking "genuine" Africa. We are to leave by bus in the morning.

Three large trucks came for us in the morning. These are trucks for carrying yams, but several rows of hardback chairs had been placed in the back of each truck. There were no roads, just overgrown trails through the jungle, and everybody in the trucks became terribly sick and coated with dust. The chairs jumbled and shook mercilessly, and after a while, we tossed them aside and huddled together on the truck bed. At times, we made hairpin turns on narrow jungle trails where one side was high rock, the other side a steep precipice, and the back wheels of the trucks hung over the cliff edge before the drivers managed to rev the engines and right the wheels. When night came, we stopped and camped along the roadside, all of us falling down from our aches and pains. None of us could have imaged this journey, or how long it would take. One night, we camped on the banks of the Luangwa River, a tributary of the Zambezi, and there were crocodiles in large numbers. Tall grasses grew over these trails—it seems a miracle that the drivers even know where they are going. They are fearless and sure of themselves.

It took five days to reach Fort Jameson. At first, we didn't notice it, as there isn't much to see except the jungle and waist-deep grass. We were told it is a settlement of about fifty-two white people, situated on a high plateau with a reasonable climate. Supposedly, there is little presence of sleeping sickness. The trucks soon arrived at a fresh clearing, and we could see that new rondavels were being built. Each had two bedrooms joined by an open living space. These structures have packed-earth floors and thatch ceilings from which all manner of insects seem to continually rain down. Water is brought by a small army of "boys," as they are called here, and everyone has been supplied with a hurricane lamp and a sun helmet. The furniture is made of paraffin tins, as any other material, we are told, would be devoured within hours by termites. We have a large communal eating and cooking hall on one side of the clearing, and our toilets, also on the edge of the clearing, are holes in the ground, covered with wooden planks. We have been cautioned to examine these carefully before taking a seat.

For the past few days, because the rondavels are still under construction, a few of us, including Edek and I, have been staying at the local "hotel," which is run by a Mrs. Knowles. She gives us a very decent dinner and afterward, we sit on the open veranda in the darkness and listen to the jungle noises. It is all so new and strange, frightening and thrilling. Such an enormous variety of insects crawling on the walls here—large, small, strange centipedes, all colors and shapes—the walls are covered in them. It is terrifying and fascinating.

November

At Mrs. Knowles', we met a man names Van Breda. He is very tall and very thin, and he comes for Fort Jameson to pick up supplies. He told us he finds it very overcrowded, and it gives him a headache, and he can't understand why anyone would want to live in such a crowded place. His wife, an Englishwoman, had been killed early in the war when a torpedo struck her ship as she sailed back home to visit their daughter, who is in boarding school in England. Van Breda owns an estate so large that he hardly knows where it begins and where it ends. He invited us to join him on his rounds of his land.

He took us by truck. We saw herds of giraffes, springboks, zebras and elands in open plains, and we drove through dozens of native villages. Some of the natives have never seen a white woman before. They gathered around me, chattering and giggling. Van Breda said that they think I am painted pink, and he encouraged them to see if the paint comes off. Several of them came over and touched my arms and rubbed gently to make sure it is not paint. Entering his private grounds, we were greeted by rows of servants and six enormous Rhodesian ridgebacks, several of which had their ears torn off, evidently from tangles with cheetahs and lions. We stayed at a guest house, and in the evening, we listened to the BBC News as drinks and dinner were served by stewards in white uniforms. There were all sorts of mixers, buckets of ice, dishes of olives, nuts, and crisps. The Germans have all of Europe and are marching through Russia like a hot knife through butter. There is no stopping them.

DIVERGENCES

By the end of 1941, the family members have dispersed across four continents—Nathan and Marysia are in Poland, Nina in China, David in Palestine, and Wanda in the British colony in Northern Rhodesia, where colonial authorities have organized a refugee resettlement program. Nathan has lost his mother and the other women in his family. Nina's hoped-for journey to the West has stalled following the Japanese attack at Pearl Harbor. David still expects to return to Warsaw when the war ends.

After many months of increasing frustration and rejection of their travel applications, Nina's parents finally secure entry permits for Curacao, a Dutch colony in the Caribbean. Associated transit visas are granted by Chiune Sugihara, the Japanese consul, who committed himself to aiding the Jewish refugees of Lithuania, in violation of official orders. With expensive tickets in hand, Nina and her parents board a train to Moscow and then Vladivostok, traveling from there to Kobe, landing eventually in Japanese-occupied Shanghai, where a colony of Jewish refugees has grown. Further travel is blocked as the United States enters the war in the Pacific. Indirectly through Nina's story, we get a panoramic view of the remarkable scale of a war now being waged on all continents, affecting many hundreds of millions of people, and the desperation of refugee efforts to find points of access to safe haven in an expanding conflict. In periods of active flight alternating with uncertain waiting—a pattern well known to refugees around the world even today—Nina and her family experience a humiliating series of rejections, a sequence of deeply disturbing signals they are unwanted virtually everywhere. We see from her writing that Nina is acutely aware of these and certainly concerned, but we also see that her parents continue to provide warmth and affirming routines that enable their now eight-year-old daughter to feel seen, heard, wanted, and protected. Nina's memoir exemplifies the immeasurable value of competent adult role models who impart coping and self-regulatory skills in times of stress. Family rituals and interpersonal patterns become a kind of portable experiential home for Nina precisely at a time when conventional "place"-based meanings of home are no longer viable. Home is a configuration in this family's mind and manner of relating, we see, and there are means for fostering and enhancing its integrity to some extent even when its physical presence has been taken away. In Nina's narrative, we get a sense of how relationships internal to the family loomed ever larger as reference points for self-definition as the surrounding structures of community and society progressively crumbled; it is a lesson in the dynamic interplay, so often referenced in theorizing about family systems, of interpersonal, community, and social environments.[1]

From the window of the room she has rented, Marysia observes emaciated Jewish children being tossed over the ghetto wall. Joining her boyfriend and circle of friends in the Polish underground, she begins her work as a resistance activist. She also discovers a new way to visit her father, who has been assigned to a slave labor unit on a construction site, where he participates in the underground trade in confiscated Jewish luxury items. Marysia, now twenty, exemplifies a core paradox of early adulthood: even as a sense of her own competence and independence grows, she still derives intense comfort and validation from her father's loving gaze.[2] So dear to her are their brief moments of mutual appreciation, she continues her searches for her him despite the immense personal risk they pose. The yearning to sustain attachments to loving figures, we see, overrides the cognitive appreciation of danger; young people go to great lengths to preserve contact with their parents.

Nathan has been enlisted in a slave labor unit in the Krakow ghetto. His mother and the other women have been taken away, but his father persists diligently in attempting to provide shelter and protection, and Nathan senses keenly that he is deeply loved. Nathan sketches in his mind an image of his mother in her final moments: vulnerable but courageous, hiding successfully until the very end but for one tiny, momentary lapse. It is heartrending to encounter this description, as we sense it must have served a taming function, a way of managing what might otherwise have seemed an overwhelming loss. Donald Spence, the psychoanalyst, wrote that the representations we evoke tend to cohere not only with what is recognizable to us but also with what we need and desire from them.[3] Emphasizing competence, capacity and effort, Nathan's picture of his mother's final moments aligns with his father's continuing messages about perseverance and hard work. Oriented to problem-solving, endurance, and self-regulation, it was a representation not only of his mother but also of the story Nathan was learning to tell himself.

Particular narratives of the holocaust are enshrined in popular culture, and as the anthropologist Erica Lehrer has written,[4] there is an understandable reluctance about noting that for a small group of people, the war offered elements of adventure. Even in the broader context of persecution and looming atrocity, we can acknowledge Wanda's remarkable journey across the African bush. Wanda traveled through the Soviet Union to Istanbul, Aleppo, and Beirut, continuing from there to Tel Aviv. She and her husband then joined a resettlement group that sailed across the Red Sea, southward along the east African coast to Durban, South Africa, from where they traveled by train through Johannesburg to Lusaka, landing finally in a hut in a jungle clearing in what was then the tiny colonial white settlement of Fort Jameson, Northern Rhodesia. From the deck of her ship, Wanda observed the global sweep of the war from which she and her husband were attempting to distance themselves: Italian prisoners staging a song-and-dance show for their British captors as wounded South African soldiers, their arms and legs missing, sat alongside bands of refugee Polish political elites. Wanda tracked the news as it unfolded. But moment by moment, she tended only to what needed tending—holding mostly at a distance any less immediately pertinent information. We see that young people cope with horrible truths at times by compartmentalizing them. Moreover, we note that the events of history can be viewed from a great diversity of vantage points: a religious minority persecuted in one setting has taken on the qualities, in a different context, of a colonial presence.[5] The identity of a refugee is context-bound, framed in reference both to local and global forces.

NOTES

1. Bronfenbrenner, *The Ecology of Human Development*; Miller and Rasco, *The Mental Health of Refugees*.

2. Rustin, "Finding out Where and Who One Is," 39–60; Erik Erikson, *Identity: Youth and Crisis* (New York, NY: W. W. Norton, 1968).

3. Donald Spence, *Narrative Truth and Historical Truth: Meaning and Interpretation in Psychoanalysis* (New York, NY: W. W. Norton, 1982).

4. Erica Lehrer, *Jewish Poland Revisited: Heritage Tourism in Unique Places* (Bloomington, IN: Indiana University Press, 2013).

5. Rothberg, *Multidirectional Memory*; Shirli Gilbert and Avril Alba, eds., *Holocaust Memory and Racism in the Post War World* (Detroit, MI: Wayne State University Press, 2019).

Chapter 4

1942

NATHAN

November

Father and I were moved to the camp at Plaszow. It was surrounded by barbed wire. We were assigned to a barracks. There were many of us. As long as we can continue to work, Father said, we are of use to them. We were assigned to a roofing unit. We left the camp every morning and headed to our assigned location. The Germans counted us when we left, and then they counted us again at night when we returned. Our kapo, the supervisor of our unit, was a Jew named Beim. Before the war, he had been a tinsman. He was small and short and energetic, and he wore a beret on his head, with little round metal eyeglasses. We liked him because he was kind to the crew. He ran around, trying to be cheerful, trying to encourage us, keep our spirits up. We knew we needed to work as hard as we could. Beim taught me to fix roofs. I learned how to climb up on a roof, and how to solder metal. I was quite interested in this work.

Winter

On the ground, I found a piece of an old rug. I took a small length of roofing metal and formed a needle from it. With the wool from the rug, I made a lining, and I sewed it into my pants. I wore that wool lining under my prisoner uniform. Everyone in the camp was cold, but not me. I stayed warm. Father was moved to a different barracks, but I continued to see him in the camp. One night, he found potatoes, and got a message to me. When it was dark, he came to get me. We sat together in a corner of the yard in the middle of the night, and we ate together. I don't know how he got those potatoes.

Chapter 4

MARYSIA

Spring

I met Julek through our resistance group. We had been running a clandestine printing press. Our friend Zbigniew had rented a room near the center of town, where we set up the equipment. When I visited, the landlord just assumed I was one of his many female admirers, and neither Zbig nor I did anything to discourage this assumption. We had started with printing leaflets at first, and later expanded to several pages of news. As we had to make ourselves inconspicuous when posting our leaflets around town, Zbig and I used reverse psychology: I leaned my back against a wall, pressing down on a leaflet to glue it, as Zbig acted out a love scene—with some conviction and enthusiasm, I must say. People are so easily distracted by couples in love! After we "finished," no one even noticed that a new anti-Nazi poster had appeared on the wall behind us. But then Julek didn't show up at the apartment where we kept the press. I waited and waited. Then I saw his name posted on an announcement—a list of people to be hanged for involvement in Underground activities. Julek had finished a year of architecture school before the war started. He was smart, sympathetic—he had worried about a Jewess like me taking risks by working with the Underground group. Is such an effort worth the lives it costs?

I kept checking the construction site, but I hadn't seen Father in several weeks. Men with armbands were working there—but no one I recognized. It seemed that a new crew had come and replaced Father's group. Finally, I saw an opportunity to enter the site and ask one of the Jews about my father. He'd never heard of him. I am in agony.

July

A worker at the railway told us about freight trains crowded with Jews. The Germans have been conducting roundups—surrounding a street, closing off exits. They shout orders for the residents to gather in the courtyards, and they shoot anyone who tries to hide or escape through basements or attics. They have been marching everyone onto the cattle trains at the Umschlagplatz. I must get my family out.

August

Father was captured in one of the roundups. My grandparents, too, are gone. But there is some good news. Lilka, my sister, managed to track down the address of a former neighbor of ours—a kind and well-off gentile named Wiktor, who had lived in our building before the ghetto was formed. She sent him a letter pleading for help. Much to her amazement, he responded. He contacted someone who knew someone else, and that person contacted a German he knew who has been secretly taking money to help people get out of the ghetto. Not only did Wiktor purchase false identity papers for my sister—he also paid the German a fee to smuggle her out through a checkpoint. Then, on the Aryan side, he took her to a church and married her! Which of course now means she has legal papers that prove she is a gentile. They have rented a nice apartment. Lilka looks very Jewish, so she never wants to leave the house. But Wiktor put himself in even greater danger, as he arranged for Mother's exit as well. This man is now harboring two Jewish women—a sure risk to his own life. Mother has put a large scarf over her head, hiding her Jewish features, and is masquerading as an old peasant woman. No one in the world is more invisible than an older woman—and Mother is taking full advantage of this fact.

My room has become a transit point. Czesław and his resistance group have been smuggling girls out of the ghetto, and they are using my apartment as a base of operations. Sometimes, he brings them here to hide for a few hours. Other times, they stay overnight and even, on occasion, they sleep in my bed. This places all of us in great danger, of course, and it completely undermines any privacy I might have hoped for. I can't allow them to wander around at night or use the toilet, as any noise will make the neighbors suspicious. I have been asking them to urinate in bags, which I take downstairs with the trash in the morning. I pretend it's all normal.

November

It seems as if this war is going on forever. At Stalingrad, Soviet forces started a counteroffensive, encircling 330,000 German troops. In Africa, the British have defeated the Germans at Alamein. I am aware of all these things, but at this point they leave little impression on me. I feel I am running out of energy. The blood center is refusing my blood because the tests show I have become anemic.

December

At the Institute of Hygiene, a program is being organized to develop an antityphoid serum. The Nazis are desperate for such a serum. Typhoid is carried by lice. From what I can gather, the serum is being produced by infecting lice with the disease. This is the Weigl Method, and I am using it to my benefit. I have volunteered for the program. The lice need to grow and multiply somehow, and the Institute needs hosts. Lice are not choosy, I guess, as my anemia doesn't seem to matter to them. The Institute pays me partly in cash and partly in hens' eggs—left over, evidently, from a different scientific experiment being conducted there. The lice are brought to me in something that looks like a matchbox, with one long edge made of very thin, fine netting. The cover is slipped off. The attendant scrubs an area of my skin with alcohol and then places the box on the skin of my thigh or on my forearm. In those places, I am told, a woman's skin is most readily penetrated. Twice a day, for about half an hour, I am strapped with ten boxes, and I allow myself to be eaten. It is disgusting—and I am carrying a perpetual feeling of revulsion. But I am kind to my lice, and they, in turn, seem to be satisfied with me. The pay is the same as from the blood center, plus the additional eggs. Lice are never fussy, and I am grateful toward my tiny charges.

Lilka has had a baby, and Mother is serving as her nanny. The landlord threatened to evict all of them if they're too noisy—so Mother carries the baby in her arms all day long. It is a unique baby indeed that never cries in its first months of life! But Mother, too, belongs to an exceptional group in our current situation: an older Jewish woman who is still alive. We are grateful for the courage of a remarkable man.

NINA

July

Everyone is frightened. Father says the Germans have told the Japanese to round us up and put us on a ship. They want the Japanese to send us out to the sea and sink us. The Germans want this to happen on Rosh Hashanah, New Year. Father says we are to be rounded up from the synagogue. We are waiting to see if the Japanese do what the Germans are asking. We are just waiting.

WANDA

January

Edek and I share a rondavel with the Epsteins, whose daughter, Lucy, is in a separate hut with three other girls. It has turned out that a couple of women in the camp used to be cooks, so we held a general meeting and appointed them as cooks to the camp. We have a committee now for buying food supplies, a committee for physical exercise, a health committee, and an entertainment committee. The chap in charge in of physical exercise, a former judge from Silesia, ordered everybody to have communal exercise, but no one paid even the slightest attention to him. The food supply committee soon got into trouble, as the Poles have complained they can't live without potatoes and onions, and they find the local mutton unacceptable. They want beef. An official was flown in for consultation. He explained that such things cannot be produced locally because of the tse-tse fly. So now the Poles have arranged for these items to be flown in from Lusaka every week. The small propeller plane lands in a clearing next to the post office. It delivers mail, food, and other supplies to the Victoria Club, a kind of Holy of Holies for the English tobacco farmers here. Some of them live 200 or 300 miles away, and they've been here for generations, but every Wednesday they come to Fort Jameson for an evening in their Club. The ladies dress in evening gowns and "mosquito boots," and the men in dinner jackets. Their Club has billiards and cards rooms, a library, a smoking room (for men only), and a cinema projector room. It is old and shabby, but it is theirs.

When they heard of the new arrivals—having made sure we are white—the members of this Club extended invitations and gave us honorary membership to their Sanctum. The very first Wednesday, we went there to see a movie. The auditorium had three rows of armchairs, each marked with a person's name. Other chairs were provided for us, but even before the English people arrived, the rude Polish yobs in our group plonked themselves in the armchairs and put their dirty boots up, muddying the seats in front. During the movie break, one of the Englishmen came over to remonstrate with our yobs, and they left him with a black eye. We sent our best English speaker, Mrs. Goldin, to apologize, but the invitation was withdrawn, and we never went there again.

February

When it rains here, it is not drops of water that fall. It is a sheet, a dense curtain, a thick, impenetrable wall of water. A bush baby has befriended us, allowing itself to be taken for walks in our pockets. It jumps on the coffee cup rim. We have a monkey, too, which we bought from a native boy. We keep it tethered outside our rondavel. Everybody gathers in the big hall before dinner. Mrs. Goldin is our official translator of the 6 o-clock BBC News. We are glued to the radio, and after the broadcast, she translates it all for us into Polish. We are following every new development. Edek and I eat and play bridge with the Kurzeskis. I found a book, "Death on the Nile." This is my first time reading something by Agatha Christie.

March

We spend our days taking long, long walks, marveling at the vivid colors of the plants and flowers. Deep blues, yellows, dazzling reds. We see beetles the size of small mice, some with unbelievable coloring, horns, eyes on long stalks, tails, and so on. There are large lizards, monkeys, deer, and many kinds of cats, but no birds. The place seems to be birdless except for parrots. Sometimes, we come across the bleached skeletons of lizards or monkeys. We had to give away our monkey. It played with itself so much, we had to get rid of it in order not to corrupt the camp's children.

We met a German hunter who is the official government elephant culler. Four times a year, he told us, he enters the bush with two native trackers and stays for a month, killing elephants. We also met another German, a Jewish refugee with a gentile wife. He is in charge of the East Africa Trading Company. His store supplies an area the size of Switzerland. His wife told me their original furniture was turned to dust by termites in a single night. Their nests are everywhere, large and thick and in fantastic shapes. Edek has applied for transfer to South Africa. He has sent around applications for work to some of the factory managers there. We have been told no South African immigration permits are being issued during wartime.

April

I developed an itch above my navel and nearly tore my skin to shreds trying to relieve it. By the time someone suggested bilharzia, I could already see the animal growing under my skin. The camp doctor, Dr. Berman, said I'd need to travel 200 miles to the hospital in Blantyre, but I fought tooth and nail against this. I nagged our neighbor, Igo Mann, who had been a veterinarian back in Poland, and I wouldn't take no for an answer. He didn't want to touch me, but when he saw it, his eyes popped out on stalks. He ran outside calling for his wife, Erika, who came at a fast gallop. I begged Erika to make her husband take the thing out, even though he kept insisting he only takes care of horses. Finally, I pointed to a small hole in my skin where the egg must have originally been planted. All he had to do was enlarge the hole and pull. He acted like a nervous ballerina, but then he brought over some tools and almost painlessly pulled the slug out. It was more than an inch in length, and very fat, and it squirmed like mad. I don't think Igo Mann was ever as proud of anything as he was of this operation, as he described it in minute detail to anyone who would listen.

I am longing for a baby. I have plastered our round bedroom's wall with placards that say "I want a baby." Edek says we will not have a baby during wartime, especially considering how badly things are going for our side.

May

Late last month, we received entry permits into South Africa. This was so unexpected—almost impossible—everybody was open-mouthed with amazement. It is not a proper immigration visa, just an entry permit, and we would have to leave right away, on the next truck that arrived in Fort Jameson. Edek will be making waterproof leather boots and shoes for the South African army. He is studying his chemistry books. The whole camp turned out to say farewell to us. I am eager for a new adventure, but sad as well. Fort Jameson has been good to us—even the climate was mostly benevolent. We climbed into the truck—this time, sitting in the cabin—and began the trek back to Lusaka. We passed many elephants, large prides of lions, zebras, giraffes, and bucks beyond number. As before, we traveled for days, and then, finally arrived at the train terminus. Compared with Fort Jameson, Lusaka seems mind-bogglingly busy, and our heads began to swim with the noise, traffic, shops, and houses. There are at least three cars on the road here. The people from our old group came out to greet us with a hero's welcome, embracing us and singing rousing Polish songs in our honor. I can't understand why all this fuss. What's more, I'm not looking forward to another endless train ride.

We'd been sitting for days, but we finally reached Bloemfontein, where we needed to change trains. I felt I could not take another single night on a train. But this feeling was momentarily relieved by a woman in a red coat at the Bloemfontein station. I have never before seen anybody dressed in red, and I couldn't take my eyes off her. We left Bloemfontein in the evening and reached Port Elizabeth, where Edek was supposed to start work. Mr. Hoffenberg, the new employer, met us at the station and took us to dinner. I was so relieved to be at the end of the journey. Then he dropped his bombshell: there was no place for Edek in his tannery, but Mr. Rosenthal, in Wellington, was awaiting our arrival with open arms. Another day and night of traveling! I cried all night until I saw the marvelous Western Cape mountain passes—a glorious sight for weary travelers who had spent almost a week on a train. We are to arrive in Wellington by mid-afternoon.

A YEAR OF TERROR

Family members' previous efforts at reconstituting life routines are undermined in 1942 by the sheer magnitude of the escalating brutality. Nathan has been transported to the infamous concentration camp at Plaszow and assigned to a work unit where he learns new skills he finds interesting. Eventually separated from his father, he continues to see him in the camp and cherishes the moments they spend together. Nathan's stories from this period are brief, but we can find in them the evidence of a significant developmental shift. Where previously he looked toward his father for comfort and protection, we see here how he has begun to turn outward—to welcome new male mentors and role models. Just as he enters middle adolescence, Nathan meets the cheerful tinsman Beim and realizes that the lessons Beim teaches can be applied to his own emerging strategies for self-reliance and self-protection. We note the awakening interest in a fifteen-year-old boy in acting independently and testing his personal skills, and we see that in the context of the concentration camp, self-care itself has become an arena for creative declarations of independence and defiance.

Before the war, Nathan's father had run a scrap yard, and Nathan spent time playing in it. When he tells us that he finds in the camp an old piece of rug and fashions a needle to sew the wool into his prisoner uniform, we sense that the very act of looking and finding small objects—of configuring his body to seek, collect, and create something new—might have conjured in Nathan something comforting and familiar. Akin to what Donald Winnicott described as a "transitional phenomenon,"[1] searching and scavenging activities are not quite home, but they are reminiscent of home, an uncanny evocation of bodily activity from the past, now set to new purpose.

Marysia oscillates between nagging discouragement and a determination to not capitulate. She tells us about the Polish gentile who has used money and social connections to smuggle her mother and sisters out of the ghetto. Her father and grandparents are lost in the roundups, and a trusted friend is captured and killed. Weakened and anemic from over-frequent blood donations, Marysia finds a new source of income, volunteering for a grotesque Nazi research experiment in which skin patches on her arms and thighs are infested with lice. We are appalled to learn she gives her body in this way, as it seems like an acquiescence to further self-harm. And yet we see that it provides, quite the contrary, a strange and subtle psychic triumph. Marysia reshapes discomfort and self-abnegation as assertions of power and self-affirmation. Her engagement with lice, along the lines of what is sometimes called the psychological "transformation of passive into active,"[2] becomes a statement in her mind about her own intactness and capacity for mastery, even in the context of what appears on the surface as a challenge to her bodily integrity.

As her small bedroom becomes a staging area for clandestine ghetto rescue operations, Marysia finds herself further enmeshed in the dangerous project of sabotage. We notice she continues to tell her story as a kind of volley—good news matched by bad, bad news matched by good. There is something significant in a young person's structuring of a narrative in this way, as it provides a clue, even years later, of the moralism that animates and invigorates the now twenty-one-year-old girl—the inspiration and energy she derives from an internal representation of struggle between forces of good and forces of evil. But Marysia admits that even as she has committed herself to this bold resistance work, she also finds herself disappointed by the loss of privacy in her apartment. We see in this that she has continued to navigate between the competing developmental demands of belonging and separating, becoming herself and becoming what others want her to be.

In the Fort Jameson settlement, Wanda's adventures continue. She meets Germans who aren't the enemy. She enlists a fellow refugee, formerly a veterinarian, to provide treatment for schistosomiasis. She and her husband eventually opt to make the long journey to Wellington, South Africa, where they settle comfortably in a small community of other Jewish refugees, all closely monitoring the grim news from Europe. Wanda's story of the whites-only social club, where Jewish and gentile Poles find themselves unwelcome, illustrates a well-known paradox of global displacement: it re-shuffles the social order. Someone who holds high status in one location can find himself, in a new place, suddenly relegated to the lower social rungs. Formerly meaningful within-group differences of status and social class, moreover, can fall away in new contexts, as the refugee community is painted in broad brush strokes by its skeptical hosts.

Nina and her parents watch and wait as conditions become uncertain in the Shanghai ghetto. They fear what the Japanese might do to in the service of their alliance with the Germans. In the very sparseness of Nina's memoir entries for this year, written so many decades later, we can still perceive a nine-year-old's sense of precarious balance, of vulnerability and hesitation—as if words themselves might tip the scales in the wrong direction.

NOTES

1. Donald Winnicott, "Transitional Objects and Transitional Phenomena: A Study of the First Not-Me Possession," *The International Journal of Psychoanalysis* 34 (1953): 89–97.

2. Sigmund Freud, *Beyond the Pleasure Principle* (New York, NY: W. W. Norton, 1961).

Chapter 5

1942 in the Warsaw Ghetto

Our story returns now to the beginning of 1942, as we meet Irene Birnbaum, the sixth of the family members whose memoirs appear in this book. Irene's family has spent the previous two years in captivity inside the Warsaw ghetto, along with almost all the other Birnbaums and their extended families. Her narrative presents a new perspectival scale, as it relays the events of a several-month period in the form of an intimate, almost day-by-day account. As will be seen, this level of detail—even filtered decades later through multiple layers of translation and editing—reveals with a disturbing clarity the internal struggle of a now fifteen-year-old girl attempting to sustain psychic continuity as the world fragments around her. Irene's memoir begins in early January.

JANUARY

We were ordered to hand over our warmest coats. They'll be sent to the German soldiers freezing on the eastern front. At school, we burned some of the wood benches to warm our classroom. More bodies have appeared on the sidewalks, swollen and stiff. People have covered them with sheets of newspaper. Last night, we heard the gestapo rushing from apartment to apartment, dragging people downstairs and shooting them. Now that the Americans have entered the war, the Germans are saying, we have invited our own annihilation. We hear these threats but don't believe them.

Father and Mother and I consider ourselves lucky, as our apartment is nice compared with most. We're just four people in a two-bedroom. Some are jealous because we still have our maid, Zocha. She's not our maid anymore, really. She was an old, faithful servant to Granny. She isn't paid, as we can no longer afford it. We moved here just before the creation of the ghetto, after our real apartment was bombed. Mother had locked all her jewelry and money in a safe at the bank, but then everything was confiscated because we are no longer allowed to have bank accounts. Granny sold some of her diamonds so we could continue to live respectably. The other tenants here are mostly upper-middle class, like us. It might have been strange, before the ghetto, to see a lawyer sweeping the stairs or a teacher mopping the patio floor. But we have been brought closer together because of the curfew. There is no longer electric light in our building, but we still have gas for the stove. The young people here have organized a youth group. We do community work. I've been tutoring and taking part in food collections. High school is forbidden, but we have found a way to continue our schooling. My old school, on Sienna Street, was excluded from the ghetto last year, when the boundaries changed and part of that block was switched to the Aryan side. Many of my former classmates then moved to Mechanic School, a clandestine architecture and design school on Grzybowska Street. I have two years left. I'm terrible at Math, but very good at Latin, Literature, and History. My Latin teacher on Sienna Street even said I should study Classics after the war! Now, instead, I'm taking Commercial Art. Professor Griffenberg says I show "imagination and taste for colors," but I lack "accuracy in execution." He thinks I'll have to become a supervisor so I can hire assistants to work for me in my future design studio. I think I would like to study fashion design at the Sorbonne. I certainly imagine myself in Paris—the capital of fashion. But France's surrender to the Germans upset all of us, and now we are keeping close watch on the newspapers. The Germans seem to be winning everywhere.

FEBRUARY

New faces have appeared at school. I already know which ones I hate! Two are plain thugs. Waisman is ugly but well-dressed and wants to impress everyone by bragging about his father's money. Typical nouveau riche. I have never liked that type. The other one, Wolman, is fairly handsome. In a different time, he probably could've played the part of Tarzan in an American movie. His brains don't match his body, unfortunately, but at least he doesn't disgust me. The worst new ones are Kadysh and Helfgot. Kadysh is the cousin of my friend Hala. It's hard to believe these two can be related! Kadysh: tall, thin, ugly, annoying. Hala: sweet, pretty, nice (though Mother says she is far too fashion-conscious). The most important thing about Kadysh turns out to be his best friend, Kuba Siemiatytzki. I would say Kuba is probably the best-looking boy in the ghetto in our age group. He is a year ahead of me. He was so smart at his old school, he skipped forward a year. This is him: brilliant, fair hair, eyes blue, very athletic. A few new girls have shown up, too. The

Rosen twins are nieces of a business associate of my Uncle Jakub, who owns the big cosmetics supply factory, Marcel. I like that it has a French name! They produce toothpaste and beauty products.

MARCH

Waisman sits next to me in class and talks to me all the time. What else can I do but respond? Talking to him doesn't mean I like him! But Helfgot and Kadysh have started spreading rumors. Now that they're editing the school newspaper, they're threatening to put "news" about me in the next issue. They are so despicable! But right now I am more worried about Father. I see him sitting in the apartment, dour and depressed, with his eyes glued to the newspapers. Since the war started, he has not earned a cent, and the war news is getting to him. It doesn't help that Mother treats him badly. She is aggressive and domineering, and I cannot believe how angry she makes me sometimes.

APRIL

Our youth group started a garden in the apartment courtyard during spring break. The goal was to plant vegetables, as fresh food and vitamins are badly needed. Mother assumed the role of "adviser." I would work under anybody else's guidance—but NOT Mother's! Everybody seemed surprised when I said I won't take part. But it didn't take long for those poor perspiring young people to see exactly what I've been going through all my life! They had quite enough of Sergeant Commander Natalia Zoltek Birnbaum!

Spring Break has ended, and on the first day back at school, on the very first page of the school newspaper, what do we find? A cartoon drawing of a couple sitting on a park bench. You couldn't recognize the girl's face, but she was wearing a red wool cap, just like the one I'd worn all winter. The boy's profile, with wolf-like teeth, left no doubt about his identity. I felt everybody's eyes fixed on me! But I will not play into their hands! I am not giving them the satisfaction of seeing me show weakness! Helfgot had the audacity to came over and ask if I am angry. Of course not! I told him. What a hypocrite. He looked so disappointed!

Today was a great day. I arrived a little late at school. Seats in the drawing studio were all taken, so I went downstairs to the architecture classroom. Kuba was there! "What did you think of the newspaper today?" he asked me. "I liked it very much," I answered, very sarcastically of course. I am quite happy to show I am strong enough to rise above this situation. I know

I made a good impression. Later in the afternoon, I pressed down too hard on my ruler, and it cracked in half. I got to ask Kuba if I may borrow his. A pianist visited our school today, and almost everyone gathered in the main hall to hear the concert. We have one of the last pianos left in the ghetto. Did the Germans overlook this one? I don't know. Beethoven is forbidden, as the laws require us to listen only to "our own" composers. But that still leaves Mendelssohn, Mayerbeer, Offenbach! We have many options. We will not allow the Germans to stop us from enjoying the beautiful things that life offers! When everyone was absorbed in the music, I slipped downstairs—under the pretext, of course, of returning Kuba's ruler. Kuba was finishing an assignment. He asked if he could walk me home. We talked and laughed as we exited the building, but when we reached the street, another boy from our class ran up. "Don't go down toward Twarda Street," he cried. "Men are being caught for compulsory labor!" Kuba and I had to go our separate ways. But at least we got to spend a few minutes together.

One of the Horch sisters has been absent from school for weeks. She is convalescing from typhus. I learned that Kuba visited her. Her sister went around bragging about it to anyone who would listen! Then I saw Kuba in the hallway, and I think he was blowing her a kiss! I had to take action, so I broke my ruler again, and then I went downstairs to see if he could lend me another one. This worked! Kuba asked to walk me home. I agreed, of course. Zocha opened the apartment door. What a thorough inspection she gave him! Full head to toe! Mother was busy in the kitchen, but I introduced her briefly. Luckily, she didn't have time to pay much attention. On the street where we had walked, some children pointed, and one said "Look, there's a couple in love!" I felt quite happy about this, because I think Kuba and I make a very nice couple indeed! I have not felt this happy in a long time!

MAY

Kuba and I have seen each other every day for almost a month. After school, we stop at my apartment to drop off our school bags, and then we go for a walk. He is unlike all other boys at school—handsome, brilliant, funny. I've never met a less conceited person! I know he will go far in life. It feels like we've known each other forever. At science assembly today, we couldn't take our eyes off one another. Unfortunately, my teacher saw us. He lives in my apartment building. This evening, Mother asked him how I have been behaving. He said "Today she wasted her time!" Both of them laughed.

MAY 8

Friends came over to celebrate my birthday, which is tomorrow. We can't host a proper party with the situation as it is. But we managed what we could, and it was great fun. Beba came, and Fredek, Stawska, Marion, and a few of my cousins. Hanka was there, of course, with yet another new boyfriend. Kuba told me at school that he probably couldn't make it, but of COURSE he was there! He invented that ploy so he could surprise me! After all the other guest left, Kuba took me in his arms. It was heavenly. He asked if I love him! Yes, I do! Unfortunately, he had to hurry home because of the curfew.

MAY 9

This is the happiest day of my life. I am sixteen today—and floating on air! At morning recess, Kuba and I snuck into an empty room to kiss between classes. I can truly say: we are in love! I am calling him Bertie now. I think this sounds American. Maybe I am a little snobbish, but I've always liked English-sounding names. He is calling me Irusia—but no one else knows about these secret names. In the afternoon in our apartment, while my parents busied themselves with a guest, Kuba and I kissed especially passionately.

MAY 16

Today we had the end-of-year party at school. There was music and dancing. Father says it is not proper for us to be dancing in the ghetto. It is a pity to see him so depressed. He used to be quite a cheerful man. Bertie has started talking about more than kissing. He says he dreamed about me—and it was much more than kisses! I am not sure how I feel about this. I know the male mind. If I delay, there's a chance I could lose him. I need to move carefully.
  Bertie and I left school early to run a charity fundraiser. We made giant donation boxes and stood outside the building collecting money for the hospital. A neighbor of Bertie's stopped to chat, but he reported us to Bertie's father, who made a giant scandal. Bertie said he was severely scolded for spending time with me instead of studying. Today I saw Bertie's apartment and met his little sister, Lula. She's ten. I was relieved that his parents weren't home. Bertie led me upstairs to show me the seventh-floor window. It nearly brought me to tears! The most amazing view of Warsaw! I hadn't seen my beloved Vistula River in more than twenty months! We are calling this place our own "Seventh Heaven." It was wonderful to be with Bertie, just the two of us, looking over the city. When Bertie visits our apartment, Mother and

Zocha find a million reasons to enter the room. It's every five minutes, as if any pretext is good enough. Today I finally confronted her. Mother has no respect for me or my privacy.

JUNE

The Germans started making a film in the ghetto. They rounded up some religious Jews with long sidelocks and black coats and brought them to Chlodna Street, where they had trucked in a lot of obviously stolen luxury furniture, carpets, and crystal ware. They forced everyone to pretend-celebrate an "evening ball" at the Jewish Council. Jawerbaum, my classmate, was picked up. At school, he told us they forced him to sing Jewish songs for six straight hours as they filmed him. They took a lot of pictures of beggars, too, and of some emaciated naked bodies from the street. People all over the ghetto are talking about this. They are saying films are being shown in Berlin—as a so-called "portrait" of our "moral values." We are hoping they've done this to make up for some military defeats. The Italians have received a beating in Africa, and we are happy about it.

The Jewish police held a parade, and Adam Czerniakow, president of the Jewish council, came to visit at school. He stopped at our piano and began playing, and Kadysh secretly sketched his caricature. With a few pencil strokes, Kadysh immortalized the bald head, the hook nose, and the enormous fold of fat on the neck! A new kindergarten is to be built on one of the bombed-out lots across from our school. The teachers asked the most talented artists from our group to paint murals for the walls. I was not chosen, but at least Bertie was there to comfort me. Disturbing rumors are spreading. We are being told that announcements will be made soon—and that we will be given forty days left to live. No one knows what to do with this rumor, except to feel frightened. I believe since we have no way of leaving here, there is no point worrying about it. Bertie is using those rumors for his own ends. "What will you gain by dying as an innocent virgin?" he wants to know. "We should enjoy life as long as we can!" I don't think this is reasonable. We are living with our parents, after all, and we are dependent on them. We barely find any private moments!

Anyone with relatives in Palestine has been told to register at the Jewish Council office. They are saying we'll be able to leave the ghetto and join our families. Some people are saying this is a Nazi trap to get our names on a list. But Father came home very excited. His parents have been in Palestine since the early 1930s. Mother says she's not going. I'm quite worried: How can I leave Bertie, especially with all the rumors about what will happen?! I am thinking of staying.

JUNE 20

Przebieg Street is soon to be switched to the Aryan side, and the wall will be moved. Also: the side streets of Muranowski Square. Bertie's family will lose their home. My grandmother, too. The ghetto is getting smaller and smaller. In preparation, the manager of Bertie's apartment building tore down all the posters and announcements. We passed him on the stairs on our way to our "Seventh Heaven." We will miss this place terribly. With his fountain-pen, Bertie wrote on the wall near the window: "On June 20, 1942, Irene and Bertie visited this place together for the last time during the war."

JUNE 21

Father's mood seems a little better. He spent the day at Marcel, his brother's firm. There is an annoying red-headed boy in our class whom nobody likes. Some of the boys finally got tired of him today and locked him in a closet behind the piano. Professor Hillf and Professor Griffenberg heard his crying and wailing and rescued him. But nobody got in trouble for it.

JULY

The new kindergarten opened across the street today, but nobody from our school was invited to the ceremony—not even the students who painted the murals. The Jewish police orchestra played a march, and the council president gave a speech. We are in a terrible heat wave, and everyone is very uncomfortable. Bertie is in some trouble at home because his father is blaming me for his poor grades in Chemistry. He registered Bertie for private tutoring at home so there won't be time to "think about women." Bertie's birthday is coming up soon. He will be eighteen!

JULY 17

In the middle of my Literature tutoring, we heard shots fired. At first, we thought it must be smugglers getting caught trying to move goods over the Biala Street wall. But the shots kept coming—many of them. Father suddenly appeared in my classroom, extremely upset and out of breath. We left together and made our way to Uncle Jakub's factory. Father said the shots came from the area of the Tribunal building, which has been our door to the outside—one of the only places where we have been able to make contact with Poles on the Aryan side who come to buy and sell our belongings. By sundown, things quieted, so we made our way home.

JULY 18

The ground floor of Marcel factory faces a garden attached to The Fountain, one of Warsaw's most exclusive coffeehouses. Today there was a live show, and the garden was full of very well-dressed people. There was an operetta, and my friend Kristina and I stood in the factory and watched from the basement window. We would hear and see everything—some of the most elegant and prosperous Jews of the ghetto. But then it started raining, and the show ended on a down note. Not long ago, I felt so happy. But everything is changing now.

JULY 19

Bertie is eighteen today! Granny gave me a nice silk dress she has been saving. I matched it with a short white jacket that Socha sewed out of lovely fabric from some trousers left over from the times when Father traveled on business trips to Italy. No one needs to know the source of the jacket fabric! I took a bicycle-rickshaw to Bertie's. The dining room was already full when I arrived. I spotted many friendly faces: Elek, Jurek, Rysiek Lindenbaum, and others. Bertie looked amazing in a blue shirt and navy pants matching his fair hair. His father didn't even greet me—just completely ignored me, which hurt a little. Afterward, we all hurried home to beat the curfew. We saw police on the block, hunting people for compulsory labor.

JULY 20

Bertie's father is demanding that he break up with me. I told Mother about this. She is furious. She thinks I should break up with Bertie first, just to show our family is above their insults. She considers this a personal affront—some private war between the parents, as if my feelings do not matter to her at all. I think that nothing besides her pride has ever mattered to her.

JULY 21

A general anxiety took hold of the ghetto. We felt it at school. News arrived at midday that members of the Jewish Council have been arrested. The teachers told us we would be allowed to use the kindergarten yard to play volleyball if we wanted. In the afternoon, we heard gunfire—the gestapo were shooting at passersby. Father's sister Gucia came running to our apartment, warning us to stay indoors.

JULY 22

An evacuation was announced. Police affixed notices on the buildings: we are to be rounded up and deported, 6,000 every day, the Germans are saying, until no one is left. We are to go by freight train. The Jewish police will collect us, building by building. They are saying we will be transported somewhere "to the east," but no one is saying where. They are telling us to bring money and jewelry. We know the Germans are planning to rob us. But certain people will not be deported: Jewish police, members of the council, and any worker at Toëbbens, Schultz, or other German firm that has set up a factory here, and their wives and children up to age fourteen. Those who are left here will be lodged in factory quarters. When the news came, everyone crowded into the street in a panic, pale and frightened, many crying or arguing, trying to figure out what to do. I spotted one of Bertie's classmates and ran to him. He and Bertie had gone to school in the morning, but when some gestapo cars passed near the entrance, they ran to hide in a top floor room. The police action started. The first to be attacked were the refugee centers housing the poorest people. We saw that even families with children and grandparents were being marched in groups toward an empty lot at the Umschlagplatz. People who refused to board the trains were shot. In the evening, I met a girl from school, Hala Parnes' younger sister. She said she had seen Bertie earlier in the day, and he asked her to reassure me, since I have looked so pale and worn recently. Maybe a solution will be found, he said. I know he did not believe his own words.

JULY 23

Very early, the police action began anew, first with apartments near the Umschlagplatz. On streets that were not blockaded, everyone ran feverishly from business to business, begging for papers to prove they are employed by a German firm. Some ran with their sewing machines, as if these will buy them a job. I went to Marcel to look for Father. Uncle Jakub was trying to transfer the title of his company to a German firm so that the workers will be protected. Throughout the day, we heard police ransacking the apartment buildings. In the evening, we all gathered in the apartment courtyard, and fatal news poured in. The neighbors shared which streets have been taken, which families have been separated. Czerniakow has poisoned himself. There was much talk about this. A policeman appeared. He told us that Mila and Zamenhof streets were being rounded up—documents not even considered. That is where Bertie lives.

JULY 24

I left the apartment early and ran to look for Bertie, but when I turned the corner, I saw Karmelicka Street had been blockaded, so I ran to school instead. Few people were there. Then I ran to Marcel. Some workers were standing inside the factory, but no one knew anything. I raced home. But when I got near our apartment on Panska Street, I saw it was blocked. A man was putting up posters: "All unemployed tenants must appear tomorrow at six o'clock in the morning at the Umschlagplatz. Bread and jam will be distributed. Volunteers will be given double food rations." I ran back to Marcel to tell the others. I passed many bodies on the street. What is happening to us? On the way, I met Helfgot and Wolman. They were cheerful, and Helfgot was wearing a white armband. He showed me his new documents with the swastika on them. He has volunteered for an auxiliary police brigade, thinking it will keep him safe. Father was at the factory trying to arrange work documents. Then Uncle Ryszard showed up. I have never seen him here before, as he is not related or connected to Uncle Jakub. He was with a young man I've never met. He told me he lived on Zamenhof Street. He knows Bertie. I asked if he knows anything. "Mr. Siemiatytzki is all right," he told me, "but his wife and children have been taken away." Something strange happened to me then. I felt as if I had been split in two. One part did not know what was happening but was trying to understand. The other part was just watching her. Everything has been lost. Father took me outside and tried to comfort me as we walked home. I could see so many others like me, who have lost someone they love.

Jarek, my second cousin, came to the door to tell us that roundups were beginning in the area between Sienna and Chlodna streets. Mother ran in with Uncle Ryszard. They used to quarrel bitterly, and I hadn't seen them together in years. Everybody started throwing things into sacks, bags, anything we could find. We loaded everything in the back of a bicycle-rickshaw, and I rode in the back, and we returned to Marcel. Father and Zocha were already there. Many others as well. A new firm, Kohn and Heller, is now in charge of the Marcel factory, as Uncle Jakub finally succeeded in transferring ownership documents. Father said these men are Nazi informants. With their names on Uncle Jakub's company, Father said, the gestapo will leave us alone. I made my first "professional" pen-and-ink poster, but it wasn't what I'd imagined for my first paid job! My sign said: "Marcel Company is placed under protection of the Nazi Labor Party." I found a blanket and put it on the desk in Uncle Jakub's office. We are "camping" here together for the night.

JULY 25

Military police and SS squadrons have moved quickly from block to block, dragging people down the staircases. People gathered on the Chlodna Bridge. From that vantage point, they could track which direction the hunters were moving. Gunshots continued throughout the day. Many freight trains arrived and departed the Umschlagplatz. We still do not understand where they are headed.

We have spent the past few days at Marcel, returning to Panska Street in the evening. Uncle Jakub and Aunt Sabina watch carefully when we work, pouring the toothpaste into tubes. They want to make sure nobody slows down, as they fear a surprise inspection from the authorities. It is hard to focus on the work. I sit in my assigned place and wonder what has happened to Bertie. Everybody has been trying to show me sympathy, but they always talk about people in the past tense—saying they "were" instead of they "are." I wonder how easy it has become for a person to get used to the loss of so many. Foreign volunteers have joined the Germans now. We see them in their special uniforms—Lithuanians, Latvians, Ukrainians, Slovaks, Romanians. People say the Germans and Ukrainians might be bribed with gold and diamonds, at least sometimes, but the Lithuanians and Latvians, if approached, will answer only with bullets. Jewish police have continued to aid the roundups as well. Some try to use their position to save their families. But I have also seen some directing their own families to the transports. A few have thrown away their insignia, joining their wives and children. I don't know how these things are even possible. A few days ago, during a blockade of Karmelicka Street, two policemen tried to subdue a woman carrying a child. When she resisted, one of them said "Let's take the child, and she will follow!" She did.

AUGUST

Many mysterious boxes and heaps of lumber were carried into Marcel. The men worked all through day. They covered up a window, and they erected a large wall of storage shelves across one of the doorways. Then they loaded the shelves with paint cans, boxes, and various containers of chemical products. The bottom shelf is our secret gate. If you push it, it flips open, forming a small doorway just high enough for us to crawl inside. Behind this passage is a narrow staircase leading us down to the basement, and at the bottom of the stairs is a corridor connecting two small chambers. Uncle Jakub directed the men to install a little bit of electric light from the factory above. This is where we will hide. I am calling this our "secret catacombs." Some of the men have been assigned as guards. They will take turns standing at the street, and they are to signal an alarm if danger nears. In our group, we have created our own police force. All the details are planned. But we can never be sure of the behavior of the children. They do not understand that life is at stake. They try to talk or cry.

The Germans have killed Kohn and Heller. When we heard the news, no one could agree what to do. Now we must find a new way to protect Marcel and our work permits. Father and Uncle Jakub went to the Schultz firm, on Nowolipie Street, hoping to secure a deal for them to take over Marcel. Schultz is a huge firm making shoes, coats, and leather goods as well as other textile products for the German army. Thousands of Jews are enslaved there. Uncle Jakub has an old friend, Dr. Hepner, who heads the chemical laboratory, and we went to see him, while Mother and the others remained in the catacombs. Hundreds of sewing machines were lined up in the Schultz courtyard. Father said they belonged to people who came begging for work permits. We spent the whole day in Hepner's small laboratory room in the attic, but without settling anything, and then we returned to the catacombs. Father and Uncle Jakub called a family meeting. It was decided that our group would divide, and some would move to Hepner's laboratory until the Marcel ownership matter is resolved.

AUGUST 7

Our first night at Dr. Hepner's, there was another family with very noisy young children. They argued all through the evening. Dr. Hepner agreed it is not wise for so many to stay there, and he arranged a room for us on the fourth floor of one of the Schultz apartment buildings. It's only for daytime. At night, we are to return to the lab in the attic. Everyone I love and care for is disappearing. My school friend Stefa and her parents were rounded up and deported today.

AUGUST 9

Around midday, Mother and Granny went to visit Uncle Ryszard, who is living near the Schultz factory. Father and I stayed in the room Hepner had arranged. Aunt Sabina was with us, as well as Cousins Alec and Liliana. Suddenly, we heard shots fired in the street—a blockade was beginning. Everyone was ordered to come out. We looked down toward the courtyard and saw bodies already on the ground. When we came out through the front door, we were met by Ukrainians pointing their guns. They ordered us to form rows, and then they prodded us toward the Umschlagplatz. A small boy broke loose from the crowd and tried running into a storefront. One of the Ukrainians ran after him. We heard a gunshot, and the boy did not reemerge. We continued, running, with the guns at our backs. A Jewish bicycle-rickshaw driver approached as we reached the entrance to the plaza. "Leave me your ration-cards," he called. "You won't need them anymore!" We saw that a large crowd had assembled at the Umschlagplatz, and we filed forward slowly, advancing along the wall toward the area where German police were inspecting papers. I saw two of my school friends moving in the crowd. Father approached a Jewish police officer, who brushed him aside, but he continued, approaching one officer after another, until finally one of them paused. Announcements were being shouted. I heard: "Felix, step forward! The employees of Felix must step forward!" Father seemed to be showing the man our papers. After a few moments, he motioned for us to follow, and together we broke from the crowd and ran down Stawki Street. We ran as fast as we could, passing broken windows and heaps of blackened corpses. There were flies swarming in the air as we ran, and the stench was terrible. Another group of Ukrainians and SS appeared, and we ran into a doorway to hide. Across the street, a woman's head appeared momentarily in a window and then vanished. We know people are hiding among these haunted buildings. We stayed in that place for several hours, hiding on the staircase and listening, with the awful smell all around us. Finally, when it seemed there was no more movement outside, we emerged. Father and Aunt Sabina led the way, and we ran to Uncle Ryszard's. Mother and Granny and the others were there! Safe! Mother said they had run to the factory and hidden inside it during the roundup, and no one had entered to search for them. Father told everyone about the enormous amount of money he's been carrying in his coat pocket. He said he paid the policeman a thousand zlotys for each one of us.

AUGUST 14

We woke up early. Our street is to be evacuated. Father tried to get Mother to leave and take refuge at the factory, but she refused. She did not want to leave Granny. Mrs. Klin, a distant cousin, was also there. We began packing, and Father sent me ahead with two suitcases. He warned me: I must run straight up to Hepner's lab and hide there if I see any unusual activity. When

I finally arrived, it did seem suspicious. I crossed the courtyards and made my way upstairs. Many people had already taken refuge. Father was there, but he had troubling news: carrying more of our suitcases, he'd left Mother and the others in the apartment. Once the blockade began, he was no longer able to return to reach them. A commotion broke out downstairs as he was telling this, with much gunfire. We sat in silence for about three hours and listened as the apartment buildings around us were emptied of people. When the street was silent again, we went downstairs and headed to Uncle Ryszard's apartment to see what had happened. The door of the apartment was open when we arrived, but no one was there. Furniture had been overturned, and clothes were scattered on the floor. In the kitchen, it looked as though someone had tried to build a barricade out of baskets and suitcases and small pieces of furniture. Mother and Granny and Mrs. Klin must have struggled desperately to defend themselves. Father found the corpse of one of the building cleaning women. We stayed there until sunset. I would give everything to wake up and find this has been only a dream.

AUGUST 15

Today I started work at the furrier unit at Schultz. I am assigned to hand-finishing, which means I put final touches on the fur-lined waistcoats. The cutters cut the fur hides. The machinists sew the pieces together. The trimmers cover the seams with silk tape. Then the coats move to the finishers section. We are on the upper floor. We sew on buttons and make the loops. Then the transport-men take our coats to the Umschlag. One of my prewar schoolmates, Edzia, is here. She is a pretty brunette, and she knows the job. She has been teaching me, but she is weak from lack of food, as the rations have been shrinking. The Toëbbens firm took over ownership of Marcel. Uncle Jakub had to pay them 40,000 zlotys for this, but at least the factory will remain open under a German name, and the staff will be protected. A permanent guard has been stationed on Leszno Street.

SEPTEMBER 1

Toëbbens canceled the deal they made with Uncle Jakub. They will not protect Marcel. Father said everyone connected with Marcel is again in danger and must quickly find someplace to work. There were new blockades today. Apartments are being looted. It is the third anniversary of the start of the war.

SEPTEMBER 3

During my shift, SS came. There was much gunfire and yelling, and we were ordered to go outside with our work permits. With large whips, they forced us to run. Police dogs were brought, but then we were stopped and told to wait. This took a long time, and everyone just sat down on the street. A few people were taken, but the rest of us were marched back to work. As soon as the SS left, I ran to find Father.

SEPTEMBER 5

A general evacuation was decreed. I fried pancakes for Father and for me to use up what was left of our lard reserves, and then we went downstairs. All the apartment doors had to remain open. Schultz workers were to report to an address on Mila Street. Workers from other firms were assigned different locations. Rumors began spreading about a selection. We heard the children would be taken first, and also any adults appearing to be in ill health. We assembled at the designated location but were sent home. They will come for us again tomorrow.

SEPTEMBER 6

Some of the women have applied rouge to their cheeks in order to look younger and healthier. Parents have been dosing children with alcohol to make them sleep, then hiding them in knapsacks. I remained with my work group, and Father joined his. In the crowd, I spotted many familiar faces—my cousin Joziek, his son Jerzyk, my friend Jarek—and I saw a policeman with a stick beating two young mothers clutching their children. We formed rows, as we were ordered, but the crowd stretched for a great distance. There are so many of us. We advanced slowly toward a checkpoint. At the end of the crowd, we could see groups being separated, some motioned toward the Umschlagplatz and others to the right, the other way. An SS officer took my papers and gestured to the right, where the rows re-formed, and we continued moving toward the next checkpoint. I passed through three selections, the last one on the corner of Mila and Zamenhof streets, just below Bertie's old balcony. That's where I finally lost my self-control. I started sobbing, and some women came and encouraged me to calm down. Those of us who had passed all the selections were ordered to return to work. We could see that another section of the ghetto had been destroyed—windows broken, their blinds hanging loosely. I was overjoyed when I saw Father.

SEPTEMBER 7

Uncle Jakub and Aunt Sabina had a close call: they spent five days in a storage closet as Ukrainians and SS temporarily occupied the adjacent room and used it as an office and for some drunken parties. They had a sack of beets with them, which kept them well nourished! Liliana, their daughter, was smuggled out of the ghetto by a Polish family. I heard they arranged for new identity papers to be made for her, and they have given her a new name, Barbara. I believe Uncle Jakub paid for this. Cousin Alec also is still alive, working at one of the "outpost" factories. All the others from our Marcel group are gone—Mrs. Rosen, Elek, Raoul, all four of their parents, Aunt Ludwiga (Uncle Jakub's sister) and her husband Bernard and their two children, Tolek and Stasia. Also Zocha. On Mother's side: the Nisenszals are gone (Ryszard's brother Maurice and his wife Natalia and their children). Also all the Wierners. Both my great aunts on the Bialer side. Jarek's mother. Joziek Trauman's wife. We heard that Dr Hepner's wife and children were shot, and also Dr Hepner himself. These are the ones we know about. But there is heartening news as well: Father has started a job in the fur-cutters' section at Schultz. Hanka and her parents were rounded up but passed all the selections and are living on Muranowska Street. We received word that Cousins Adam and Ludwik escaped over the wall, as did Heniek, and they are living under false identities on the Aryan side. Jarek, too, is still alive, we have heard, passing for an Aryan laborer. Uncle Ryszard and Aunt Lola also are alive. They were helped by a Polish family living on Wolska Street and are living on the Aryan side. Lola's father, my great uncle Bronek, is also there. We count what blessings are left for us. Father and I have sold Mother's remaining dresses, though of course we could not get much for them. The two of us are sharing a room in a two-room apartment. Father works the day shift at Schultz, and I work the night shift. I try to keep the apartment clean while he's at work, and I prepare whatever food we have so it is waiting for him when he returns in the evening. Our shifts are about 11 hours, so we don't see much of one another except on Saturday nights, when we both are free. He and I have invented a ritual: we listen for the other's footsteps on the stairs. When I return from my shift, he stands at the door and says "Is it you, my Iruchna?" And I do the same for him.

At the factory, everyone receives one meal: potatoes with one eighth of a loaf of dark bread, spread with a bit of turnip jam. We also have a bowl of watery broth. Once a week, we are given a slice of meat and a boiled egg. Those who finish 11 waistcoats, instead of 10, may receive an additional 250 grams of sugar and 20 grams of margarine. But a new word has appeared in our conversations: Treblinka. People are talking about "gas baths." They say thousands can be murdered in minutes. They say the corpses are burned in large ovens. Not everybody believes these tales. Some even laugh. But I see what is happening here, and I believe. How else would it possible for so many thousands of people to disappear in such a short time? We can see what the Germans are capable of doing. I have started suffering from dreams. I imagine Bertie pressed inside one of the freight cars that leaves from the Umschlagplatz. I see the fear on his face. I see my mother going to the "baths," followed by Granny, weak and helpless. I imagine them carrying their towels and soap, and then I hear a sound, like the moaning of cattle driven to the slaughterhouse. These scenes merge into a big black mass that whirls before my eyes.

NOVEMBER

A knock on the door woke me up. It was Father. He had to the apartment in the middle of his work shift, putting himself in great danger. He said there are rumors of another blockade. I quickly dressed and returned to the factory with him, trying to make myself small in a corner, since I wasn't supposed to be there. One of the workers showed me a leaflet he found in the street: "Coreligionists! We are calling you! Don´t believe the Nazi propaganda tricks! All the deported have been murdered and incinerated in the crematories of Treblinka, Majdanek and Belzec. Don't let yourselves be driven passively to death! The heroic 3 days of resistance of Krzemieniec's Jews may be an example to you! You must resist and die honorably if necessary! Let's change every house into a fortress! Death to the German bandits!" (Signed) Z.O.B. (Jewish Fighting Organization). Military police have been posted at both ends of Nowolipie Street. Father is saying that people outside the ghetto are helping smuggle explosives to these fighters.

A man named Edek, whose brother-in-law is an influential foreman in the cutters' section at Schultz, has been walking me home after my shift. Today, as we reached my front door, he grabbed me and forced a kiss on me. It happened so quickly I didn't have time to resist. Because of his brother-in-law's influence, he has been able to secure extra food, which he has been lavishing on me. He even gave me a box of machine-needles, which are so difficult to obtain but so helpful. He made me a pair of splendid, fur-lined gloves and embroidered them with my initials. I don't like him and do not want relations with him, but I know he is useful to me. The foremen are being given meat cans with the inscription: "Schweiner fleisch" ("pig's meat"). We are suspicious about the sudden appearance of these cans in such great quantity. Some are suspecting cannibalism. I wonder: is there any crime the Nazis are not capable of? We've had air raid alarms, as Soviet planes have started flying overhead. It seems they have marked the factory as a military objective.

A small bomb fell next door, though it failed to detonate. When the alarm sounds, we switch off the lights, and the younger workers sit together in the dark, singing and reciting poems. Marcel has closed. Uncle Jakub could not find any way to keep it going. He and Aunt Sabina took jobs in the chemical branch at Toëbbens factory and have moved to a Toëbbens-owned room on Leszno Street. They believe that our only hope now is to flee to the Aryan side, even if it means we risk being shot at the wall.

Schultz is producing gloves now instead of coats. Gloves have to be cut from big fur hides, and each machinist must sew ten pairs, plus one huge sheet made out of all the scraps. This is terribly tiresome work, especially at night, so we started deceiving the management by taking fur strips directly from the cutters and sewing them together, making it look as though they had been pieced from scraps. In this way, production was diminished, even as our official output was not. In our own way, we have embraced the spirit of sabotage. I have been quite happy with this arrangement. But they have begun to suspect us. The manager arrived with a guard and began a roll call. At 3 a.m., we were ordered downstairs to pick up huge piles of fur pieces. Every machinist's name was written down so each pile could be tracked to a specific person. Then we had to sew all the pieces together directly under the eyes of the supervisor. By 6 a.m., when our shift usually ends, we were made to start a second load. I was so sleepy that my head kept nodding onto my sewing machine. Finally, by 8 a.m., they let us go. A crowd had gathered, as the day shift had already reported for work. Father cried out with joy when he saw me emerging. Everyone worried that a blockade had been imposed.

DECEMBER 31

New Year's Eve has arrived. Some people are saying they feel thankful to have lived to see another year. But not all.

A PSYCHIC GEOGRAPHY OF FRAGMENTATION

Irene's story opens with the drama of high school. We find her consumed with gossip and with competitions over boys, fashion, beauty, and social events. She attends parties and complains about students in her class. She fusses over her clothing and grouses about an overly controlling mother and a boyfriend's strict father. We see, in the beginning, that teenagers even in the ghetto attempted to reestablish norms of social life that would be recognizable to adolescents elsewhere—with the peer group serving as a reference point for self-esteem, self-definition, and playful social experimentation.

Gossip is the teenagers' tool of power and influence in a context where other means of self-expression are mostly inaccessible, in the ghetto as elsewhere. Thoughtful and sensitive teachers reinforced this configuration to the extent they were able by providing an environment of conventional school rules and familiar, predictable routines. Even in the ghetto, we see, while surrounded by scenes of death and destruction, good teachers recognized the profound value for children of art, sport, and play. A growing body of research points to the persistence of play activities even in the midst of the most crushing circumstances of the war.[1] When Irene tells us about a classmate's caricature of a reviled school visitor, we understand that the teenagers, among themselves, have endeavored to give voice and form to their own ideas and judgments.

But the story soon changes tone, and we enter the whirlwind of death and destruction that followed from implementation of the Final Solution in mid-1942. With work documents, some of the family members are able temporarily to avoid execution and deportation by affiliating with a small manufacturing facility that has been converted to supplying hygiene products for German soldiers. Underneath the little factory, the men build a secret bunker behind a false wall. Irene and her parents take refuge there as the Nazis and their collaborators step up their sweeping raids. The "cleansing" of the ghetto begins, and thousands of Jewish residents each day are forced onto freight trains and delivered to the death camp at Treblinka. In the ensuing weeks of this mass slaughter, Irene loses her mother, her grandmother, and many of her closest friends, including the handsome young classmate with whom she has experienced her first love. Her telling of this atrocity tears at our hearts, as it reveals so much about the psychic experience of an acute trauma. We can pause here to consider what we have read.

We might notice, first, Irene's quite stunning description of the threat of breaking apart—the feeling of being "split in two" on hearing news of the capture of her beloved Bertie. But her subsequent narrative turns rapidly to family and community—to a description of her father's offers of comfort and the scene of fellow mourners experiencing similar loss. We see in this brief pivot the child's mode of anchoring herself by reasserting links to others and to membership in a social group. We note, as well, Irene's descriptions of running—from the factory to the apartment, from the apartment to the school, from the school to the factory, and so on. As terror and confusion escalate, these frenetic descriptions serve as something more than a mere recounting of locations. Rather, we are met by the child's panicked effort to find her bearings. We see that in struggling to reconstitute a feeling of containment, she triangulates, literally, among familiar data points. The writer Suzanne Kaplan, who spent many years studying affect regulation among child victims of the genocide in Rwanda and also among Jewish holocaust survivors, referred to a phenomenon she called "space-creating"[2]—a process by which children construct containing spaces in their minds where a semblance of rationality might be secured against the backdrop of surrounding senselessness. Irene's struggles can be considered in this framework. We also see illustrated here the closely related general principle that a geography of social life is also a geography of psychic life. Writing on the experience of immigration and refugee displacement more generally, both Vamik Volkan[3] and Salman Akhtar[4] have suggested that the physical environment—landmarks, topographical features, and other characteristics of space and place—is taken up in narrative representations of internal emotional life in times of transition. Even years later, we can feel viscerally the horror that Irene describes—a perforation in the logical order of things. But we marvel at how the metaphorical intertwining of physical and psychic space infuses the fifteen-year old's quest for sense, solace, and refuge.

Having secured positions as slave laborers in a firm manufacturing coats and gloves for the German military, Irene and her father find themselves among the rapidly dwindling population of the ghetto. As the mass deportations continue and the death toll mounts, Irene learns what a growing number of historians have observed: that being female has both costs and benefits—and even the experience of survival in the ghetto had fundamentally gendered aspects.[5] We learn there are men among her own community who expect and demand sexual favors in exchange for offers of smuggled food and other supplies. Entering adolescence, we see, Irene must navigate intersecting vulnerabilities and structures of power and powerlessness.

Under the weight of destruction around them, Irene and her father turn to one another. In the mounting chaos, their relationship itself serves as a small zone of comfort and safety, and they devise rituals that clarify and amplify what remains of their capacity to care for one another. Irene's narrative presents us with details that in a different context might seem mostly insignificant: how she prepares a meal, how she and her father listen for one another on the stairs, how they assign one another special new nicknames. In the context of massive and unrelenting violence, however, even these smallest gestures take on a much larger import. We see that they serve as profoundly meaningful statements of integrity and self-affirmation — illustrations of how the capacity to care for others is a tool by which young people cling to their own humanity, even in the context of inhumanity.

NOTES

1. Daniel Feldman, "Children's Play in the Shadow of War," *American Journal of Play* 11, no. 3 (2019): 288–307.

2. Suzanne Kaplan, "Children in Genocide: Extreme Traumatization and the 'Affect Propeller'," *International Journal of Psychoanalysis* 887 (2006): 725–46; Suzanne Kaplan, *Children in Genocide: Extreme Trauma and Affect Regulation* (New York, NY: Routledge, 2018); Suzanne Kaplan and Andreas Hamburger, "The Developmental Psychology of Social Trauma and Violence: The Case of the Rwandan Genocide," in *Psychoanalysis and Holocaust Testimony: Unwanted Memories of Social Trauma*, eds. Dori Laub and Andreas Hamburger (New York, NY: Routledge, 2017), 104–24.

3. Vamik Volkan, *Immigrants and Refugees: Trauma, Perennial Mourning, Prejudice, and Border Psychology* (London: Routledge, 2018).

4. Maria Teresa Savio Hooke and Salman Akhtar, *The Geography of Meaning: Psychoanalytic Perspectives on Place, Space, Land, and Dislocation* (New York, NY: Routledge, 2007); Akhtar, *Immigration and Identity*.

5. Agnes Grunwald-Spier, *Women's Experiences in the Holocaust: In their Own Words* (Amberley: Amberley Publishing, 2019); Elizabeth Baer and Myrna Goldenberg, *Experience and Expression: Women, the Nazis, and the Holocaust* (Detroit, MI: Wayne State University Press, 2003); Andrea Peto, Louise Hecht, and Karolina Krasuska, eds., *Women and the Holocaust: New Perspectives and Challenges* (Warsaw: Central European University Press, 2015); "Holocaust and the History of Gender and Sexuality," *German History* 36, no. 1 (March 2018): 78–100; Zoe Waxman, "Unheard Testimony, Untold Stories: The Representation of Women's Holocaust Experiences," *Women's History Review* 12, no. 4 (2003): 661–77.

Chapter 6

1943

NATHAN

When a newcomer arrived at Plaszow, he received eating utensils—a metal spoon, a cup. We tied them to our belts so they didn't get lost. At night, we lay in our bunks, and we heard the sound of people being marched past the window. The utensils struck one another like small bells. We heard these things, and then, some minutes later, the machine guns. Then silence, maybe for ten minutes. And then the revving of bulldozer engines. We stayed inside the barracks and listened. We could not tell how many prisoners were led past our barracks, but this went on for many nights, night after night. We did not want to go outside, not even to use the toilets.

Inek Tenser was about my age. One day we were walking together in the camp, and we got behind the fence of the kitchen. We saw that the cooks had just thrown out some rotten potatoes. Inek ran over to pick up something to eat, because we were so hungry. The guards fired on him from the tower. I held him in my arms as he died.

Two of the men escaped from the roofing crew. When we got back to camp, Kapo Beim acted like nothing happened. We lined up to be counted in the usual way, but we moved around, and somehow the guards didn't realize two were missing. Beim didn't say anything. The next day after the shift, we were stopped on the way back into the camp, and they recounted everyone. The next morning, we were not sent to work. They took us to the yard. Many guards and dogs were already assembled there, and a gallows had been erected. We were arranged in a rectangle around the gallows, and then they brought Kapo Beim with his hands tied behind him. We could see how much smaller he was than the large men in uniform standing around him. They put the rope on his neck. But at that very moment, with the rope around his neck, he shouted out to us in a loud voice, in Yiddish: "Take care of my wife and children!" The guards kicked away the stool, and Beim was hanged there. One of the guards went over and fired a bullet into his head.

I was sick with diarrhea, but one of the prisoners taught me a way to cure it: charcoal. The Germans burned weeds around the edges of the camp sometimes, and I saw that a few fenceposts were charred at the bottom. I scraped off the charcoal from the fenceposts and I ate it, and my diarrhea stopped. I was beaten only once in this period—during an inspection. I was in the bunk with my feet facing out. The kapo lashed me because he said my feet are too dirty. It didn't hurt much, but I told myself I would not give him another chance to do this to me.

Father and I were moved to a smaller camp near Plaszow. The camp was attached to a factory that was making oil coolers for airplanes. There were only a few buildings, and we were in a small barracks. There were even some children in this camp. I don't know who they were, or if their parents were there with them. I didn't know what they were doing there. I was selected to work the night shift. The work was good, because on the night shift, there were fewer guards, which meant we had some independence. No one was there to constantly look over my shoulders. I started making cigarette boxes and hair combs out of the aluminum pieces, and I was able to sell some of these to the gentile workers in exchange for bread. When the supervisor came near me, I simply loosened the vise and let the pieces fall to the floor. There were some Polish workers who came from the outside, and they gave me bread or sometimes a potato as a trade for the items I made—and they didn't tell anyone what I was doing, making hair combs for their wives and daughters. I made my pants leg into a pouch by tying a string around the bottom near the hem, and I could hide the extra food inside there. No one noticed it.

There was girl in the camp, maybe ten years old. Her name was Nina. She had long black hair. I struck up a friendship with her. In the shop, I made her a little necklace with a pendant in the shape of a heart. I carved letters in it— shin, dalet, yud—which stand for the name of God. I gave her that necklace to show her that God will take care of her. But in the barracks, there were some religious Jews. They took the necklace away from her. They said if she hangs the necklace around her neck, she will be carrying the name of God into the toilet with her, and to other dirty places. That girl cried very much when they took the necklace away. Then one day the Germans came and rounded up all the children and put them on a truck. I was asleep in my bunk at first, because I had worked overnight, but I woke up from the noise, and then I watched them from the window of the barracks. When the day workers returned from the factory after their shift, all the children were gone. Nina was among them. There were no children left after that.

Through the body of the oil cooler, we had to insert two long screws that had nuts on either side. My job was to tighten the nuts and solder around them. But I started to sabotage the machines. I undercut the threads on the screws so the nuts would loosen easily. When I soldered over them, nobody could see anything wrong with them. Some of the coolers were brought back to me to fix. But not all. They made it past the quality-test station. I hoped they were exploding on the planes. A few times, coolers were returned from the field. They came with repair tags. I recognized some that I had made. Whenever I saw them, I had hope in my heart. I hoped they caused great destruction.

One of the Germans walked up to me and pointed his gun. Demanding I follow him, he led me to a pile of coal and motioned for me to climb on it. For a moment, I thought I might have a chance to kill him. We were alone, just the two of us, and I could grab his gun. But when he directed me to jump up and down on the pile, I realized he was after the rats. I jumped on the coal and the rats scurried out, and he shot at them for target practice, and then he let me return to my barracks.

One day, nobody went to work because the tattooing crew came. They lined us up, and they put the letters KL on our wrists—Koncentration Lager. I tried to hide in the back of the group, where no one would see, but eventually they caught me and tattooed me. That night, in my bunk, when no one was looking, I used my teeth. I scraped the tattoo for many hours until I made a bloody mess on my arm. They tattooed us so that escapees could be found and returned. I covered my wrist with a rag so that no one would see what I did. Another man here taught me to urinate on my wound, because urine fights infection. I urinated on the wound whenever I could. No one knew what was under the bandage I made, so I was able to continue to work.

I was wheeling some sheet metal on a cart at the factory, and the sheet metal slipped. It cut me deeply on two fingers of my left hand. I soaked the wound with my urine, as I had done with the tattoo. The camp was full of spider webs. I collected them and used them to form a dressing to cover my wound. There were Jewish doctors, prisoners in the camp, but they couldn't help anybody. We had to take care of ourselves.

Chapter 6

MARYSIA

January

Frozen potatoes cost next to nothing. If I combine them with the eggs I get from the lice experiments, I can make a delicious potato dough which is easily boiled or fried. I'm eating a lot of sauerkraut, too, as there is plenty available, and it's affordable. I am not hungry. For weeks, I had been able to keep my new livelihood a secret from Czesław. He would be disgusted if he knew about the lice—and of course he'd make me stop. I don't want him to suspect how desperate I am for money. But bright red rectangles appeared on my thighs and arms. This posed a problem. But with some effort and searching, I managed to find a long-sleeve dress that fits me well. It's sexy and suggestive, with a low neckline, and it perfectly covers the red patches so no one can see them. Czesław has no idea why I've suddenly taken an interest in this kind of thing—but he's not complaining. We finally found an apartment together, though he continues to bring the ghetto escapees to stay with us. I was hoping for some peace and privacy, but I don't want to seem selfish or look like I'm not willing to make sacrifices for the movement. He brought a new girl this week, Ida. She's nice-looking—a little too interested in him, frankly—and she's going to be staying for a while, helping us in the resistance. I don't like her around, and I certainly don't want her in my bedroom. I tried to bring this up in a conversation with him but it didn't go well. He jumped immediately to the issue of how we need to sacrifice. He is so moralistic, it's almost impossible to talk about anything without making myself look selfish and petty. I am keeping an eye on that relationship.

February 5

The Russians have pushed back the Germans at Stalingrad. We are all feeling a faint hope. The biggest news is, I'm pregnant. I know this baby doesn't have much of a chance. But in this place where so many people are dying and there is such utter contempt for humanity, I feel responsible for the life growing inside me. This new life is a rebuke to everything that is hateful and inhuman.

February 24

Czesław did not come home in the evening. But soon after the curfew started, my younger sister, Ina, knocked on the door, crying and out of breath. Soon after, three uniformed gestapo men showed up and pushed their way in. They asked which one of us is Czesław's wife. "No such person living here," I said. We never had a wedding, anyway, and according to my identity card, I am single. One of the men then approached my sister, caressing her face. It was disgusting. The second approached Ida—the escapee girl who was staying with me. The third came over and surveyed me. They told us to wait in the apartment and said they'd return in half an hour. We listened to their footsteps receding on the stairs, and as soon as they were gone, we started madly throwing things into suitcases. But soon we heard their footsteps returning—and this time, they opened the door with a key. I realized immediately what must have happened: Czesław must have been captured, which is why he hadn't come home, and they must have taken his apartment key. One of the men grabbed me and pushed me with such force that I flew back through the hall into the bathroom and struck my head against the wall. Then they hounded us downstairs into a waiting van. Ina began to speak but was slapped hard. In one swoop, without knowing it, these men had rounded up three Jewish women.

We arrived at the gestapo headquarters on Szucha Street and were ordered to run to the basement. A guard opened a gate, and there we saw the cells. There were benches in the basement, and people seated with their backs to the entrance so only the guard had a full view of what was happening. My sister was led to a seat two rows ahead of me. She turned and murmured quickly: "We met last year during our holidays in Ciechocinek." This was an important message, because they would certainly ask what our relationship was, and of course we couldn't admit to being sisters, since our identity cards show different names. After a few minutes, she turned again and uttered another sentence: "I came to visit you, and we were so engrossed in our chatting, we overstayed the curfew." One of the guards heard her talking and grabbed her. He dragged her out to the corridor where I couldn't see. I heard him ordering her to lift her skirt and pull down her panties. Then I heard the sound of his rod as he beat her. After a few minutes, she was brought back in to the cell, and then I was then taken out to the corridor. I told the guard I am pregnant, but it made no difference. The rod did not hurt. But now I am afraid. My sister gazed at me afterward with quiet tenderness and love, but neither of us could say a word.

We were taken upstairs. On the way up, we saw long corridors with many doors. Everything was quiet. We were brought to an office with a desk. The officer asked a lot of questions about the resistance. We denied everything. But after the questioning, he pulled out one of the leaflets my group had printed. I told him I knew nothing about it. My sister and Ida said the same. But the interview was soon disrupted by the sound of repetitive pounding. The doors opened, and Czesław was dragged into the room. He was covered with blood. "Which one is your wife?" one of the men asked. Czesław pointed weakly toward me. "Do not torment her," he begged. "She is pregnant."

We were returned to a basement cell, and after some time, to our great relief, led outside to the courtyard, where snow was falling. Then we were shuffled onto a truck, but the windows were tightly covered so we could not see outside. It was very dark. When the doors finally opened, we found ourselves at Pawiak, the German prison. We were asked the usual questions at the reception desk: mother's name, father's name, date of birth, and so on. We told them what was listed in our false documents. Then I was separated from my sister and Ida and placed in a cell. Solitary confinement. I was so exhausted, I slept deeply in my bunk.

I lost track of the time. It must have been some weeks. Previous prisoners before me had scratched graffiti into the wall of the cell, and I gazed constantly at one particular message just at my eye level: "Boris, my beloved husband—I shall never see you again." My cell had a small window covered with a thick metal grate. By jumping up and grabbing the bars, I could catch brief glimpses of the courtyard. I saw that spring had arrived, and the sky was bright blue. I saw my sister and Ida in the courtyard, and I knew they were alive. Once, my sister glanced to the window just as I was holding myself there, and she saw me. But then I stopped being able to sleep at night. I kept thinking about how I would react when they came to beat me. I began to imagine other tortures. Day follows day, all the same: silence most of the time. At evening roll call, we were counted. I heard the sounds of the keys turning in the locks, and some shouting and footsteps, and then silence again.

Then one night, I heard loud howling—as if from many animals. I could not move my body. In the morning, the German guard came, and then a doctor, and I was transferred to the prison hospital. The hospital seemed to be staffed with Polish doctors and nurses who were themselves prisoners. I understood from them that my illness looked like typhus. The Germans feared this disease like a terror. My lice! I suddenly felt intensely grateful to them! They are my benefactors!

My fever subsided after a few days. It wasn't typhus. But then I was granted another reprieve: when the doctor prepared my discharge papers, he asked for my name. But I had forgotten it! He realized immediately what the problem was. I didn't have to say anything. Quietly, he handed me a pencil and a scrap of paper and asked me to write a note for someone on the outside who would know the name on my false identity papers. He said it would be a few days before the gestapo approached—they wouldn't bother me until doctors certified that I am typhus-free. I wrote to Wiktor, my brother-in-law, who is no stranger to these manipulations. Within a few days, Wiktor's response was smuggled back to Pawiak with my so-called name. My spirits were buoyed to see that even under the noses of the gestapo, there is an Underground organization!

Guards then came to my cell and brought me downstairs, and I was put in a truck. My sister and Ida were on it. We were overjoyed to be together, but we could not rejoice. To see my beautiful sister and sit alongside her, even touch her—these brought me such exquisite happiness. Soon we arrived at a new location and were placed in a room with benches. Hours passed. More prisoners were brought in—so many from my group that had been publishing the Underground newspaper. They were not in good shape. Several had been beaten up badly. After some time, we were returned to Pawiak.

March

I was finally transferred out of solitary confinement and placed in a communal cell in the women's section. In the communal cell, I had companionship and conversation; my pregnancy was advancing, and the other women treated me with great care. At certain times, we were permitted to receive visitors. One of my old friends, Jerzy, came to see me. The Polish guard at the door recognized him because they used to socialize together before the war, so he let him in. Jerzy explained what had been happening: once they had the key, the gestapo began using my apartment as a trap. An agent had been stationed there for two solid weeks, arresting everyone who came to the door. One after another, the members of our group had been caught—so many of our fellow resistance fighters.

April

The air around the prison filled with thick smoke, and an intense smell of burning permeated the cell in the women's section. We couldn't figure out what it was. But soon the girls were all talking about the uprising in the ghetto: all the buildings left there, we learned, had been incinerated, and no residents were left. Everyone had been rounded up. I passed out when I heard this. I don't know what my cell mates thought. I hoped they did not suspect that I am Jewish. I hoped they blamed my reaction on the pregnancy. After that day, we spent our days in the prison calculating our chances and missing our families. We tried hard to remember what life was like before this.

I was taken out to the prison yard in the morning, where I saw my sister and Ida were already there. We were pushed through the gate and made to run. Outside the prison wall, we saw what had happened to the ghetto. It was nothing more than a stinking, smoldering pile of rubble—total devastation. A gestapo directed us to a building near the Umschlagplatz and left us there.

The ground was littered with strange objects: toys, clothing, some pieces of furniture. There were so many photo albums. Everywhere, I saw photo albums scattered along the ground. I sat down and began to look at them—so many friendly and happy people, weddings, newlywed, elegant receptions. But soon another gestapo appeared, shouting, motioning us toward a cattle car on the track at the other side of the plaza. It was crowded, with room only for standing. A small amount of sunlight entered through the bars of a window. Hours passed. A stench grew inside, and I must have fainted, but I woke when cold drops of water hit my face. They were falling from the ceiling—our breath had condensed in the darkness of the night. In front of me was a very old man with a long white beard. I could tell he was blind. Standing beside him was a young girl, whom I assume was his grand-daughter. She tenderly wiped his brow and spoke soothingly to him. She will hold his hand and lead him like this, I thought, to their deaths. Then the train began to move, and a stream of air flowed from the window, making it easier to breathe. The train stopped. Then moved again. Then stopped. I could not see through the crowd, but I could hear my sister's voice. She and some of the young men had started talking about forcing open the door—waiting until dark. A great commotion rose in the crowd because of this discussion. "When they see broken doors, they will kill us all," someone screamed. "We want to reach the camp." But as the train moved, the young men started to work at the doors, and soon we could feel the blast of cold air. I pushed my way toward my sister's voice. "I will go first," I heard her say. "I will go second," I heard Ida's voice. I pushed my way to the opening, and then my sister disappeared. Ida followed. I heard shots. And then I jumped.

When I woke up, I was on a sand embankment. It was dark. I felt sharp pangs in my abdomen—my child was awake. I couldn't see my sister or Ida. I tried to think: if they jumped out before me, they would be behind me. But which way was that? The tracks looked the same in both directions. I stood to walk, and then a young man appeared. He looked dazed. I thought perhaps he'd been thrown from the train and hit his head. He grabbed me like a child clinging to its mother, but I pushed him away and ran, leaving him on the tracks in his misery and vulnerability. Soon I came across my sister and Ida together. Her legs were covered with blood, and she was crying for water. Ida and I lifted her from the rails, but she cried in pain. I left them there, Ina and Ida, and walked along the tracks until I came upon a small village.

By now it was early twilight, and I could make out the outlines of a building. Then a few more—maybe twenty cottages in all. There were no lights, no sounds. Not even a dog barking. I walked from door to door, knocking, but no one answered. Perhaps these people had found ways to shield themselves from knowing the reality. I myself had just abandoned a young man on the tracks, after all. I noticed a large brick building and moved closer: German police insignia. Perhaps nobody answered my knocks because the Germans were watching. I gave thanks for the darkness.

Outside the village, I found a cottage with a well and a pail chained to it. I knocked on the door and asked for a vessel, but no one answered. I continued to knock until finally a voice called out: "There is a bottle beside the shed." I found it and filled it, and then headed back along the rails to my sister. Not far from where she lay, there was a dense cluster of bushes emerging from a deep hollow. Beyond that was a small patch of forest. Ida and I carried Ina into the gully, and we hid. It was raining, but we slept until we were awakened by gunfire. We thought escapees probably had been rounded up in the forest. We heard the voices of the Germans, but no one approached our hiding place. A full day passed. Then a night. Then another day and another night. We had periods of light rain and periods of sun. After three days, a man came walking through the forest, and he arrived at the edge of our hiding place. He was carrying eggs. By his boots, we could see that he was a civilian, and that he was poor. When he came upon us, he panicked and crossed himself: "In the name of the father and the son," he said, his eyes fixed in terror. Short and of slight build, he seemed to be about thirty years old. We told him we had run away from the transport, and that one of us was wounded. When he saw my beautiful sister in her crumpled skirt, with her golden hair, he seemed to get control of himself. We talked for a while and thought of a plan: he would go home and return with paper and pencil. We would write the name and address of our family in Warsaw, and he would go there and inform them, so they could organize help for us. Ina pulled out a gold chain with a cross. She had been wearing this to look like an Aryan. Where had she hidden it while we were at Pawiak? I only imagined. She handed it to him, and he promised to return. Indeed, a few hours later, he did return, and we wrote a letter to our brother-in-law and gave the young man the delivery address.

Wiktor must have paid him generously, as when the man returned, he was in good spirits. He managed to help Ina get up from the gully, despite her injuries, and we reached a barn near his cottage. Finally, we were dry and warm, surrounded by the smell of hay. The man gave us milk, bread, and boiled eggs.

Some days later, a friend from Warsaw came for Ina. He brought fresh clothing and a summer coat. This was important for looking respectable on the train. We didn't want her standing out. She combed her hair and washed up, though she moved slowly and needed to rest frequently, as her leg and back were injured. Our host moved us out of the barn to a small storage hut farther out in the field. The next day, more help arrived. Jerzy, my old friend from the resistance movement, brought new identity cards. We walked to the train station and hid with him in the bushes and waited, and at just the right moment, when the train arrived, we boarded the first car, just out of sight of the German guard. The train soon stopped again, however, and Germans boarded and began checking papers, removing some passengers off the train. I fainted. When I woke, I saw two distressed male faces. "This gentleman cleared a place for you when you fainted," Jerzy announced, gesturing toward the German. When the German realized that someone had noticed his courtesy, he asked why I had passed out. Jerzy told him in perfect German: "My wife is pregnant." The German then ordered all the passengers out of the nearest compartment and helped to find me a comfortable spot on a bench. I had seen the friendly eyes of the enemy. That man could have made a different choice.

When the train finally arrived at the station in Warsaw, we saw that police were checking documents, and people were being detained. I went to the toilet and locked the door. Jerzy made a paper sign that said "out of order," and we arranged to meet after the curfew. At the appointed hour, I left the bathroom and flagged down a rickshaw driver, who took me to Czesław's mother's apartment. I took a bath. I ate. I slept. Another friend from the resistance came and took a picture for a new identity card. The most important thing: I learned that Czesław was still alive. At Majdanek concentration camp. His father had made contact with a plumber working inside the camp, smuggling letters and food. This plumber was being paid, of course. But it was a priceless service performed at great risk. Czesław's mother spent many subsequent nights standing at the window, behind the draperies, watching for Germans. Not everyone could get used to the idea of harboring a Jewess, especially a pregnant one. I didn't want to endanger her—or anybody. I needed to find someplace else to stay.

September

My son's name is Piotr. He is small and skinny and weak. He sleeps when brought to me for feeding. But I am producing a lot of milk, which gives me hope. I gave birth to him at the charity hospital, which then sent me to Father Badouin's Home for Foundlings and Unwed Mothers. It is financed by the municipality but managed by the Sisters of Mercy, who live there. In the admissions office, the nun asked a lot of questions about my so-called seduction into sin. I invented a wonderful story about a university classmate of my supposed brother. The nun wanted details: what did he look like? what did he say? what did he promise me in exchange for seduction? I told her about his vow to marry me, his method of gaining my trust, my feelings of safety in his presence—everything she wanted to hear. Never before had I delivered such a tale of nonsense. When I finished, her face was flushed! So was mine!

Several women share a room at the home for unwed mothers. Each room has a few beds and cribs, a table, chairs, a wardrobe. There is even a flower vase on the window sill. To be a Jewess here would be a death sentence. But an unwed mother with a new infant and no home—if she is a gentile, she is safe here.

NINA

Our British teachers at school have been disappearing. Even our headmaster, Mr. Holland. Father said Mr. Holland was sent to a prisoner-of-war camp. Now we have Mr. Kahane, a Russian. We had an assembly, and it was announced that we will begin learning Japanese. Our teacher will be Mr. Suzuki. He knows very little English, but he says we can teach him English as he teaches us Japanese. On the blackboard, Mr. Suzuki drew a picture of a bird. He taught us to say "Tori."

As usual, I am a good student. I am always first or second in my class. At recess, we play hockey or run relay races around the synagogue next door. Boys who misbehave get their hands slapped with rulers, and sometimes they are made to stand on one leg. Sometimes, they are made to write 500 times "I must learn to behave" or "Shanghai Jewish School, 544 Seymour Road."

Now that we are in Hongkou district, Father is no longer working. When I am home, he and I spend a lot of time together. We examine the atlas and play geography games. Father has taught me to read and write Polish and Russian. When I listen to Father's stories about all the great places he has traveled, I feel part of this big world, even though our lives here are so limited. My best friend is Anna (Niusia) Szpiro. She is from Bialystok. After school, we buy snacks from the Chinese vendors at the side gate.

IRENE

January 20

More selections have been announced. The Germans are saying they will "cleanse" everyone remaining in the ghetto. Jewish fighters have started throwing grenades. The ghetto is ablaze. At 6 a.m., Father and I ran into each other on the dark staircase—one returning from the factory and the other on the way to work. We talked for a short time and decided we would hide together for the day, and then we went to look for a place. We made our way through Toëbbens territory, through the passageway, toward the secret catacomb at Marcel. The building was in poor condition, with its windows smashed, but we were able to enter through a broken door in the back. It was freezing down in the catacombs, but we spent the day there waiting together in the darkness. By about 6 p.m., when we emerged to the street, we learned that a massive deportation had taken place at the Schultz factory. In the underground passage, I came across a machinist who had worked with me. Eight hundred people had been rounded up. He said Father and I were lucky: half of all the workers in the fur section had been taken, including every one of my coworkers—all the women in the finishers' unit. Father and I decided to return to spend another day in the catacombs at Marcel. It was quite cold.

The fur section at Schultz grows emptier every day. Many of the workers have attempted to cross the wall to reach the outside, but few have succeeded. A Polish laborer smuggled in a letter for Father—a long letter from Uncle Ryszard on the Aryan side. Uncle Ryszard has made arrangements for me, the letter said. There is a place to stay and a person who will help me cross the checkpoint. This cost him a lot of money. But Uncle Ryszard feels I must come now, as time is running out. My heart is torn in two. I know that escape might be my only chance to live. But how can I abandon Father here? Uncle Jakub? Aunt Sabina? Father acted very stoic when we read the letter together. He said he will give me 24 hours to think it over. We visited Uncle Jakub together and talked about it. He and Aunt Sabina encouraged me take the risk of an escape. "At least you'll have a chance," they said.

January 31

The plan is that I will join the Ostbahn work group when they travel to one of the outpost factories. I am to disguise myself as one of them and make my way to the military checkpoint, where I will merge with the group as they pass through the gate. It lifts my spirits to know that today was my last day at Schultz factory. In the evening, Father and I crossed the underground tunnel, and I bade farewell to Uncle Jakub and Aunt Sabina. They were crying. They made me swear I would try to find their daughter, Liliana, and take care of her if they do not make it out of the ghetto.

February 1

I woke up at 4 a.m. I dressed carefully, pulling on as many layers as I could fit: three layers of underwear, two good blouses, a skirt, a dress, two heavy ski-sweaters, a blazer, and my coat. I took an old ring of little value and stuffed 100 zlotys in my stocking. I separated three zlotys, just in case, and put them in my coat pocket. Then Father and I walked toward the checkpoint at Leszno Street. Father ducked behind a building as I approached the gate. There seemed to be a misunderstanding. I couldn't cross. I watched the group leave without me.

February 2

We tried again. This time, the guide met us on Leszno Street. The moment of separation arrived. I embraced Father. We looked at each other's faces. We both cried. This was his last word to me: "Persist!" I left him there and stepped away to join the group. Near the checkpoint, the darkness was slightly illuminated by a burning heap of some kind. I was the only woman among the 200 men, and therefore conspicuous. The plan was to say, if asked, that I am to be working in the kitchen. The men took me to the inside of the group to protect me, in case the guards started thrashing their whips. Each of us was searched. The military policeman took the three zlotys I had prepared in my coat pocket. I carried a photo of Mother and another of Bertie, but I didn't dare carry a photo of Father because of his Semitic features. The policeman looked at the photos but gave them back to me. Then there was a signal, and the group filed forward. I saw Father's silhouette grow smaller until it melted into the darkness.

The guide had prepared me: at a signal, I was to turn calmly and walk toward Chlodna Street, continuing straight ahead until Wolska. The others would continue to the Central Rail Station. "Now," said the group leader. So I walked. I walked as casually and as calmly as I could. I crossed streets where I hadn't set foot in almost two and a half years. Then, almost at Wolska Street, I was stopped by a group of young men. "What a lovely day!" one of them said. "But in Treblinka, it isn't so lovely, is it?" I had been warned about the extortionist gangs—preying on men and women attempting to escape from the ghetto—who rob their victims and turn them over to the police. The men grabbed me and dragged me to a house. On the stairs, they tore off most of my clothing and took my shoes, my money, and the cheap ring, leaving me with a single dress and an overcoat. And then they let me go. I continued walking but tried to cross streets in a zig-zag fashion, to confuse them in case they followed. Finally, I reached Uncle Ryszard. He was waiting for me.

Uncle Ryszard and Aunt Lola escorted me to the home of his former chauffeur, Bolek, and Bolek's girlfriend, Natala, who used to be an obstetrician before the war. The apartment is nice and in a residential quarter of Warsaw. I noticed that Bolek was calling Uncle Ryszard by his first name—a social revenge that makes me smile.

Natala is very pleasant. The main inconvenience is her large family. She trusts very few of them to keep quiet about me. If anyone visits (other than one trusted brother and one trusted sister), I must run to the attic. One of the "untrustworthy" sisters and her husband visit frequently, unfortunately, and quarrel ceaselessly. Sometimes, when they arrive, I don't even have time to dress, and then I spend hours in the attic shaking with cold. Bolek brings his work friends sometimes. They laugh and drink. I don't complain, though: after the guests leave, I am treated to hot tea and snacks. I have my poems that I recite to myself, and I do not feel alone. Natala and Bolek both work at a German factory. They steal and sell everything they can get their hands on—even spare car parts! They talk about these exploits among their friends and laugh and laugh. From time to time, Uncle Ryszard and Aunt Lola visit. Lola uses her new name, Agatha. They bring me letters from Father. "You must endure anything and obey Ryszard absolutely if you want to survive," Father has written. I notice he does not write about himself. I can only guess how bad it must be for him now. Should I have stayed with him? I yearn for him and blame myself for leaving him alone. I can't stop thinking of him.

April 19

From my window, I heard rumbling and thunder from the direction of the ghetto. I am reminded a little of September, 1939, when the first bombardment began. My heart is bursting with pain and wrath. I hope so desperately that Father is holding on. It is the start of Passover.

May

Everyone was talking about the remarkable Jewish resistance—with grenades and gasoline bombs. Even the "friendly" Poles shook their heads in disbelief. They believe the Polish resistance must have helped. In retaliation, Bolek said, the Nazis set fire to every building in the ghetto. Bolek heard troubling rumors at work: the Nazis are going to search the entire city of Warsaw. They will go from house to house, rooting out Polish resistance fighters and Jews in hiding. I still have no identity papers. Uncle Ryszard says he is working on it, but he is running out of money.

June

I have moved to a new place—a one-room apartment. The man here, Yurek, is kind and easy-going, but his wife is stubborn and makes negative comments about Jews. They leave for work in the morning and return at night. My job is to keep the place clean. But I am not to go out or show my face near the window. I spend hours reading on the couch. If visitors come, I lock myself in the bathroom. My hosts apologize and say that it is out of order. I listen for voices on the street outside, and in this way, from my couch, I learn the news. "Well, now, here's to Pantelleria!" I have heard. And "here's to Lampedusa!" I know these are Italian islands, near Sicily. They have been taken by Allied forces.

September

My false identity documents finally arrived. I have moved out of the city to Ostrow, a small provincial town. My new name is Kristina, and I am working as the servant for two women who live in a large country house. Mrs. Taczanowska is a very elderly lady, and her daughter must be about fifty, though she still looks pretty good for her age. Her husband does not live here, but he is an acquaintance of Uncle Ryszard, who has paid for this arrangement. Mrs. T. has turned out to be kind and intelligent. From the garden, I have milk, flour, groats, and vegetables. There are hens, geese, ducks, and plenty of potatoes. I am better nourished now than at any time in years. In return, I work from dawn until dark. I wake early to light wood in the stove. I have learned to clean the poultry and cook it with potato peels. I wash and iron the sheets. Sometimes I am so busy, I don't even have time to comb my hair. But I am not complaining one bit, as this is nothing like the forced labor of Schultz. To some extent, I have noticed, Mrs. T. feels herself a victim because of her daughter's hostility. This has given us a certain shared feeling, and we have struck up a friendship. She is a former schoolteacher, and we spend every free moment chatting, discussing literary subjects. We heard that Allied forces are nearing Rome.

December

Cousin Heniek and his wife are dead. Someone denounced them to the Nazis, and their Jewish identities were found out. It is a reminder that we remain in constant danger, despite our new papers. We celebrated Christmas with great solemnity. Mrs. T and her daughter used all the sixty eggs she had been keeping for the occasion. We baked enough cakes, biscuits and tarts to fatten a regiment. Guests came. They finished every last crumb.

ENDURANCE, RESISTANCE, TERRIBLE CHOICES

As 1943 ends, the war rages. At Plaszow, in the nighttime darkness, Nathan lays in his barracks and takes in the grim rumblings of gunfire and bulldozers just outside. Even decades later, we note in his telling, he continues to be haunted by the strange, delicate notes of metal utensils that knock one other like bells. We see what a generation of trauma scholars has observed: that a child's memory of catastrophe affixes itself to minute details of somatic experience, to small remembered fragments that hold back great submerged expanses of terror.[1] In the sparseness of Nathan's story, moreover, we see the child who does not bring himself to articulate what his mind knows—the familiar interplay of knowing and not knowing, of telling but also refraining from telling. Even in relaying the story decades later, Nathan reiterates that he is speaking from indoors behind a barrier of separation from what is happening outside. It is as if he is continuing to remind himself, even years later, of whatever remains of the possibility of refuge and containment. This is, again, the child's creation of a "sense-making space."[2]

A young friend is shot and dies in Nathan's arms, and his work-unit supervisor is hanged in a brutal display of camp discipline. But Nathan reports that the vulnerable man, despite his small stature, possesses a large and bold voice—a voice that rings out defiantly even at the edge of death. This clearly makes an impression on Nathan, and we see that he responds with a change in his own voice—a voice that reflects a growing sense of agency and self-determination. With increasingly bold assertions of defiance, Nathan begins purposefully and deliberately to sabotage the factory machines and harness his energy to undermine the enemy. In an act that under other circumstances might seem like florid psychosis, moreover, he uses his teeth to tear and carve his own skin, disfiguring the Nazi registration mark that has been tattooed on his arm. It is difficult to allow ourselves today to imagine such a profoundly disturbing image—the near-starving sixteen-year-old boy in his bunk, chewing his arm in the darkness. And yet we understand that in the hideous language of rage, Nathan is erasing the sign of his subjugation. Reclaiming symbolically the integrity of his disfigured body boundary, he announces the fundamental and unassailable intactness of his right to remain alive and in charge of himself. This is a stunning development in Nathan's story—a pivotal juncture in his evolving pathway to adult identity and capacity.

As the Russian army pushes back the Germans in Stalingrad and hopes rise for the war to end, Marysia learns she is pregnant. Separated from her boyfriend in a gestapo trap and then sexually assaulted by prison guards, she is thrown into solitary confinement in a cell at the notorious Pawiak Prison, where she sinks into a delirious fever. Weeks pass, but Marysia comes to see that even deep in the prison, a community of Polish activists continues its clandestine work of resistance. When the prison yard air fills with smoky ash and word spreads about the ghetto's destruction, Marysia hides her agony. She cannot begin to count by now the numbers of her family who might have been slaughtered just on the other side of the prison wall. Pregnant but rounded up for deportation, she leaps from a boxcar. A strange accident of luck—a Polish peasant wandering near the forest—enables her to reestablish contact with her network of supporters in the underground, and her Polish brother-in-law provides remarkably astute assistance that ultimately saves multiple lives, including her sister and a fellow resistance fighter.

Deception has evolved into an art form for the surviving Jews of Warsaw, we see, and for their gentile allies—a creative enterprise requiring constant alertness to moments of emerging opportunity. These creative aspects of resistance seem to energize Marysia, demanding her attention and strengthening her engagement with the tasks of survival. When her son is born, Marysia deploys quite creatively and in a curated way the prevailing Polish Catholic cultural narrative of female victimization, convincing some nuns that she has descended into sin. In exchange for her appealingly lurid story, they provide refuge for Marysia and the infant boy. Passing as a poor girl unwittingly seduced, but hiding the real source of her persecution, Marysia secures a safe place where she and her baby can wait out the rest of the war.

Irene and her father observe their life chances diminishing rapidly. But Irene makes an agonizing and momentous decision when an opportunity emerges for her to escape from the ghetto. Her decision means abandoning her father and her remaining aunt and uncle. Just before she slips, disguised, into a crowd of workers crossing the checkpoint, she receives her father's final gift, a message: "persist." It is a talisman she will hold long after the war ends. Irene's story reminds us that persecuted children make impossible choices; their titanic acts of courage and realism carry unspeakable personal cost. Irene follows carefully the instructions she has been given; she accommodates to new conditions and remains open to new relationships. But yearning for her father, she is heartbroken and wracked by guilt. When she tells us that guests have come to the farmhouse where she is hiding and have eaten "every crumb" of a Christmas dinner, we understand that she herself feels almost completely consumed.

Nina's father spends more time at home after the refugee families are confined within the Hongkou district. Father and daughter enjoy their time together and study an atlas of the world. It is a message of hope, in a sense, as it enables Nina to continue to feel that she knows a place in the world—a literal place—and that the world is in some ways still comprehendible if seen in the right light.

NOTES

1. Bessel van der Kolk, *The Body Keeps the Score: Brain, Mind, and Body in the Healing of Trauma* (New York, NY: Penguin Books, 2014); Vamik Volkan, Gabriel Ast, and William F. Greer, Jr., *The Third Reich in the Unconscious* (New York, NY: Brunner-Routledge, 2002).

2. Kaplan, *Children in Genocide*; Suzanne Kaplan and Andreas Hamburger, "The Developmental Psychology of Social Trauma and Violence: The Case of the Rwandan Genocide," in *Psychoanalysis and Holocaust Testimony: Unwanted Memories of Social Trauma*, eds. Dori Laub and Andreas Hamburger (New York, NY: Routledge, 2017): 104–24.

Chapter 7

1944–1945

NATHAN

1944

We were marched back to Plaszow. We didn't know why the work was stopped. They kept us in the camp for a few days, and then we boarded a freight train. Many people were inside. It was crowded. Eventually I was able to lay on the floor with my face down near a small hole in the planks, where I could get some air. Some people died next to me, but I did not move because I didn't want to lose my spot. Days passed, but when the doors opened, we were at a new camp—Mauthausen. I jumped out onto the platform, leaving bodies behind me on the train. Father survived the trip, weak but still able to stand. We found ourselves in the middle of a wide, clean street of neatly painted white buildings. It looked pleasant at first—with colorful flowerbeds. Then we were arranged by alphabetical order, and a selection started. The officer looked us over and motioned with his white glove, assigning each person to a group, some to the right, some to the left. I noticed that a young boy in my group, younger than me, had the same name as my father—Avram Gutman. Father had been sent to a different group, but he was able to move in in the crowd with no one noticing, and he found his way back toward me. We could see what was happening. Some men were being loaded onto trucks; the others were being led toward a building. Another selection started, and Father and I once again were separated. But again he found his way back to my group and stood next to me. We kept trying to do this, but eventually, the numbers in the crowd were getting smaller, and it became impossible for Father to continue switching without being noticed. I nodded my head to him across the platform—trying to assure him that I would be ok. I wanted to tell him I would be ok. But he was taken away, and I was loaded onto the back of a truck.

In the truck, we traveled some distance over a rough road, high into the mountains, before arriving at a new camp. This was St. Valentin. At the factory attached to the camp, they were building parts for German tanks. I was put to work at the turret lathe. My left hand was still injured, but I had kept it wrapped so no one could see. I knew I must continue to work. I used my right hand.

Every morning at dawn, we were marched to work, surrounded by armed guards with dogs. We moved six in a row—we were like skeletons in our striped uniforms marching through the streets of the village of St. Valentin. I saw people peeking through the curtains of their houses sometimes as we passed. We made a strange sound with our wooden clogs on the cobblestones. In the evening, we were returned to the camp, but not everyone returned. When someone was too slow or weak, if he stumbled or fell, the guards shot him, and then his body was dragged to the side of the road. There was a work unit at the camp—prisoners assigned to retrieve the bodies of these fallen men. In the camp, we stood in line and receive a piece of dark bread and a cup of watery cabbage broth. Then we were locked in the barracks again until the following morning.

Inside the factory, it was comfortable. The machines were arranged in rows. They made a clattering sound. My job was to move a big wheel. I moved it two revolutions clockwise, then two revolutions counterclockwise. I caught the finished piece and advanced the stock. I needed to repeat the cycle every minute or so. We got half an hour for a midday break. The movement of the wheel was monotonous, so sometimes as I worked, I dreamed. I thought of Mother and Father, my home. I dreamed of food.

Some of the prisoners were saying it was Yom Kippur. When they handed out the piece of bread in the morning, I didn't eat it. I hid it inside my pants. Grandmother taught me to fast on Yom Kippur. So I stood at the lathe, and I recited to myself: *Sh'ma Israel, Adonai Elohenu.* I said this over and over, quietly to myself, as I worked. When we returned to the barracks, I sat in my bunk, and I said *Sh'ma Israel* one more time, and I took out the bread that I had been hiding in my pants, and I ate it.

WANDA

January 1944

I had wanted a baby, but Edek said we'd need to wait to see how the war goes. Soon after the Battle of Stalingrad, last spring, we started to make an effort in earnest. We are at the hospital in Cape Town. Erica, my daughter, was born on my mother's birthday!

IRENE

January 1944

The Soviets have crossed the Bug River! A tenant rented one of the spare rooms, but I never got to know him, since he stayed only briefly. Nazi officers came searching for him last week. Mrs. T. told me he had been a Polish officer and was using a fake name (just like me). Out of caution, the women have invented a story to "explain" my presence to the neighbors in town: they are saying my father is being held prisoner in Auschwitz, and I am working to raise money for mother and little brothers and sisters. In support of this tale, I have started attending church and praying where everyone can see me.

October 1944

Germany is in retreat. Transports from the eastern front have been passing daily. The soldiers rent our rooms, but thankfully they are exhausted—not much interest in women. This is quite unlike the insolent and shameless "master race" that invaded our country five years ago. My Uncle Bronek and my cousin Ludwik are dead. I received word that they were shot during the Warsaw Uprising. The Nazis burned house after house, destroying every quarter of the city. The Russians watched indifferently as Warsaw fell to ruins. Millions of people, Poles and Jews alike, are dead.

NINA

Spring 1945

I have been given an important part in the school play! I am "Little Miss Buttercup." I am also going to sing in the school choir. I have visited some of my friends. They are Russian Jews. The Soviets are not at war with Japan, so the Russian Jews are permitted to live outside the refugee district. They live splendidly! with large homes, cars, chauffeurs, and Chinese helpers. I am taking ballet lessons. My teacher is very strict. She hits our knees with rulers to make us strand straight! At school, we are studying Shakespeare's plays. I have memorized parts of Hamlet and Julius Caesar. Father and Mother marvel when I recite for them. Father has put up a map. He is using pins to show how things are moving. We are glued to the radio for reports about the war. Father and Mother are rarely leaving Hongkou now. The entrances to our district are being carefully guarded. Father says the Japanese are getting worried about how the war is going.

July 1945

American B-29 planes dropped bombs on Shanghai. We heard there were some dead and wounded in Hongkou district. They are saying it was not far from our apartment, near the Ward Road jail. On the streets, we see many homeless and sick people now. I have seen a disease called elephantiasis. It is quite terrible. Several organizations have been distributing food. The Jewish Joint Distribution Committee, UNRRA, IRO. In our district, there is a large central kitchen, and families have been given permission to take food home. Father says our family has exhausted most of our money supply. We are listening closely to the radio. The Japanese have started to leave the city.

September 1945

The war is over! The Japanese have surrendered, and Americans have entered Shanghai. They are playing American music in the movie theaters now! I know some of this music! We have received news about our family. Many are dead. We are beginning to realize how lucky we have been. Father and Mother visited the US Consulate. Finally, they were able to get visas for us. We are looking forward to things to come.

IRENE

Early Spring

The regional military postmaster rented a room at our house. Last week, he got himself drunk and announced he wanted me as a "date." I ran into the kitchen and piled up the tables and chairs to barricade the door. He banged and banged at the door, like an animal, and I ran into the garden to hide. He chased me and pulled out his gun and started shooting randomly into the air, crying my name. Nobody came to help—they were too scared! He finally retreated to bed. In the morning, he pretended nothing happened. But before he left, he stole a few of our ducks.

Russian rockets began roaring overhead, and we stayed four days in the basement while an artillery duel raged outside. The Nazis dynamited a few buildings nearby, and the town was full of smoke. We all emerged to cheer the "Kosciuszko Division" of the Soviet Army, our liberators in their Polish uniforms. Mrs. T died soon afterward. I think it was all far too much for her. I was sad. We had a series of guests after that in the spare rooms: some

Russians, then a friendly doctor from Tashkent, who brought with him a Jewish servant, and then a troupe of folk singers. They left the rooms in a terrific disorder, but I didn't mind. I stood in the kitchen corner and enjoyed their beautiful songs.

March 17, 1945

Warsaw has been liberated. I returned to the city as a free person. It seemed others had the same idea as me, and several of us met each other on Florianska street, at mother's father's home. We found an entire Soviet Army unit camping in the yard. There was a sergeant occupying the kitchen and an officer in grandfather's former office. The surviving Bialers met us there. Uncle Ryszard was there with Aunt Lola (now Agatha), and cousins Adam, Lili (now Barbara), and Zosia Klin, whose mother had been taken away with mine. Lili has a new husband, who also came. The next day we gathered at the Jewish cemetery to see grandfather's grave, and then I went on to Panska Street. Nothing was left of the ghetto—just a heap of bricks and rubble and bone and ash.

NATHAN

1945

Some Austrian civilians were working at the factory. My supervisor, the tool-setter, was one of them. He was an old man with shoes that were old and worn, and his little wire glasses that kept falling down his nose. He bent at the grinding wheel sometimes to adjust the controls or sharpen one of the instruments. His hands were large and strong, with long fingers stained black from the machine oils. He walked among the machines and sometimes picked up a finished piece to inspect. At his lunchtime, he sat in a corner and opened a box. He took out a package wrapped in brown paper and unwrapped it with great care. I could smell the fresh bread, and I couldn't take my eyes off him as he ate. When the last bite seemed to be gone, I watched him slowly crumple the wrapper into a ball. Then he stood up and walked to the nearby trash barrel. But when he raised his hand to throw in the paper ball, he held it in the air just an instant longer than necessary. At that very moment, he looked at me. It wasn't a long look. It was just a moment. But after he walked away, I felt that he had told me something. So I bent down into the barrel and grabbed the brown paper ball. The guard did not notice when I quickly hid it in my clothing. At my work station, I could smell it: the tool-setter had given me a piece of soft, fresh bread.

Every day after that, the tool-setter brought me bread. He never said anything to me or even looked at me. I waited for him to move away from the garbage bin so that no one would suspect anything. I don't know anything about this man, but I am so grateful.

The Germans expected a certain output from the machine. I took a piece from the pile on the right, put it the machine, and then moved the finished piece to a pile on the left. At the end of the day, the finished pieces were counted. But as soon as the counting was done and the guard walked away, I took a whole bunch of pieces from the left and put them back on the right. This way, I already started the next day with 100 or 150 finished pieces—and, even more important, the Germans got less work. They did not know, but I was doing my best to slow them down. I was getting very thin, but still strong enough to stand on my feet and keep working.

It was bitterly cold. The sirens were going off frequently, as we were having air raids. When we heard the alarm, we rushed to an underground shelter. We recognized a strike by the flickering of the lights and by the dust falling from the ceiling. When the bombs exploded very close by, we felt the tremor of the walls, and we cheered. Then the bombings became more frequent and more accurate. The factory was quite badly damaged, and we could see the sky, gray and snowy, through big holes in the roof. Some of the walls collapsed, and not all the machines were working anymore. But we continued with the ones that were left. One day, the guards stripped us naked, even though it was freezing outside. Two men grabbed me and dipped me into a vat of cold freezing water, supposedly with some kind of disinfectant. They were saying this would rid us of lice. Food was growing more scarce.

May 5, 1945

After the factory at St. Valentin was closed, we were returned to Mauthausen in trucks and unloaded in front of Barracks 6. The guards locked the doors, and then we were in darkness. The boy next to me died. He was delirious and cried for a few days, calling out to me. His body was cold and stiff alongside mine, and it was difficult to breathe because of the smell. I lay in my bunk, thinking of the Austrian tool-setter, imagining he is watching me from behind his little wire glasses. I don't know how much time passed. A loud sound came, almost like an explosion. It shook the barracks. I heard the doors sliding open, and I knew that light was flooding the room. I could make out the silhouette of a helmeted figure, and I heard his words. They were in English: "Oh my God."

Chapter 8

Young People in the Confrontation with Disaster

In a period of less than six years, World War II reconfigured the world. It reshaped political boundaries, governments, national ideologies, and economies. It shattered cherished conceptions about morality and forced a painful reckoning with the human capacity for gross brutality. One-third of the world's Jews were exterminated, including 90 percent of those who had lived in Poland, once home to Europe's largest concentration of Jews. Among the murdered were my great-grandmother Ester and almost all of my father's many dozens of aunts, uncles, and cousins and their spouses, children, and extended families: Jakub, Mala, Gustava, Ludwiga, Barbara, Janina, Helena, Stefania, Julius, Bernard, Stasia, Zygmunt, Tolek, Sabina, and so on. They included Irene's mother, Natalia, and her father, Stanislaw; Marysia's father, Josef, and Wanda's sister-in-law, Nina. They included Hadas and Avram, Nathan's parents, and also Hadas' mother, her sisters, and their extended families. The stories collected in this book are those of a uniquely small minority.

Young survivors can be among those most profoundly affected by war, as war disrupts so many of the conditions for normal physical and psychological development, and at a time in life when they matter greatly. All the more so for young people who are the targets of a genocidal ideology—who come to know they are objects of widespread hatred. But there is evidence, nonetheless, that during and following even the most profoundly depriving conditions, many young people continue the developmental journey relatively successfully.[1] Indications of this emerged in some of the earliest postwar writing, when Anna Freud and colleagues described remarkable work in England with a small group of children who had forged intense social bonds with one another during their captivity in Terezin concentration camp.[2] Studies of "alternative avenues" for development might have significant implications for contemporary theorizing about processes of growth and change in children, as Anna Ornstein has written.[3] Much can be learned in this regard from the stories collected here, as they document, albeit in highly filtered form, many important elements of the developmental arc traversed by each young person through the years of the war. The memoir entries illustrate strategies that each young person deployed in attempting to extract affirmation, protection, nourishment, and validation from an environment where these were severely compromised. Underscoring the uniqueness of each young person's developmental journey, the stories here reveal, at the same time, more general patterns and capacities in the processing of loss, separation, humiliation, fear, and violence. This is a key to what the stories can tell us about development and resilience in the context of a world that is today again in chaos. The material here is moving to us not only because of the grotesque historic evil it records. It is moving, as well, because of the intimacy and immediacy of the evidence it provides for the diversity of experiences of loss and strategies of psychological self-preservation across different ages and life stages, even within a family.

Nina, at age six when the war began, was the youngest surviving member of her once-sprawling family. Her escape from death can be attributed to the actions of a courageous Japanese consular official—an agent of the enemy— who defied the orders of his commanding officers and granted travel permits to the panicked Jews of Kaunas.[4] But that man's bold acts are not at the center of Nina's story. Rather, beginning in Wilno in 1940 as her parents' desperation mounts while their visa applications are repeatedly rejected and hopes dashed, Nina presents us with a bright, optimistic, and confident six year old—sociable, friendly, and eager for adult approval. She understands at a certain level that her family is in danger; she knows they have been repeatedly rejected in their applications for safety. But she adjusts to temporary quarters and is shielded from the worst news. Even as they subsequently flee across continents, we see, Nina's parents retain sufficient resources to provide a cushion of familial warmth and daily routine that foregrounds stability and predictability despite the surrounding and encroaching chaos. Appropriate to her age, Nina finds refuge in mastering her school subjects and pleasing her teachers, and in the familiar rhythms and configurations of her parents' continuing social contacts with their neighbors and friends. There is reciprocity in this provision of comfort: in the songs and poems she learns at school and brings home to share, Nina bears important gifts for her parents: tokens of mutually reassuring continuity in a time of discontinuity. Nina remains the solid student, the good girl, the enterprising youngster from the good family. She is seen and heard, and she herself sees and hears and continues to affirm this for her parents. The reciprocity in this relational structure takes the place of home, even in the context of homelessness; for both parents and child, it sustains containment and psychic continuity and provides a link to the prewar order.

Young children measure the danger and threat to themselves by gauging the reactions of those around them, especially their parents and teachers, as much research has shown.[5] In this context, against a backdrop of cultural unraveling and panicked movement across continents, we find in Nina's six-year memoir the image of the child who gazes vigilantly into the eyes of her able parents, monitors what she finds there, and aligns herself with their abiding competence. Nina reports many times about her parents' moods, their opinions, their activities, and their expectations for her. We can see she is observing them closely, alert to the signals their bodies and tones might send. Her story speaks to us about the way parents impart core ego skills even in hard times. It demonstrates the profound psychological benefits for refugee children not only of intact families but also of access to peer groups with shared experience and understanding, and of structured, normalizing routines offered by schools and other familiar cultural institutions. We note that support for parents—for their sense of competence and capacity—has urgent bearing on the health of their children. Generations of research on the experiences of children in war testify to the importance of adult responses to danger as a mediating factor in children's responses.[6]

David is a coddled and overly dependent seven year old when we first meet him in the living room of his parents' Warsaw apartment. He is doted on by servants and barely dresses himself without the assistance of a governess. External circumstances, foremost among them his father's great wealth and social connections, converge to enable his flight from the approaching storm. But we see in David's brief memoir, which covers a time period of only half a year, an arc of great developmental transition—a transition that occurs not despite the war, but also because of it. When the bombs start falling and confusing news arrives, David finds he can experiment in self-governance in ways previously unavailable. Surrounded by explosions and burning buildings, with his nannies in flux and his parents tense and distracted, David senses, vaguely at first, that much is amiss. He assigns himself the task, in this context, of acquiring detailed information. He asks endless questions, takes inventory of new cultural artifacts, investigates what lies behind forbidden doorways and around dark corners, and checks his maps as he tracks the family journey under aerial bombardment. He registers the sights, sounds, and smells in the milieu, memorizes place-names, notes precise dates on the calendar, and acquires fragments of several new languages. When his parents arrive to check on him in the butcher-shop cellar where he has been briefly hidden, he is proud to show that he has found a means, quite literally, to stand up by himself and look outward. In accumulations of data and detail, in the activity of information-gathering, David builds for himself the image of a masterful young man in the know, an able and industrious young person who is no longer a baby. We see that he creates, in this way, an alternative both to the prevailing atmosphere of violence, chaos, and humiliating rejection and, at the same time, to his previous helpless dependency. Erik Erikson, in his classic book about child development,[7] noted that the primary developmental task for children of David's age is to learn to participate actively and meaningfully in society, to achieve a first taste of proficiency and mastery. In David's stories, we see that under conditions of danger and profound uncertainty, simple curiosity and information-seeking can serve for some children as important tools in achieving this core developmental task.

But we see that David also practices what the Israeli psychoanalyst Shamai Davidson[8] called "awareness control." Even as he is vigilant and answer-seeking, he manages to avoid a direct confrontation with certain kinds of knowledge. He is moved, for example, when bullets fly just meters from his own body and a child his age is murdered, but his story, we see, focuses not on the boy but on the actions of his own father, who has pulled him out of the line of fire. David diverts from consciousness some particularly disturbing information about his own risk and the reality of being hunted. He smells the burning orphanage but does not dwell on what was lost there—although the sensation will return to him in later life, as my sister and I found when we cared for him in his final months. We see in David's story, also, how particularly horrifying realizations can be compressed into the more tolerable packaging of passing observation: David notes that one of his cousins has been turned away from the car window on the morning of the escape from Warsaw; with little fanfare, he registers from his mother's lap the conflict this has aroused in the group. He also reports, but briefly, on the birthday gift of an expensive land parcel in British Palestine that ultimately elevated his own family's prospects for survival above those of so many less fortunate others, including his closest cousin. His guarded way of telling these cataclysmic truths, even decades later, reminds us that children balance knowing and not knowing, vigilance and denial, dissociation and attention. They take up new information selectively, allowing it to enter their consciousness in self-preserving ways—though their strategies of parsing and packaging might not last forever.

The next oldest of the group, Nathan, is torn from a comfortable middle-class life and thrust, at age twelve, into a six-year vortex of monstrous violence and degradation. He loses his friends and his community and is separated from his family as he is buried in a hole under a barn. He hears, at close range, the barking of search dogs. When the situation becomes unsafe for the farmer who has taken him in, he is sent to walk alone to find his family. Soon, in the Krakow ghetto, he loses his mother, his aunts, and his grandmother, hearing from a neighbor the violence to which they have been subjected. Subsequently conscripted into slave labor and transferred among a series of concentration camps, he holds in mind his father's advice: that labor will be the key to survival.

Separated from his father in the concentration camp, Nathan continues alone. But we see, in a sense, how Nathan finds ways of feeling un-alone. Precisely at a time in life when children open themselves to new role models, Nathan realizes there are skills to be learned from other men in the camp. Stumbling upon a scrap of wool and an odd bit of wire, he shapes a small needle and sews a lining for his prisoner uniform. He uses found pieces of string to rig secret hiding pouches in his clothing and forms random chunks of rubber into soles for his shoes. Free momentarily from a factory guard's gaze, he hides away an extra piece of metal and solders a gift for a fellow inmate. He learns to treat wounds with urine and spider webs. In a setting where no secure or permanent allies exist, we see that Nathan discovers a way to turn found objects into allies. The very act of rummaging for objects might itself have evoked for Nathan a familiar configuration—a bodily memory of the comforting feel of playing in the scrap yard his father had operated before the war.

Day upon day, as the death toll mounts around him, Nathan labors at the tasks to which he is assigned. Starving, ill from exhaustion and disease, and surrounded by bodies of the dying and the dead, Nathan makes use of the single element of the environment over which he retains personal leverage—activity itself. Over time, he comes to sabotage the factory machines whenever opportunity arises. He makes small combs and other personal items to exchange for food. Even in the form of debilitating and degrading slavery, we observe, physical labor itself has a paradoxical effect: though it saps his physical strength, it requires attention and concentration; it keeps him thinking. Moreover, it stands as evidence in his own consciousness of an intact capacity for life-affirming acts of defiance and self-definition. Labor itself calls his father's guiding voice to the active present. Nathan sustains through his own hard work a kind of living tie to the loving protector he has lost, a protector whose words and presence he has internalized deeply.

We see in Nathan the preadolescent with deep wells of creative capacity to imagine circumstances different from those given to him. His story shows us that some children are able to sustain inside themselves the idea that standards of humanity from the previous world can still exist, apart from the current situation. Holding inside themselves not only the image of lost loved ones but also the feeling of love and safety with which these lost objects are connected, such children retain the capacity to affirm the continuity of a moral order even in the midst of disorder—sustaining a memory of what is right and good. As if to prove this to himself, Nathan uses his teeth to carve the message into his own body: in an act that in any other circumstances might seem like florid psychosis, he bites off his own skin to disfigure the Nazi tattoo. Exorcizing the emblem of his subjugation, the teenage boy asserts, in this way, the intactness of his bodily self and the irreducibility of his own claim on a right to be alive. Preserving his skin, symbolically, as his own domain, it is an act of stunning self-affirmation. We note, in this, that young people engage sometimes in the language of symbols: even bizarre behaviors can take on profound private meaning and become expressions of intense emotional and developmental significance.

We also see in Nathan's story that children are capable of astute and fine-tuned judgments of even small changes in the landscape of risk and opportunity. Nathan recognizes the benefits to himself of being chosen for work. Even as the broad prognosis deteriorates, as the bodies pile up, he gravitates to whatever opportunities of luck and chance emerge on a day-by-day basis, and he puts himself to the task of making use of them. Some children, moreover, seem to possess the ability to attract the interest and emotional investment of adults. We see this in Nathan—a capacity that enables complete strangers to feel they are deriving something meaningful from their interactions with him. Nathan remains open to relationships with a series of mentors and protectors—he seeks and finds competent adult male figures who contribute to his survival, find something good in him, and consolidate his sense of himself as a young man who is valued and worthy.

The psychologist Robert Sternberg[9] has proposed that human intelligence consists of elements far more complicated than mere possession of analytical skills. Rather, it includes the creative capacity to apply prior knowledge to new situations and, equally important, the everyday practical intelligence of being able to adapt in concert with the demands of changing circumstances. In Nathan, so battered by loss over an extended period, we see this triad of remarkable gifts. We see that in the transition from comfortable twelve-year-old boy to eighteen-year-old adult, alone and near death but still clinging to consciousness, Nathan manages to build for himself a private understanding of the world as sustained by individual acts of diligence, conscience, and moral fortitude.

Irene's memoir begins as the war is already well underway. At first, we find in her a sassy fifteen-year-old desperately embracing the distractions of normalcy. As is appropriate to her age, Irene immerses herself in the lush and baroque dramas of adolescence—in competitions for the attention of handsome young men, in playful rivalries over beauty and fashion, in the new thrill of sexual desire, in music and art, and in teenagers' strange mix of yearning and distaste for the meddling of overbearing mothers. Rich gossip serves in the clandestine Warsaw ghetto school the same role it serves elsewhere: casting scathing judgment on the transgressions of peers and adults, Irene and her circle of teen friends feel briefly authoritative, capacitous, able to conjure meanings of their own, even in a milieu that is disabling and humiliating. With their rules of discipline and their classroom demands, moreover, Irene's teachers add to the semblance of stability and order.

Irene watches attentively as her Uncle Jakub (the brother for whom my own grandfather pined in his late-life war nightmares) tries desperately and ultimately unsuccessfully to use his social and professional connections to prolong the lives of his extended family. But in mid-1942 an announcement is made: block-by-block roundups will commence and continue until the ghetto is liquidated. Everyone is to be deported "east," to some place they do not know. Terror grabs hold of the remaining ghetto captives. Bodies accumulate rapidly on the sidewalks, and Irene grieves as the adults around her grow increasingly desperate and despairing and her network of friends is decimated in a matter of days. In an atmosphere of escalating confusion and desperation, she loses her mother, her grandmother, and her new boyfriend, among many dozens of others, and we see that she struggles desperately to sustain a sense of her own continuity and coherence in a milieu of massive and rapid social disintegration. Irene's description of the unfolding chaos provides an intimate view of psychic fragmentation, and we see in her story what Salman Akhtar observed about the intertwining of internal landscapes and external ones.[10] Irene races from place to place, desperately triangulating among familiar landmarks; we witness in her story a child's frenetic efforts to build a boundary of refuge—to find a space of containment in a landscape of senseless horror.

In the ensuring weeks, the death toll continues to climb, but Irene and her father cling to one another. With limited tools, they create collaborative rituals that evoke and confirm continuity in their family life: listening for the sounds of one another's feet on the stairs, greeting one another with special new nicknames, arranging their shared room to be as clean and orderly as possible, and having meals together when they can. With routines of giving and caring for another, cultivating what small elements remain of their family life, Irene and her father attempt to create order and rationality in whatever diminished form these might still be found. They sustain hope as a collective project of mutual validation.

The desire and capacity to care deeply for another life, we see in Irene's story, is itself life-affirming for young people—a source of vitality and nourishment that reminds them of their own goodness in a broader context of hatred. An expression of purposefulness and humanity, reciprocity stands against abjection. But Irene soon confronts an impossible choice: she must grapple with the limits of love and compassion. Understanding that she needs to leave her father to a certain death, she ventures alone, in the end, toward the possibility of survival. In a risky and daring last-ditch effort, she escapes the ghetto just days before its final destruction. Her story reminds us that children navigate wrenching paths between hope and despair—and make achingly painful choices between them. The courage of their realism propels them toward adulthood but carries unspeakable personal costs.

Fresh from high school graduation at age eighteen, Marysia is a study in the bristling, defiant moralism of late adolescence, and her responses to the war's challenges reflect clearly her developmental position at the brink of adulthood. She receives the war as a massive affront, not only to herself personally and to her family but also to the broader social principles with which she has aligned—rationality, justice, decency, fairness. Connecting her situation to the general human picture, she is able to attach personal feelings of fear and loss to the much larger power of moral outrage and to a sense that right is on her side. Making use of the blessing of blonde hair, she refuses at first to enter the ghetto, choosing instead to remain with her gentile boyfriend outside the ghetto walls. An eighteen-year-old's opting for independence over childhood, the decision comes at great cost, as it means she loses contact with her parents and sisters. Finding ways to deceive the Nazi authorities, however, she soon discovers ways of sneaking past the guards, even in plain sight.

With limited access to money and food, Marysia makes use of the resources of her own body. At first, she sells her blood for transfusions. When that becomes impossible, she volunteers her skin for a Nazi medical experiment that erodes the surfaces of her arms and legs. This effort is disgusting, but she frames it as a triumphant act of self-sustenance and self-affirmation. Wrapping her wounds in appealing clothing, she announces outwardly her claim of mastery over her subordination and shows us how the young person's quest for independence and selfhood takes a variety of simultaneously physical, psychic, and symbolic forms.

Despite what she learns are complicated attitudes about Jews among some of the members of the resistance movement, Marysia joins the Polish national fight against Nazi domination, risking her safety to run a printing press in the heart of the Nazi-occupied city. Her activities and associations land her in a political prison, where she is sexually assaulted by guards. But even in prison, she finds weapons of self-affirmation: the power to keep silent, to protect her secrets, and to reveal nothing to her captors. Behind bars, she finds means by which to continue the work of sabotage. Creative and dogged acts of defiance remind her that remnants can still be found of the capacity for self-determination, and these are her sustenance despite her decreasing physical strength and the near death of her newborn son. We see in Marysia's story what Erik Erikson observed[11]—that oppositionality taunts despair. We also see that a sense of moral connection—of feeling one's fate linked inextricably to that of global others—can strengthen young people when they are most alone, and we acknowledge the significant assistance provided in this by more than one heroic Polish gentile. We note that young people's acts of aggression and defiance are attempts, at times, to remind themselves of the possibility of hope. We can note, as well, the clever deployment of cultural tropes as a survival resource: in order to gain admission to the convent shelter for unwed mothers and shield her son from further harm, Marysia hides the real source of her vulnerability — her Jewishness — under a victimhood story of sin and seduction that is far more marketable in the setting.

Particular narratives of the holocaust have been enshrined in popular culture, and there is an understandable taboo about noting that for a small group of people, the war provided elements of adventure. Against the backdrop of a mass murder that exterminated millions of Jews and wiped out most of her extended family, Wanda journeyed thousands of miles across Europe and Africa. She had barely turned twenty, a year past her dislocation from the city of her childhood, when her scientist husband answered a British government call for volunteers for an experimental refugee resettlement program. The choice created an unusual backdrop for the transition from late adolescence to new motherhood. Before 1939, Wanda's life had been organized around exceptional comfort and privilege, and even after the war began, she was shielded by an abundance of material resources. (She had graduated high school just a year ahead of her less lucky younger cousin Marysia.) Old enough and sophisticated enough to understand the grave threats surrounding her, and aware of the losses to her network of friends and kin, Wanda tracked the news as it unfolded. Moment by moment, however, she tended only to what needed tending—protecting herself by holding at a distance any less immediately pertinent information. We see in Wanda the young person who copes with loss by compartmentalizing—by paying attention foremost to the immediate and urgent present and one's own affairs in it. We also observe that withering sarcasm and irony are tools, in war as in peace, by which vulnerable people shore up a sense of self when the self is under humiliating assault. We see, as well, that a religious minority pursued and slaughtered in one setting can take on the quality, in another setting, of a colonial presence. Wanda's story reminds us that identity emerges always as a construct within a specific historical context.

Running from bombs, buried in holes, imprisoned, enslaved, crouching in secret basement rooms, or waiting years in states of uncertainty and transit, the young people whose stories are collected here confronted at extremely different levels the realities of loss, cruelty, deprivation, and separation that the Nazis imposed. Nathan lost everything and everyone, witnessing unfathomable atrocity over a period of many years of unrelenting violence, physical labor, and emotional assault. Irene and Marysia, survivors of a different type, observed their comfortable worlds corroded in a series of progressively more humiliating deprivations and losses. Irene chose between loyalty to her father and a chance at own survival. For David, there was merely a brief period of chaos, and for Nina, there was long-term uncertainty, accompanied, throughout, by a buffer of thoughtful parenting and family stability. At the other extreme, Wanda explored marvelous new landscapes under the protection of British colonial authorities, holding at a certain distance her awareness of what was happening to the rest of her family.

The range of experiences is both striking and disturbing. But what unites all these stories is that they illustrate the fundamental alertness of young people in the encounter with violence and humiliation—their active agency and remarkable instinct for creative self-preservation. None of these young people were passive recipients of what the war brought. Rather, with whatever resources made themselves available by history and happenstance, each in his or her own way and at his or her own developmental level endeavored to create sense and order in what otherwise was senseless and disordered. Each found tools embedded within ordinary and mundane situations to extract the affirmations necessary to continue the developmental journey. They found means to continue growing toward adulthood. The women, we see, faced dangers uniquely connected to their gender. Pregnancy and motherhood, sexual assault, and pressure to exchange sex for food and supplies all figured into a uniquely gendered landscape of opportunity and risk.

To note these young people's physical and psychological achievements is not to minimize the unspeakable atrocity of genocide or to divert attention from the reality of mass murder that extinguished the vast majority of Poland's less privileged Jews. Rather, it is to observe that even within the young person who experiences catastrophic losses and disruption and who recognizes that his society despises him, certain internal resources can remain available for the sustenance and organization of selfhood. This is a lesson that reverberates far beyond the immediate context of a single family's stories, as it speaks to the nature of childhood and youth more generally. It is a lesson about people in the past, but it contains a message worth revisiting in the context of the current era.

Against what have become commonplace and reductive popular understandings of "trauma" and victimhood as explanatory frameworks, the stories here offer a far more dynamic picture of the processing of violence, separation, and loss. They provide a portrait of the active agency of young people in seeking what they need psychologically even within a broad climate characterized by deprivation and assault. The stories show us that resilience is emergent, a property of shifting intersections between people and situations. A blend of capabilities and opportunities, of possibilities and limitations, it is born in young people's instinctive efforts to continue trying to meet their own developmental needs under changing circumstances and differential resource landscapes. It is important to note, as well, that the stories here provide brief and fleeting glimpses of dozens of elusive and mysterious figures—aunts and uncles, infants and grandparents, neighbors and lovers, strangers and friends, gentiles and Jews—who contributed to each young person's situation during the war. These figures are long lost to the world, but some trace of their contributions will forever emerge at least partially from the darkness by virtue of their presence in these stories.

NOTES

1. Jennifer Bonovitz, "When Mother Isn't There: Finding Alternate Pathways to Development," in *The Mother and Her Child: Clinical Aspects of Attachment, Separation, and Loss*, ed. Salman Akhtar (Lanham, MD: Jason Aronson, Inc., 2011), 121–33; Kaplan, *Children in Genocide*.

2. Anna Freud and Sophia Dann, "An Experiment in Group Upbringing," *The Psychoanalytic Study of the Child* 6, no. 1 (1951): 127–68.

3. Ornstein, "Childhood Losses, Adult Memories," 117.

4. For more on the history of this episode, see Hillel Levine, *In Search of Sugihara: The Elusive Japanese Diplomat Who Risked his Life to Rescue 10,000 Jews from the Holocaust* (New York, NY: Free Press, 1996).

5. Simon and Apfel, *Minefields in Their Hearts*; Garbarion et al., *Children in Danger*; Mollica, *Caring for Refugees*.

6. Helen Bass-Wichelhaus, "Resilience in Child Survivors: History and Application of Coding of the International Study of Organized Persecution of Children," in *Children in the Holocaust and its Aftermath: Historical and Psychological Studies of the Kestenberg Archive*, eds. Sharon Kangisser-Cohen, Eva Fogelman, and Dalia Ofer (New York, NY: Berghahn Books, 2017), 170–86.

7. Erikson, *Childhood and Society*.

8. Charny, *Holding on to Humanity*.

9. Robert Sternberg, *Beyond IQ: A Triarchic Theory of Human Intelligence* (Cambridge, UK: Cambridge University Press, 1984).

10. Hooke and Akhtar, *The Geography of Meaning*.

11. Erikson, *Identity and the Life Cycle*.

Chapter 9

Resonances of War

Clinical research about the war's long-term psychological effects on survivors and their subsequent postwar families began accumulating in the 1960s, largely in response to the Eichmann trial and initiation of the German reparations program. It became clear that impacts varied and that multiple factors likely played a role: Had the survivors spent time in concentration camps, or in ghettos? Had they been in hiding, or in flight? Alone, or with others? For how long? How old were they? Had they participated in resistance activities? Had they found moments of solidarity or mutual aid? Had they found surviving family members in the postwar years? Multiple perspectives were brought to bear in the research: biomedical scholars focused on long-range physical and health outcomes; sociocultural theorists studied postwar parenting and socialization; family-systems theorists examined problems of individuation and separation in survivors' children; psychodynamic theorists emphasized unconscious communications, traumatic repetitions, and issues of self-object differentiation in subsequent generations; others searched for evidence of long-term biological and epigenetic effects. Some of those who had survived the war, it was found, insisted on silence about what happened, which erected barriers of secrecy that aroused in their children feelings of shame, envy, fear, or inadequacy. Others were prone to bouts of depression or rage, generating in their children a yearning for recognition and acknowledgment. Others created household climates of hyper-attachment and overprotectiveness, enacting a terror of separation that left their children struggling for a sense of independence. Among the children of survivors were some who felt a burden of needing to compensate for what had been lost, to live as "proof" of the Nazi defeat or take the place of dead loved ones (from whom, in some cases, they had been named). Others felt a need to engage in unrelenting rescue—to shield their parents from further harm by providing constant assurances of love and displays of outward optimism, repressing their own anger, or subordinating needs and desires that seemed shamefully trivial compared with what the parents had endured. A science of trauma and trauma transmission emerged in the early years of research. Those who had lived through the war had transmitted information not only by what they later said, it was found, and by how they said it but also by what they did not say, by the conversations they avoided, and by what they allowed or welcomed as elaboration or questioning.[1]

It is complicated, however, to draw straight causal arrows between painful experiences and long-term effects, both in individuals and in families, as a person's outlook is never predetermined by events of the past; people find a great many ways of living with and accepting a painful legacy. Psychologists Hadas Wiseman and Jacques Barber and a growing cadre of other scholars[2] observe that characterizations of holocaust trauma and transmission have tended to some extent to be overly dichotomous, treating the impacts of the war as if they are a clear-cut, straightforward, or predictable "package" of pathologies either passed down to others or not. An emerging body of literature points to great variability qin the picture of what is retained over time or what has impact across generations, however, and writers across a variety of academic disciplines increasingly suggest that multiple elements intertwine in nuanced ways in the holocaust's psychological legacy.[3] Experiences from the past, these writers find, reconfigure themselves over time, appearing in subsequent generations sometimes, but not inevitably, as pathology.

The memoirs in this book all end abruptly, as if the stories stopped precisely at the moment when their authors began in earnest to confront the reality of their losses and reorient themselves to the postwar order. It is as though the narratives are structured so as to seal off the war. Like most of the small group of Polish Jews who survived and escaped, the writers of these memoirs did well. They went on to live creatively, hold jobs they enjoyed, and raise children they loved. But traces from the past wound their way like threads through the fabrics of their later lives and the lives of their families.

For David, my father, the war loomed not only as a story of sudden uprooting and blatant property theft but also as a nagging illustration of what follows from great inequalities of privilege and wealth. Following their arrival in Palestine, David and his parents settled in Tel Aviv, in an apartment building where there were many other refugees. In summers, Dad worked on the farm his parents owned. Despite the family's secularism, he even had a bar mitzvah—"just for spite," he later said—"to show the Germans they had failed." In 1948, he was withdrawn from school and enlisted in military training, along with all the other eleventh graders, as the Jewish state's declaration of independence that year generated a multifront war necessitating rapid national mobilization of all able-bodied fighters. Like many teens of his generation, he was already seasoned in matters of running and hiding. Dad later attended college in the United States, where he studied civil engineering and ran on the cross-country team (though Jewish students were not yet allowed full membership). He married and took a lucrative job. But throughout his adult life, notes of the war reasserted themselves. Following his brief stint of hiding in the cellar under the butcher shop, Dad never ate meat. His diet, a source of amusement to family and friends, consisted almost entirely of eggs, raw vegetables, and dried fruit. He licensed as a hobby pilot—a nod, perhaps, to the memory of the Riga plane crash and a rebuke to the frightened child in himself who had once begged to remain in Europe. He devoted his free time to environmental causes long before these were popular and was an activist in the early environmental movement. Rescued animals filled our house—injured turtles, newly hatched chicks fallen out of nests, puppies snatched from burning buildings. My sister and I adored Dad's bedtime stories, most of them about baby animals who had lost their way in forests but ultimately reunited with their families, always by magic twist of plot. Only years later did we come to recognize the deep-seated wishes that our father perhaps unconsciously conveyed with these tales of exquisite family reunification and babies rendered safe. Dad organized family hiking and canoeing trips and late-night stargazing, and when we sat with him under the night sky, he would marvel about the very existence of a sun and moon that can shine simultaneously in so many lands—in New York and Los Angeles and Paris and Tel Aviv, over Treblinka and Auschwitz, and even through tiny soot-covered windows of a subcellar in a small Polish town. "If you lose everything else," he would say, "you still have the sun and moon," which gave us a clue about the thoughts that must have comforted the seven-year-old boy in him for whom the memory of hiding lay just below the surface.

In social gatherings with neighbors and friends, Dad often wondered what might have happened had there been a different combination of passengers in the limousine on that September day on Jaworzynska Street in 1939. Had the car been larger. Had his parents accommodated one more body—a little cousin, perhaps, a girl wrapped in blankets and presented at the window by her desperate father. Had there been a few more days to secure additional arrangements. What had happened to Mr. Lambert, from the Chamber of Commerce, to whose advice my family will remain forever profoundly indebted? He wondered about his second-grade classmates and teachers at the Wilno YIVO school, though he knew how the story ended for most of them. He wondered about his nannies—did the beloved Chinga survive to have children of her own? Did Tita? He wondered about the military wives, and the chauffeur's son, and the Yiddish-speaking families and their charming wooden outhouses in the beleaguered towns of Eastern Poland. But in their cases, too, he knew the likely outcome. Dad wondered sometimes what might have happened had his father not purchased that little piece of property in a faraway land as a birthday gift for a newborn son. My mother observed that in his richly active and love-filled postwar life, Dad had built for himself a kind of conversation between past and future, between grief about what had happened in his world, on one hand, and themes, on the other hand, of reparation, reconstruction, renewal, and rebirth. When my sister and I were teenagers, after our grandfather moved into our house, he and our father spent hours deliberating over details from the past, and my sister and I came to understand how gratefulness and mourning, joy and despair, can grow intertwined, from the same vine.

Guilt is the penance one pays, it is said, for the gift of survival, and ghosts of guilt inhabited Dad's world as a multitude of looming unanswered questions. He read voraciously about the holocaust—as if the act of absorbing so much information about its victims might lighten or retract somehow the reality of their millions of deaths. He scoured libraries, phonebooks, and agency databases—before the days of the Internet—hoping that additional family survivors might turn up. He charted the family tree as far back as he could remember it, marking carefully the names of those who had been murdered. There is something unsettling in such diagrams, my sister and I sensed. They secure the living in their places but highlight, at the same time, the proximity of the living to the dead. They call attention, in a strange way, to the near-miss of a small space in a chart, celebrating the abundance accruing to some lines but directing our eyes, as well, to the emptiness attaching to others. My sister and I prepared for the possibility of a new cataclysm. We memorized maps, addresses, and phone numbers, and on occasion, at the dinner table, we would sketch our escape routes. We planned secret code words because "they can take everything away from you," Dad would say, "but they can't take your thoughts," which made it all the more painful and sad for us when he began showing signs of dementia.

Dad loved the ocean and was a great swimmer, and one of the greatest joys was seeing him with his five grandchildren, especially at the beach. My two kids would clamber gleefully onto his back, giggling and holding tight as he dove with them into the waves. When they were young and I taught evening classes, my parents sometimes came to babysit them. While Mom prepared dinner, Dad would arrange dollhouse furniture with my daughter and move bulldozers on the carpet with my son, marveling about the power of giant machines and the comforts of home, now seen through new, young, American eyes that radiated confidence and optimism. Just as negative effects can be transmitted downward from one generation to the next, as the Israeli psychiatrist Dan Bar-On[4] has found, so, too, can healing effects be transmitted "upward." My father did not train my children in the rituals of planning for escape; they never memorized phone numbers or practiced hiding in the yard. It seemed that in them, finally, Dad had found a feeling of home. Perhaps it was the reflection he saw of himself in their eyes that no longer looked to him like the face of a refugee.

It would have brought immense pleasure for Dad to have met the person whose name appeared some years later, basically by chance. My daughter had returned from Hebrew school one day with an assignment to create a family tree. As the Internet by then had made such things so simple, we searched on our home computer for some of the names in Dad's meticulously organized charts. A manuscript appeared. Written in Spanish by a certain Irene, it had been donated to the famous YIVO Jewish history archive. I phoned the librarian there to ask about it. Nobody knew much about the author, but a staff member was able to provide the name of the donor. I tracked him down to a film production company in Santiago, Chile, and I wrote to the company's general e-mail address: "My name is Shira Birnbaum. I am researching my family. Is this Stanley the son of Irene Birnbaum, grandson of Shayus, brother of Wladek, formerly of Warsaw, Poland? If so, please contact me via email. Thank you for your time."

Within less than fifteen minutes, I received the following reply: "Hi Shira, Yes, I am Stanley, only son of Irena, daughter of Stanislaw (Shayus). I just called my mother and she confirmed this. All my life I dreamed I'd find you!"

And so began a remarkable international friendship between the daughters of David and the son of Irene, newfound second cousins enriched profoundly by our connection. Stanley sent me a copy of the photograph his mother had stuffed in her coat pocket on the day she exited the ghetto. We exchanged our parents' memoirs and retold the stories of their escape and survival. Irene's story confirmed my father's deep source of mourning: the unevenness of the war's impacts on the fate of our family's many dozens of members.

Europe lay in ruins by the spring of 1945. Soviet and Allied troops entered the concentration camps as liberators, and horrific reports began emerging, imprinting themselves slowly on the imagination of a world already hardened by years of war. American military officers ordered German civilians to line up in their villages, marching them through the camps and forcing them, at gunpoint, to view what their nation had wrought. The Germans were led through barracks where sick and dying inmates lay in narrow tiered bunks, and through the crematoria where the stoves were still full of fresh human ash. Our family and most of the other Jews of Poland had been turned to soil and dust in those spaces—burned in the crematoria of Treblinka and Auschwitz and other camps, their bones crushed into fine powder as a space-saving measure because the sheer mass of all their millions of bodies exceeded the capacity of the ground to contain them. On May 7, in a schoolhouse in Rheims, France, German military representatives signed an unconditional surrender. Allied forces divided up occupation zones across the continent, humanitarian aid efforts were organized, displaced persons camps established.

Tens of millions of people were homeless. They stood in long lines for food aid and roamed the cities of Europe, huddling in piles of rubble and scavenging abandoned buildings. Those lucky enough to have a roof over their heads lacked heat, running water, electricity, and furniture. Complex international negotiations were launched regarding the management and resettlement of the millions of people who now wandered the landscape. Such was the level of upheaval that neither military authorities nor relief agencies were able to maintain an accurate census of displaced persons. Refugees slipped in and out of officially designated camps, migrating in search of their lost loved ones.

Particularly problematic was the question of the Jews. Jews continued to be targets of violence after the war ended, as they were attacked, in some instances fatally, as they attempted to reclaim confiscated property and return to their former homes.[5] Poland was an epicenter of destruction. In the final months of the war, the Nazis had obliterated much of Warsaw, brutally slaughtering upward of 150,000 of its remaining residents and reducing the city virtually to rubble. The Jewish population at that point was a hodgepodge—consisting of some who had survived the camps, others who had been hidden under false identification documents, and still others who had survived the war in the Soviet Union and had returned after the Nazi defeat.[6] An array of Jewish political and civic groups united under a common umbrella to coordinate the distribution of relief supplies, and a semi-organized multifaceted Zionist movement emerged, beginning in the fall of 1945 and reaching its peak in the spring and summer of the following year, to facilitate young survivors' clandestine efforts to reach Palestine. Irene and Nathan were among this unique group.

Irene moved to an apartment with her uncle and a small group of other Jews. She enrolled in courses at the newly reopened University of Warsaw, where she soon encountered Pawel Gonczanski, a former neighbor several years her senior. In November 1946, they crossed the Polish border together to the American occupation zone in Czechoslovakia and continued from there to Austria, where they found temporary shelter with a small group of other refugees on the floor of a former Hebrew school in Vienna. As winter arrived, they moved to a refugee camp in Linz, where they stayed for a period of weeks, and then continued on foot to a camp in Steyr, in the north of Austria, where they spent several months. Eventually, they slipped out of the camp and made their way to Saalfelden, in the Tyrolian Alps, where they joined another small band hoping to sneak into Italy and sail from there to the port of Haifa, in Palestine, where Irene knew she could find surviving family members—my father, his brother and parents, and the paternal grandparents who had emigrated before the war. They crossed the Alpine border at Brenner in

April 1947, but found that border patrols had doubled down on efforts to prevent further movement, as in Palestine, another kind of vulnerable population was also increasingly at risk for displacement, and British colonial authorities were attempting to tamp down political conflict. Stopped again, this time for another half year, Irene and Pawel settled in a refugee camp outside Milan and awaited news. Bolivia opened its doors—among the few nations granting visas to Jews in that period. With assistance from the American Jewish Joint Distribution Committee, the largest aid organization supporting Jewish refugees at that time, the young couple boarded a ship in Bordeaux, France, in January 1948, and headed for La Paz.

Stanislaw Birnbaum's final message to his daughter had been about persistence, and persistence indeed remained a central theme in Irene's nearly three-year postwar odyssey out of the refugee camps. She and Pawel had hoped to reach Argentina, which had a large, centuries-old Jewish community, and where Pawel had cousins. Their ship indeed made a stop there, but immigration officials confiscated the young couple's passports, as the anti-Semitic Peronist regime was attempting to block Jewish entry, and they were escorted directly back to the train heading for La Paz, where their passports finally were returned. After a few months, the couple tried again to enter Argentina, accompanied this time by a small group of other Polish-Jewish refugees. Caught by border police, Pawel was returned to Bolivia, but Irene, wrapped in blankets and hidden in a suitcase compartment, successfully finished the trip. Pawel joined her some months later by hiding himself in a wooden shipping container stuffed with international mail. Restrictions eventually were lifted, and the two settled openly in Buenos Aires, where Irene became a language teacher and, later, wrote her memoirs. Her son Estanislao (Stanley), named for her father, grew up to be an artist, as Irene had once dreamed of becoming. Stanley and his wife Barbara raised two daughters, both born in Santiago de Chile.

By 1945, when Nathan and his father Avram were loaded into a boxcar and moved to Upper Austria, Mauthausen was already one of the largest concentration camp complexes in the Reich, with an extensive underground tunnel system and more than 100 subcamps for German arms and munitions manufacturing and fighter-plane assembly plants. It is estimated that almost 198,000 people passed through the camp between August 1938 and May 1945, at least 95,000 of whom died there.[7] Following the liberation of the camp, Nathan was taken to an American military field hospital, where he was enrolled in a controlled-feeding recovery program and received medical care for tuberculosis. Eventually well enough to walk, he was returned to Mauthausen, which had by that time been converted to a displaced persons camp for survivors awaiting international resettlement agreements. Nathan was defiant. Under cover of night, he and two dozen other refugees climbed into the bed of a truck and were smuggled across national borders to a Zionist training camp in southern Italy, where they studied Hebrew, amassed weapons, and rebuilt their physical strength as they prepared to make the illegal journey to Palestine, determined to fight for the establishment of a Jewish national homeland. Nathan forged deep and lasting friendships with the other young men in this group. All were alone, having lost everyone to whom they had once been connected, but their losses reconfigured into new bonds of profound brotherhood. A novel kind of family, the group arrived in Tel Aviv in 1948 on the ship *Altalena* during an infamous several-week period of near civil war in the newly created nation of Israel—a rich story for another day.[8] Nathan returned to school, married another survivor, Zahava, and had three children—one of them named for his father, Avram, whose words of love had nourished him through the war years. "When the war ended," Nathan later wrote, "There was a Marshall Plan to build Germany. There was a GI bill to help the American soldiers. But we survivors . . . we were not given anything." When an opportunity became available to attend college in the United States, the young family emigrated so that Nathan could complete an education. His friends from the refugee group pooled their money for a loan so that Nathan could pay rent and tuition fees.

Long after the war, Nathan's independence and industriousness continued to dominate the household pattern. Woodworking lathes and machine tools cluttered the basement of the family's Connecticut house, where the garage was piled with stacks of wood and scraps of metal. Nathan built much of his own furniture and crafted elaborate wood toys for his children and sculptures as gifts for his friends. He sewed his own drapery and a significant portion of his own clothing, started a photography business, registered patents for several small inventions involving tractor engines, lectured about the holocaust at high schools and universities, and published several short stories that paid tribute to the fatherly hero figures who had sustained him—the kindly Kapo Beim, with his beret, who was hanged and shot at Plaszow, and the anonymous Austrian factory foreman, with the oil-stained hands, who provided the secret, steady supply of bread that had saved Nathan from starvation in the St. Valentin airplane factory. Nathan's children learned to cook, play piano, and fix small engines, and Nathan had them take after-school jobs so that they would learn how to work, even when the family did not need the extra income and even in a country where they were surrounded by plenty. Thirteen grandchildren were born, and after Nathan died, his first great-grandchild was given his name.

Life was not easy for Wanda and Edek after they reached Wellington, South Africa. They lived with their infant daughter, Erica, in a diaper-festooned single room in an English hotel. Edek worked long hours and was promoted after a few months, after which they moved to Stellenbosch, a university town in the heart of what is now South Africa's wine country. Wanda found friends among the small community of Jewish refugees there. She became a master bridge player and learned to solve English cryptic crossword puzzles, quite a feat for a non-native speaker. Her second daughter, Barbara, was born in May 1948, after which they moved again, this time to the much larger city of Cape Town. For the most part, her daughters report, the war never came up. The girls attended a Catholic school, mostly out of convenience, as the school bus stopped at the corner directly in front of their house, but partly in a gesture of acknowledgment of Polish nuns who have taken in and protected a small niece of Edek's, who survived the war because of their care.

Things soon started changing, however. Having witnessed the introduction of racial laws once before in her life, Wanda was determined not to be swept up by them a second time. As the nationalist government further codified its apartheid program, she began agitating strongly to leave South Africa. Departure had served her before, and she was determined it would serve her again. For Edek, the move would mean once again having to abandon a successful career. For the girls, it would mean leaving school. There were strains in the marriage. But Wanda was adamant. In April 1961, they sailed for Southampton, England. They spent the remainder of their lives in London and had three grandchildren and five great-grandchildren.

In November 1947, as a result of the new Displaced Persons Act, which temporarily opened US borders to some categories of previously excluded refugees, Nina and her family were finally permitted to enter the United States. They departed Shanghai on the *SS General William H. Gordon*, a former military transport ship converted to refugee resettlement, arriving in San Francisco with a boatload of other Jews on December 17, 1947. The journey included a typhoon—"just for good measure," as Nina would later tell it. She was fifteen years old by then. After a brief sojourn together in a San Francisco hotel room, she and her parents headed for New York City, where they rented an apartment in an affordable neighborhood popular with refugee families. Nina enrolled in high school and took a job working the cash register at a Woolworth's store near Times Square. She remained an excellent student and finished graduate school some years later at the University of California at Berkeley, where she also met her future husband. They moved to Israel, where Nina took an active role in the business and arts communities. Throughout her adult life, Nina led efforts to commemorate the work of Chiune Sugihara, the heroic Japanese consul to Lithuania, without whose assistance she surely would have perished along with most of the other Jewish refugees in Wilno. She was active in the establishment of a museum on the site of the former Jewish ghetto in Shanghai. Well into her eighties at the time of this writing, she continues daily to sustain the orderly life of civilized routines that her parents had modeled: she wakes promptly at the same time each day to check the political and business news from Asia. She has two children and four grandchildren.

In the summer of 1944, tens of thousands of Poles mobilized a final uprising against the Nazi occupation. Resistance leaders, among them some of Marysia's former compatriots, expected the fight to last only days, as the Soviet Army was camping just at the edge of town, on the banks of the Vistula, preparing to enter the city. Threatened by the prospect of Polish postwar nationalism and hoping to thwart Polish ambitions for self-determination, however, the Soviets offered no assistance. Instead, halting combat operations, they abandoned the Polish citizenry to fend for themselves and enabled the Nazis to brutally massacre tens of thousands of civilians in a matter of days. The city of Warsaw was razed to the ground in door-to-door searches over several ensuing weeks, during which thousands of the remaining Jews were rooted out of hiding. Public executions were staged of the Poles who had sheltered them. At the convent home for unwed mothers where Marysia had brought her infant son, soldiers soon arrived, demanding that the nuns provide women. When the nuns insisted that Marysia offer herself, she took her new baby and fled, hiding first in the forest and then moving to the countryside, where she was taken in by a farm family from whom she continued to hide her Jewish identity. When the Nazis surrendered, she thanked her protectors and returned to Warsaw in search of Czesław.

Imprisoned first at Majdanek and later at Sachsenhausen, Czesław also survived the war. The couple married, and eventually Marysia gave birth to a second child. But decades of Soviet occupation were difficult for Marysia, as for all the Poles. She sustained her wartime stance of trusting no one and keeping secrets to herself, and for years she continued to hide the truth about her past. After the collapse of the Soviet Union, however, when free elections were finally held, in 1989, and Poland opened again to the West, my father turned his sights once more toward finding his lost family. Motivated in her own way by the sweeping political changes transforming her country, Marysia began writing a memoir. "I felt as if I were lifting myself from under a gravestone," she later said. For her sons, Marysia's revelations provided a shocking first encounter with their Jewish past.

In 1991, my father and Marysia and her sisters reunited in Warsaw. There were children and grandchildren—a new generation risen from the ashes of the city. The reunion was exquisitely joyous for my father, as it spoke to his dreams of reconnection with lost family. But it was also complex, as it challenged some of his cherished images of Poland. He had conceived of the country as a graveyard, an unmitigated anti-Semitic hell where ghosts of the dead roamed and property was confiscated. But in his long-lost cousins and their lively, extended Polish families, he found a significantly more nuanced Poland—a Poland with deep if complex ties to its Jewish past, where the division between Pole and Jew is neither as comfortingly stark nor as simple as he had imagined. No one today can estimate the proportion of Poles who might have in their past a Jew, like Marysia, who slipped quietly into Polish society under false papers. No estimates exist on the number of Polish young people who might have heard, at some point in their lives, about the grandparent or great-grandparent who once loved a Jew, harbored a Jew in hiding, or served alongside a Jew in the Polish resistance movement. My father came to see that the Poles, who had suffered breathtaking losses at the hands of the Germans, had never found a venue on the global stage to give clear voice to their suffering: the Soviets had imposed a propaganda narrative that erased both Jewish and Polish history by characterizing the war as a communist triumph over fascism. On the global stage, moreover, the postwar narrative had been dominated by the singularly tragic near-extermination of the Jews. This history of silencing contributes fuel to Polish anti-Semitism and is a core element in its virulent contemporary resurgence.[9]

My grandfather Wladek, the sole survivor among eight siblings, had first returned to Warsaw in 1946. Entering the centuries-old Jewish cemetery on Okopowa Street and finding his own grandfather's grave intact, he erected a small stone marker for Ester, Julius, Barbara, Helena, and Janina—the mother-in-law for whom he had once built a lovely new apartment house, and the family of his closest brother-in-law. He then filed a lawsuit to recover his many stolen commercial and residential properties, a gesture more of defiance than of real hope for resolution, as Soviet authorities promptly reminded him that private property does not exist under communism. Jewish property claims remain to this day largely unresolved in Poland, as a variety of legal, legislative, and financial obstacles have been erected to prevent repatriation—even in cases such as my family's, where original land deeds are still accessible. The resurgence of right-leaning and anti-Semitic ideologies makes it even less likely now that claims such as these will ever reach a resolution that satisfies the former Jews of Poland. When Marysia died, her birth and death records needed to be registered with local authorities. Her son handed over three different birth certificates— each one incorrect. Such was the life, her son observed, of a generation that had learned never to stop running, never to stop hiding, never to reveal anything of their innermost secrets, and always to be prepared for tragedy. Marysia had given her memoir to my father. I'd found it in the attic with his other papers.

My sister and cousins and I, like many of our generation born in the postwar years, lived in intimate contact with the imprints the war left on our parents. We grappled with grief, awe, rage, relief, and so on, but above all, as the writer Helen Epstein and others have observed,[10] with an awareness of looming absence, a sense of something having been lost. Eva Hoffman referred to ours as the "hinge" generation:[11] suspended between polarities of intimacy and distance, we show a tendency even today to conflate certain stories from our parents' pasts with feelings about our own private travails. I told a friend once that I was "going back" to Poland for a vacation. "Why do you say 'going back?'" she asked, "since you've never been there before?" In that slip of the tongue was revealed the illogic that asserts itself at times in my own sense of place, a feeling of still being attached somehow *there*, in that *other* home—the one that inhabits my mind. Scholars refer to this phenomenon as "post-memory"—living in close psychological proximity to events that happened before we were born, sons and daughters wrestle with boundaries of ownership.[12]

The relationship between Jews and Poles is fraught today in part as a consequence of this legacy of conflation and struggles over ownership—struggles over which narratives are most true, most accurate, or most worthy. The relationship is particularly strained as nationalist governments in Poland, Russia, and Israel all attempt to rewrite a complex story in terms that are far simpler and more self-servingly heroic than real history. Significant evidence indicates that Poles betrayed us to German authorities, stole our property, engaged in acts of murder and terror, and complied willingly with certain aspects of Nazi policy toward the Jews. But it was Poles, too, who sheltered many thousands of us, hiding us in barns and attics and in their own homes, as the memoirs here remind us. It was Poles who risked their lives helping to smuggle us through checkpoints and secure our false documents, and who staged one of world history's most significant anti-fascist rebellions.[13] My sister and cousins and I would not exist but for the efforts of my grandfather's Polish best friend, whom we know only as the elusive gentile "Mr. Lambert," who organized and safeguarded my father's escape from Warsaw during the first days of the German invasion. We owe him our lives. My grandfather searched for him desperately after the war, to no avail, and talked about him frequently in later life, virtually to the day he died. If he had survived the war, he must have needed to hide from the Soviets his capitalist past. So many years later, this is all we know. The memoirs collected here remind us that there is no simple story to be told about Polish-Jewish history, even though most of us prefer simple stories to complicated ones. There is nothing that lends itself here to easy reduction or comforting generalization.

NOTES

1. Natan Kellerman, "Transmission of Holocaust Trauma: An Integrative View," *Psychiatry* 64, no. 3 (2001): 256–67; Robert Krell and Marc Sherman, eds., *Medical and Psychological Effects of Concentration Camps on Holocaust Survivors* (New Brunswick, NJ: Transaction Publishers, 1997); Yael Danieli, ed., *International Handbook of Multigenerational Legacies of Trauma* (New York, NY: Plenum Press, 1998); Yael Danieli, Fran Norris, and Brian Engdahl, "Multigenerational Legacies

of Trauma: Modeling the What and How of Transmission," *American Journal of Orthopsychiatry* 86, no. 6 (2016): 639–651; Henry Krystal, ed., *Massive Psychic Trauma* (New York, NY: International Universities Press, 1968); Miri Scharf and Ofra Mayseless, "Disorganizing Experiences in Second and Third Generation Holocaust Survivors," *Qualitative Health Research* 21 (2011): 1539–553; Bergmann and Jucovy, *Generations of the Holocaust*; Dina Wardi, *Memorial Candles: Children of the Holocaust* (New York: Routledge, 1992); Daniel Bar-On, *Fear and Hope: Three Generations of the Holocaust* (Cambridge, MA: Harvard University Press, 1995); John Lemberger, ed., *A Global Perspective on Working with Holocaust Survivors and the Second Generation* (Jerusalem: Brookdale Institute of Gerontology and Human Development and National Israeli Center for Psychosocial Support of Survivors of the Holocaust and the Second Generation, 1995); Laub and Hamburger, *Psychoanalysis and Holocaust Testimony*; Robert Prince, *The Legacy of the Holocaust: Psychohistorical Themes in the Second Generation* (Ann Arbor, MI: UMI Research Press, 1985); Brenner, *The Handbook of Psychoanalytic Holocaust Studies*; Paul Marcus and Alan Rosenberg, eds., *Healing their Wounds: Psychotherapy with Holocaust Survivors and their Families* (New York: Praeger, 1989).

2. Wiseman and Barber, *Echoes of Trauma*; Hadas Wiseman, Einat Metzl, and Jacques Barber, "Anger, Guilt, and Intergenerational Communication of Trauma in the Interpersonal Narratives of Second Generation Holocaust Survivors," *American Journal of Orthopsychiatry* 76, no. 2 (2006): 176–84; Hadas Wiseman and Jacques Barber, "The Core Conflictual Relationship Theme Approach to Relational Narratives: Interpersonal Themes in the Context of Intergenerational Communication of Trauma," in *Healing Plots: The Narrative Basis of Psychotherapy*, eds. Amia Lieblich, Dan McAdams, and Ruthellen Josselson (Washington, DC: American Psychological Association, 2004), 151–70.

3. Natan Kellerman, *Holocaust Trauma: Psychological Effects and Treatment* (Bloomington, IN: iUniverse, 2009); Natan Kellerman, "Transmitted Holocaust Trauma: Curse or Legacy? The Aggravating and Mitigating Factors of Holocaust Trauma Transmission," *Israel Journal of Psychiatry and Related Sciences* 45, no. 4 (2008): 263–70; Yolanda Gampel, "Postmemories of Joy? Children of Holocaust Survivors and Alternative Family Memories," *Memory Studies* 12, no. 1 (2019): 74–87; Dov Shmotkin, "Vulnerability and Resilience Intertwined: A Review of Research on Holocaust Survivors," in *Between Stress and Hope: From an Disease Centered to a Health Centered Perspective*, eds. Rebecca Jacoby and Giora Kelnan (Westport, CT: Praeger, 2003), 213–34; Abraham Sagi-Schwartz, Marian Bakermans-Kranenburg, Shai Linn, and Marinus Van IJzendoorn, "Against All Odds: Genocidal Trauma is Association with Longer Life-Expectancy of the Survivor," *PLoS One* 8, no. 7 (2013): e69179; Rachel Yehuda, Amy Lehrmer, and Linda Bierer, "The Public Reception of Putative Epigenetic Mechanisms in the Transgenerational Effects of Trauma," *Environmental Epigenetics* 4, no. 2 (2018): 1–7; Lotem Giladi and Terece Bell, "Protective Factors for Intergenerational Transmission of Trauma among Second and Third Generational Holocaust Survivors," *Psychological Trauma: Theory, Research, Practice, and Policy* 5 (2013): 384–91. Robert Krell, "Resilience," in *The Handbook of Psychoanalytic Holocaust Studies: International Perspectives*, ed. Ira Brenner (Abingdon: Routledge, 2019), 41–50.

4. Bar-On, *Fear and Hope*.

5. Anthony Polonsky and Joanna Michlic, eds., *The Neighbors Respond: The Controversy Over the Jedwabne Massacre in Poland* (Princeton, NJ: Princeton University Press, 2004).

6. Snyder, *Black Earth*.

7. US Holocaust Memorial Museum, "Encyclopedia of Camps and Ghettos, 1933–1945," retrieved from https://www.ushmm.org/research/publications/encyclopedia-camps-ghettos.

8. David B. Green, "This Day in Jewish History—1948: The Altalena Arms Ship Reaches Israel, and Is Attacked with Friendly Fire," *Haaretz*, June 22, 2015, retrieved from https://www.haaretz.com/jewish/.premium-1948-altalena-arms-ship-sunk-by-friendy-fire-1.5373581.

9. Lehrer, *Jewish Poland Revisited*; Stanislaw Krajewski, *Poland and the Jews: Reflections of a Polish Polish Jew* (Warsaw: Wydrawnictwo Austeria, 2005).

10. Helen Epstein, *Children of the Holocaust: Conversations with Sons and Daughters of Survivors* (New York: Putnam and Sons, 1979); Alan Berger and Naomi Berger, *Second Generation Voices: Reflections by Children of Holocaust Survivors and Perpetrators* (Syracuse, NY: Syracuse University Press, 2001); Erin McGlothlin, *Second Generation Holocaust Literature: Legacies of Survival and Perpetration* (Rochester, NY: Camden House, 2006); Aaron Hass, *In the Shadow of the Holocaust: The Second Generation* (Cambridge, UK: Cambridge University Press, 1990).

11. Eva Hoffman, *After Such Knowledge: Memory, History and the Legacy of the Holocaust* (New York, NY: Public Affairs, 2004).

12. Marian Hirsch, "Surviving Images: Holocaust Memories and the Works of Post-Memory," *Yale Journal of Criticism* 14, no. 1 (2001): 5–37.

13. For a fascinating account, see Adam Michnik, "Poles and the Jews: How Deep is the Guilt?" *New York Times*, March 17, 2001.

Epilogue

Conversations across the Generations: Finding a Vocabulary of Remembrance

It is relatively easy to learn *about* the painful past, as the educator Roger Simon and others have observed,[1] but difficult indeed to learn *from* it, as different kinds of remembrance carry different conceptions of what should be remembered, by whom, and to what ends. Millions of people annually visit Auschwitz-Birkenau or other former extermination camps and make pilgrimages to the US Holocaust Memorial Museum in Washington, DC; holocaust education is mandated in public schools in many US states; the United Nations has designated an annual International Holocaust Remembrance Day; and in popular culture virtually worldwide, the holocaust has come to serve as a benchmark for talking about injustices and human rights abuses across a great many contexts. Yet, as Shirli Gilbert and Avril Alba[2] have suggested, the effects of all this have not been simple or straightforward. Multiple genocides have taken place in the years since World War II—in Rwanda, in Cambodia, in Myanmar, in Bosnia, in Congo, in Iraq, and in Somalia, among other places. War, corruption, crime, ethnic conflict, and ecological degradation have generated massive global population displacements, separating families and transforming millions of young people once again into refugees. Anti-Semitic and anti-immigration candidates have won elected seats in houses of government across Europe, and white supremacists have paraded on the streets of US cities. Far-right nationalists command a growing international social media following,[3] and synagogues and Jewish schools and cemeteries are being attacked with increasing frequency in Europe and the Americas.[4] On college campuses, Jewish students and faculty have found their spaces vandalized and their work ostracized by both the right and the left,[5] and surveys indicate that millions of young people know very little about the holocaust or harbor significant misconceptions.[6] The forty-fifth president of the United States has made frequent overtures to Jewish trauma and holocaust commemoration, baiting votes and donations, even while courting the allegiance of neo-Nazis and retweeting ultranationalist and racist tropes.[7] In a survey asking what it means to be Jewish, a majority of American Jews ranked "remembering the Holocaust" near the top of the list, and yet more than a fourth of the small population of remaining Holocaust survivors in the United States lives at or below the federal poverty level, according to social-services agency estimates.[8] We live in an era of a "crisis of memory," as Susan Suleiman has called it.[9] As the voices of actual survivors recede into the past, a multiplicity of meanings attaches to their experiences. We can ask, in this context: what does it mean to remember? To remember respectfully? To remember constructively? How, in fact, should we remember? This book has been my attempt to answer these questions. This final chapter begins with the questions themselves, as they warrant a closer inspection.

The unprecedented brutality of the holocaust forced people in the middle of the last century to acknowledge collectively the reality of the human capacity for atrocity. It challenged previously held myths about modernity and morality and forced a widespread reckoning with Europe's many centuries of anti-Semitism. On the level of individual experience, the holocaust was understood to be inexplicable, beyond the capacity for art or words to describe and explain, unfathomable in its extremity. But narratives are never fixed in place; they are subject to dynamic forces. In a profusion of cultural products—movies, books, websites, commemorative paraphernalia, and memorials of many kinds—images of holocaust trauma have come to saturate public life since the postwar years. Some refer to this shift as an "Americanization"[10] of holocaust memory, and sociologists have coined the term "prosthetic memory"[11] to describe the phenomenon by which almost anyone can now access the stories of the past, claim them as personally meaningful, and reshape them to new purposes. This can foster empathy and understanding across continents and communities. But it can lead, as well, to hyperbolic and sometimes bizarre narrative manipulations. Christian religious activists have talked about abortion as a kind of "holocaust."[12] Animal rights groups have described meat-eating as a "holocaust."[13] Anti-vaxxers and gun activists have deployed holocaust imagery to connect state health and safety codes to the idea of Nazi repression.[14] When US congresswoman Alexandria Ocasio-Cortez in June 2019 compared German concentration camps with US immigration detention practices at the Texas border, she reminded the nation that large social wrongs tend almost always to begin with smaller ones, but she also launched a heated national debate by presenting a holocaust image cleansed of Jewishness and voided of industrialized mass murder, cast instead as metaphor for universal human suffering.[15] Though it stood once as the ultimate illustration of the necessity for a Jewish homeland in Israel, the holocaust has been tethered to nationalist political projects only tangentially related to Jewish self-determination;[16] right-wing Israeli educational leaders in 2019 went so far as to characterize secularism and religious intermarriage as a new kind of contemporary "holocaust."[17] On television and in movies, some writers have lamented, a smothering sentimentalism turns the story of industrialized mass extermination into a transcendent redemption tale.[18]

The cacophony of metaphoric representations embodies what Michael Bernard-Donals[19] has called a tendency toward "displacement" of memory—a disjoining of fact from feeling that has the potential to trivialize genocide even while posing as commemoration. So moved are we by symbolic images of trauma, as Jeffrey Alexander and colleagues have written, so invested in expressions of the idea of suffering, we neglect to consider the specific historical, political, and policy steps that created them in the first place.[20] Jewish organizations have themselves trafficked in tropes, by many critical accounts, as, in the current era of social media, iconic images of generalized victimization make more effective outreach than do admonitions about rigorous study and serious practice.[21] Literary theorist Gary Weissman has written thoughtfully about the yearning among so many contemporary nonsurvivors to seek vicarious media-based "experiences" of holocaust suffering—to "feel" what it must have been like to "be there." Such "fantasies of witnessing," he writes, reveal the enormous distance that separates us now from the horrific reality of the actual event.[22]

Further complicating questions about holocaust memorialization is the emergence of what Michalinos Zembylas and Zvi Bekerman have called a global "politics of trauma"[23]—a tendency in contemporary culture to wield injury as the language of politics. In a Christian culture where suffering is imbued with moral meaning, woundedness itself is often taken to confer moral authority on descendants of the wounded, as the philosopher Lawrence Thomas once suggested,[24] and articulations of trauma indeed have become an almost universal civic vocabulary—a means by which marginalized groups petition for resources and compete for attention and recognition. Locked in zero-sum resource wars, social groups attempt to demolish the narratives of their competitors, as Wendy Brown and Michael Rothberg have written,[25] which means simplified, weaponized versions of the past become privileged over more complex and nuanced versions. Writing on the psychological aspects of this cultural shift, Dominick LaCapra has argued that an attachment to injury has come to replace more substantive ways for people to find connection to their cultural pasts; narratives of grievance and trauma become ritual objects that substitute for more reflective and complex explorations of the meaning of tragedy and painful history.[26] Psychoanalyst Vamik Volkan coined the phrase "chosen trauma" to describe how historical experiences of humiliation can be harnessed as rallying cries, transformed into a banner for group identity centered in a shared sense of eternal suffering—as if injustices of the past could be punished or undone by the sheer force of ongoing animosity.[27] Ultranationalist movements throughout the world today derive their popular allure from this toxic leveraging of the wound, as Timothy Snyder and others have written, even in such disparate places as Poland, Hungary, France, Britain, Ireland, Germany, Italy, Brazil, India, Pakistan, and throughout the Middle East, particularly among Israelis and Palestinians of a certain stripe and among their respective entrenched allied camps in the West.[28] Even in the United States, white nationalists wave the flag of victimhood, claiming mistreatment at the hands of Jews or of multicultural society more generally.[29] Jews in this context increasingly find themselves accused by both right and left of having a "surfeit" of holocaust memory—of cynically using the holocaust to obscure or erase the suffering of others.[30] In the current climate, as historian Carolyn Dean has observed, there is a sense that trauma narratives ought to be "performed" in a certain way—that people enjoying economic or social success no longer deserve the right to talk about genocide.[31]

Between what is exceptional and particular about the mass murder of Jews and what is universal about violence, suffering, and persecution more generally, a young generation today navigates fraught terrain as it attempts to make sense of the stories of the past. It might be tempting indeed to treat narratives of the war as if they are talismanic links to ancestors—to carry our grief like an eternal loyalty oath to the dead, an oath that excludes anyone but ourselves. But it might be tempting, at the same time, to feel entitled about the stories of the past—to feel they can be mobilized loosely and appropriated symbolically on behalf of virtually any contemporary cause. The first kind of remembering is obsessional—it denies the detail and complexity in our own stories, blinds us to the suffering of others, and locks us in cycles of endless repetition. But the second kind of remembering is equally unsatisfactory, as it is a form of erasure. It subsumes our ancestors under someone else's agenda, speaks in the name of those who aren't present to speak for themselves, and denies to real people the right of ownership of their actual history. Neither is a tribute to people we have loved. Neither honors the dead.

In this book, I have attempted to find a different path. Interrogating family memoirs for what they reveal about the internal developmental arc of young people, their unique resourcefulness and strategies for psychological self-preservation, I have tried to find a vocabulary of remembrance that retains connection to real people and real voices—that does not devolve into abstraction and reductive generalization—while also presenting the past in a form that can be read against the backdrop of new concerns. An emerging generation of holocaust scholars—Jacob Lothe, Thomas Trezise, and Michael Rothberg, among others[32]—proposes that we concern ourselves not only with the content of holocaust stories but also with the meanings we assign to them and the purposes to which we put them. Daniel Levy and Natan Sznaider[33] advocate what they call "rooted cosmopolitanism"—a linking of universalist and particularist lenses in an orientation to global human rights and collective social action. Such an approach requires a balance of empathy and reserve, Thomas Trezise has written, compassion and cautious restraint, an identification with others tempered by keen awareness of the moral limits of identification. I have endeavored here to contribute to this emerging conversation.

Parenthood, it is often said, is a dialogue among childhoods past and present. Raising children, we reconsider memories from our own childhood experiences, and we find traces, as well, from our parents' more distant pasts. With this in mind, we can return to the Salvadoran girl in the Texas detention center, the one who appeared briefly at the start of this book, forcibly separated from her family and pleading desperately over the radio for an adult to make a phone call. The story of that girl, who was united with American aunts following the media attention, was the place from which this project was launched. We find in that story a reminder that young people at different ages and life stages confront in different ways the challenges of loss, persecution, and social dislocation. They try their best to make sense and order in terrible, incomprehensibly painful situations, and to reach for whatever internal and external resources are available to them.

The stories collected here might be said to constitute what educators sometimes call "difficult knowledge."[34] They are not given as iconic representations of eternal victimhood. Nor are they offered up as metaphors open to any manner of interpretation or application. Rather, they are presented as a conversation about learning. It is a conversation about my own family, but also about the world outside the family, a world where Salvadoran girls continue today to struggle and search for separated loved ones. It is not only about a specific historical episode of massive violence and injustice but also about conditions that continue today to give rise to violence and injustice, and, above all, about the capacities of young people who are their targets. The material compiled here represents my efforts to straddle the dual obligations that my generation owes our survivor parents, on one side, and our children and grandchildren, on the other. These are the obligation to honor and remember—but also to allow a new generation to hear the stories of the past with its own ears and explore them in its own way, in conversation with the present. I have endeavored here also to acknowledge my own investment in these stories—to admit that the act of collecting old stories grows from yearnings, anxieties, and hopes, reflecting as much about the preoccupations of those who transmit the past as about those who actually lived it.

In the memoirs collected here, we meet six young people from a once-large extended Polish family most of whose other members were murdered at Auschwitz and Treblinka in the Nazi genocide that wiped out 90 percent of that country's Jews in a period of half a decade. They ranged in age from six to nineteen when World War II began, and on the eve of the war, in September of 1939, they lived, with one exception, within a handful of city blocks of one another. Less than a decade later, they were scattered across five continents. Tracing the arc of a remarkable global diaspora, their memoirs reveal not only a stunning diversity of experiences of survival and escape but also a diversity of strategies of self-preservation. In each story, we find evidence that development did not come to a halt under circumstances of profound disruption. Rather, each young person was driven in his or her own way to continue to travel the developmental journeys of childhood and young adulthood. They continued to navigate the competing demands of belonging and separating, attaching and individuating, becoming themselves and becoming what others wanted or demanded them to be. We also see the differential framing effects of age, gender, personality, family structure, community institutions, social connections, previous life experiences, and access to material resources. Each young person encountered dynamic on-the-ground circumstances in the experience of persecution and dislocation, and each endeavored, sometimes in remarkably creative ways, to make the most of the resources available.

We find an alternative in the stories here to the often reductive, generic images of the holocaust that tend to dominate popular media, and also to some of the broad generalizations about trauma, trauma transmission, and the refugee experience that circulate in contemporary popular and mental-health discourses. The overwhelming majority of Jews in Poland met the fate of death. But among the small minority who were lucky enough to escape and survive, there is evidence of great diversity of psychological experience; no singular overarching narrative can "explain" the resilience trajectory. Precisely in the diversity of details presented in these pages, we find lessons for those who work today with young people who are the objects of persecution and social upheaval.

David, my father, recounts a half-year odyssey of chaotic flight across continents. His story incorporates unlikely elements: limousines, cruise ships, candy machines, and luxury hotels, but also bombings, shootings, and nights of hiding among charred and smoldering buildings. His story traces the illogic of the refugee experience seen through a child's eyes. But we also find in David's story a seven-year-old's developmental transition, as David enters a phase of relative self-regulation and newfound independence precisely as disaster unfolds around him. We see that his development does not stop because a crisis has begun; rather, it continues within new contextual constraints and is in some ways even propelled by them. We can observe how a natural intellectual curiosity attached itself to his search for stability, and how information itself became a raw material from which he endeavored to build for himself the feelings of accomplishment and mastery that are core developmental achievements for children his age. David's story also reveals the mechanisms of emotional self-protection that can be activated in school-age children. We see that certain especially disturbing forms of knowledge can be shut out of the child's conscious awareness, and, moreover, that such knowledge does not disappear. It lingers and sometimes reemerges in later life—as haunting questions about guilt and responsibility, yearning and shame. Millions of refugee children hold inside themselves today the complex and painful secrets of their own quiet non-awareness. My father's stories reveal that persecution's outcomes are to a great extent sequestered and deeply private.

Nina, whose story traces a multiyear journey from first grade to middle adolescence, recounts the long series of repeated rejections, years of lingering uncertainty, and growing despair. But we find that hers is also a story about the messages that very young children can absorb from able parents, even in crisis. It is an illustration of the way intact families and thoughtful preservation of school and household routines can create a semblance of home, even when there is no home left. Reciprocity in social relationships, we see, is itself a kind of "holding" structure. Mutual reassurance is a collaborative project providing comfort and refuge among family members at a time when conventional community and milieu supports are inaccessible or unavailable. This, too, is a lesson for the current era.

Nathan tells the story of a twelve-year-old boy's stunning six-year ordeal of hideous and relentless cruelty. But we find that it is also a story about the child who summons from within himself the guiding beacon of a loved one's voice, even long after its original source has been violently extinguished. We see a child's capacity to take in and sustain inside himself a series of loving adult figures who continue to speak to him about caring and belonging—affirming the possibility of something better than what has been given by outward circumstances. Housing and shelter configurations, even short-term arrangements during periods of hiding and flight, it is evident, can serve important developmental and affirming functions, as they can enable children to feel capacitous, to acquire new skills, and to contribute meaningfully to family and community. We see also that children remain alert and attentive to choices and opportunities in their surroundings; their active engagement in challenging work and pragmatic decision-making might itself contribute to their cognitive intactness.

Irene recalls the terror and torment of survival in the Warsaw ghetto, and we encounter in intimate detail her experience of the several-week period that followed announcements of the ghetto's liquidation. But we see what can be preserved of personal humanity in small daily rituals of ordinary forbearance—in measured acts of care for self and others. In her story we witness at close hand what it means for a world to disintegrate, but we also see that young people cling tenaciously and creatively to the whatever remains of rational order and routine, even in the worst circumstances.

Through the prism of adolescent rebellion and activist resistance, Marysia's story reminds us of the cleverness of young people —the way they can connect themselves to larger moral narratives that amplify their courage and fuel their endurance. Creative engagement, we see—in work, in learning, in the arts, and in acts of subterfuge, trickery, and mutual aid—serves almost as a kind of psychic engine that animates and invigorates, reminding young people of power and hope, even in times of discouragement and physical exhaustion.

In Wanda's story, we find the remarkable exception to the war's wider arc. But we see, as well, the familiar psychological uses of compartmentalization, sarcasm, and irony—small means by which the weak can still dominate the strong.

The material collected here shows that these young people turned, where possible, to the reassuring gaze of available caregivers, to the predictability of school rules and work routines wherever these remained, to the safety and camaraderie offered by peer groups, and to small moments of ordinary accomplishment and triumph where these were the only satisfactions available. Deeply sustaining affirmations flowed from the activity of learning new things even in times of intense danger, and from using old and new skill sets to contribute to the well-being of others. Acts of sabotage and defiance—aggression turned outward in measured quantities—can become, for some young people, a nourishing well of hope, as the stories here show. The problem-solving challenges posed by work demands, moreover, can facilitate sustained cognitive engagement. Children are not passive victims; they do not blindly accept what outrageous circumstance imposes. Rather, within evolving frameworks of opportunity and access, they can retain fine-tuned sensibilities about risk and benefit and make sensible if breathtakingly painful choices that preserve and enhance their life chances. Physical survival can involve miraculous shifts of luck and chance, but survival in the psychological sense also involves dynamic processes of repair, reconstitution, and recalibration. We see that refugee aid and resettlement policies can repeat and reinforce the traumatic experiences of persecution and disempowerment, adding to children's physical and psychic burdens. Based on the stories collected here, we can understand why refugees in some circumstances today might continue to circumvent and sabotage the rules they are given.

Children in violent situations navigate a balance between knowing what is happening around them and submerging their awareness of it. But like many who have cared for aging refugee parents, my sister and I came to see that such acts of balancing may be time-limited and precarious. In our grandfather's end-of-life hallucinations about his dead brother, and in our father's return, in dementia, to the smell of burned children, we witnessed what a number of scholars have observed in research on aging survivors:[35] even the longest-lived defenses can be undone by age and time. We have no choice but to accede to the limits of memoir and testimony: we acknowledge where these have smoothed over, deceptively, some of the more deeply submerged and painful elements of the past.

The stories here present side by side six very different versions of the war. Differences in experience connected to social status and access to resources are especially disturbing. But we must not turn our eyes away, as these are the undeniable reflections of the reality of social inequality's impact on children in times of strife. This is a truth that cannot be undone, and my sister and I eventually came to understand why our father remained so haunted by the aching knowledge of it. It cannot be denied that my own deep-seated need to interrogate this strange legacy was a fundamental factor in the creation of this book.

Only two members of the original prewar generation of my family remain alive at the time of this writing. I cannot predict what meanings will be sustained in these stories as I pass them to the next generation. But I can hope they are engaged deeply, ethically, and creatively. Beyond the matter of acquiring knowledge, however, is the more difficult matter of what to do with it once it has been acquired. Beyond knowing the story, as the educator Jonathan Jansen[36] has written, is the question, "What shall we do next?" This book ends with that question, as it is a new generation's to answer.

NOTES

1. Roger Simon, Sharon Rosenberg, and Claudia Eppert, *Between Hope and Despair: Pedagogy and the Remembrance of Historical Trauma* (Lanham, MD: Rowman & Littlefield, 2000); Roger Simon, *The Touch of the Past: Remembrance, Learning, and Ethics* (New York, NY: Palgrave Macmillan, 2005); Roger Simon, "The Paradoxical Practice of Zakhor: Memories of 'What has Never Been My Fault or Deed'," in *Between Hope and Despair: Pedagogy and the Remembrance of Historical Trauma*, eds. Roger I. Simon, Sharon Rosenberg, and Claudia Eppert (New York, NY: Rowman & Littlefield, 2000), 9–26.

2. Shirli Gilbert and Avril Alba, eds., *Holocaust Memory and Racism in the Postwar World* (Detroit, MI: Wayne State University Press, 2019).

3. A. C. Thompson, Lucas Waldron, and Christopher Mathias, "Despite Crackdown, White Supremacist and Neo Nazi Videos Take Stubborn Root on You Tube," *ProPublica*, March 15, 2019.

4. Eva Cosse, "The Alarming Rise of Anti-Semitism in Europe," *Human Rights Watch Dispatch*, June 4, 2019.

5. Jonathan Greenblatt, "It's Time to Call Out Anti-Semitism by Both the Left and the Right," *Washington Post*, October 26, 2018.

6. Julie Zauzmer, "Holocaust Study: Two Thirds of Millennials Don't Know What Auschwitz Is," *Washington Post*, April 12, 2018.

7. Ben Kharakh and Dan Primack, "Donald Trump's Social Media Ties to White Supremacists," *Fortune*, March 22, 2016.

8. Matthew Fishbane, "Soon There Will be No More Survivors," *Tablet Magazine*, January 27, 2014, https://www.tabletmag.com/jewish-arts-and-culture/160324/soon-there-will-be-no-more-survivors.

9. Suleiman, *Crises of Memory*.

10. Gary Weissman, *Fantasies of Witnessing: Postwar Efforts to Experience the Holocaust* (Ithaca, NY: Cornell University Press, 2004); Hilene Flanzbaum, *The Americanization of the Holocaust* (Baltimore, MD: Johns Hopkins University Press, 1999); Peter Novick, *The Holocaust in American Life* (New York, NY: Mariner Books, 2000); Alan Mintz, *Popular Culture and the Shaping of Holocaust Memory in America* (Seattle, WA: University of Washington, 2001).

11. Alison Landsberg, *Prosthetic Memory: The Transformation of American Remembrance in the Age of Mass Culture* (New York, NY: Columbia University Press, 2004).

12. Associated Press, "Pope Calls Abortion 'White Glove' Equivalent of Nazi Crimes," *The New York Times*, June 16, 2018.

13. David Sztybel, "Can the Treatment of Animals be Compared to the Holocaust?" *Ethics and the Environment* 11, no. 1 (2006): 97–132.

14. Helene Sinnreich, "Anti-Vaxxers are Comparing Themselves to Holocaust Victims—Who Relied on Vaccines to Survive," *Washington Post*, April 10, 2019; Daniel Moritz-Rabson, "Gun Rights Group Criticized for Using Holocaust Pictures to Attack Rabbi Backing Gun Control Legislation," *Newsweek*, October 30, 2018.

15. Omer Bartov, Doris Bergen, Andrea Orzoff, et al., "An Open Letter to the Director of the US Holocaust Museum," *New York Review of Books Daily*, July 1, 2019, https://www.nybooks.com/daily/2019/07/01/an-open-letter-to-the-director-of-the-holocaust-memorial-museum/; Timothy Snyder, "It Can Happen Here," *Slate*, July 12, 2019; Danya Ruttenberg, "Never Again' Means Nothing if Holocaust Analogies are Always Off-Limits," *Washington Post*, June 19, 2019.

16. Jackie Feldman, *Above the Death Pits, Beneath the Flag: Youth Voyages to Poland and the Performance of Israeli National Identity* (New York, NY: Berghahn, 2010).

17. JTA and TOI Staff, "Rafi Peretz Says Intermarriage among US Jews is 'Second Holocaust,'" *Jerusalem Post*, July 10, 2019.

18. Lawrence Graver, *An Obsession with Anne Frank* (Berkeley, CA: University of California Press, 1995); Alvin Rosenfeld, *The End of the Holocaust* (Bloomington, IN: Indiana University Press, 2013); Lawrence Langer, *Using and Abusing the Holocaust* (Bloomington, IN: Indiana University Press, 2006); Jeffrey Shandler, *While America Watches: Televising the Holocaust* (New York, NY: Oxford University Press, 1998); Gavriel Rosenfeld, *Hi Hitler: How the Nazi Past is Being Normalized in Contemporary Culture* (Cambridge, UK: Cambridge University Press, 2015).

19. Michael Bernard-Donals, *Figures of Memory: The Rhetoric of Displacement at the United States Holocaust Memorial Museum* (Albany, NY: SUNY Press, 2016);

Michael Bernard-Donals, *Forgetful Memory: Remembrance and Representation in the Wake of the Holocaust* (Albany, NY: SUNY Press, 2008).

20. Jeffrey Alexander, *Remembering the Holocaust: A Debate* (New York, NY: Oxford University Press, 2009); Jeffrey Alexander, *Trauma: A Social Theory* (Malden, MA: Polity, 2012); Jeffrey Alexander, Ron Eyerman, Bernhard Giesen, Neil Smelser, and Piotr Sztompka, *Cultural Trauma and Collective Identity* (Berkeley, CA: University of California Press, 2004).

21. Mintz, *Popular Culture*; Flanzbaum, *The Americanization of the Holocaust*.

22. Weissman, *Fantasies of Witnessing*.

23. Michalinos Zembylas, *The Politics of Trauma in Education* (London: Palgrave Macmillan, 2008); Zvi Bekerman and Michalinos Zembylas, *Psychologized Language in Education: Denaturalizing a Regime of Truth* (London: Palgrave Macmillan, 2018); Michalinos Zembylas, *Emotion and Traumatic Conflict: Reclaiming Healing in Education* (Oxford: Oxford University Press, 2015); Snyder, *Black Earth*; Pankaj Mishra, *Age of Anger: A History of the Present* (New York, NY: Farrar Straus and Giroux, 2017); Alison Cole, *The Cult of True Victimhood: From the War on Welfare to the War on Terror* (Stanford, CA: Stanford University Press, 2006); Sarah Ahmed, *The Cultural Politics of Emotion* (Edinburgh: Edinburgh University Press, 2004).

24. Lawrence Mordekhai Thomas, "Suffering as a Moral Beacon: Blacks and Jews," in *The Americanization of the Holocaust*, ed. Hilene Flanzbaum (Baltimore, MD: The Johns Hopkins University Press, 1999), 198–210.

25. Wendy Brown, *States of Injury: Power and Freedom in Late Modernity* (Princeton, NJ: Princeton University Press, 1995); Rothberg, *Multidirectional Memory*.

26. Dominick LaCapra, *Writing History, Writing Trauma* (Baltimore, MD: Johns Hopkins University Press, 2000); Dominick LaCapra, *Representing the Holocaust* (Ithaca, NY: Cornell University Press, 1996).

27. Volkan, *Immigrants and Refugees*; Vamik Volkan, "Transgenerational Transmission and Chosen Traumas: An Aspect of Large-Group Identity," *Group Analysis* 34, no. 1 (2001): 79–97.

28. Snyder, *Black Earth*; Mishra, *Age of Anger*.

29. Mitch Berbrier, "The Victim Ideology of White Supremacists and White Separatists in the United States," *Sociological Forum* 33, no. 2 (2000): 175–191.

30. Cole, *The Cult of True Victimhood*; Walter Benn Michaels, "You Who Were Never There: Slavery and the New Historicism—Deconstruction and the Holocaust," in *The Americanization of the Holocaust*, ed. Hilene Flanzbaum (Baltimore, MD: The Johns Hopkins University Press, 1999).

31. Carolyn Dean, *Aversion and Erasure: The Fate of the Victim after the Holocaust* (Ithaca, NY: Cornell University Press, 2010).

32. Trezise, *Witnessing Witnessing*; Jacob Lothe, Susan Rubin Suleiman, and James Phelan, eds., *After Testimony: The Ethics and Aesthetics of Holocaust Narrative for the Future* (Columbus, OH: Ohio State University Press, 2012); Diamond and Sklarew, *Cinematic Reflections*; Victoria Aarons, ed., *Third Generation Holocaust Narratives: Memory in Memoir and Fiction* (Lanham, MD: Lexington Books, 2016); Victoria Aarons and Alan Berger, eds., *Third Generation Holocaust*

Representations: Trauma, History, and Memory (Evanston, IL: Northwestern University Press, 2017); Esther Jilovsky, Jordan Silverstein, and David Slucksi, eds., *In the Shadow of Memory: The Holocaust and the Third Generation* (London: Vallentine Mitchell, 2016); Daniel Mendelsohn, *The Lost: A Search for Six in Six Million* (London: Harper Perennial, 2008); Maria Roca Lizarazu, "Remembering the Holocaust: Generations, Witnessing, and Place," *Holocaust Studies* 24, no. 1 (2018): 128–30; Maria Roca Lizarazu, "Third Generation Holocaust Narratives: Memory in Memoir and Fiction," *Holocaust Studies* 24, no. 1 (2018): 124–28; Esther Jilovsky, "Holocaust Generations of the Past and Future," *Journal of Modern Jewish Studies* 9, no. 2 (2010): 275–78; Esther Jilovsky, *Remembering the Holocaust: Generations, Witnessing, and Place* (New York, NY: Bloomsbury, 2017); David Slucki, *Sing This at My Funeral: A Memoir of Fathers and Sons* (Detroit, MI: Wayne State University Press, 2019); Liat Stier-Livny, *Remaking Holocaust Memory: Documentary Cinema by Third Generation Survivors in Israel* (Syracuse, NY: Syracuse University Press, 2019).

33. Daniel Levy and Natan Sznaider, *The Holocaust and Memory in the Global Age* (Philadelphia, PA: Temple University Press, 2006).

34. Deborah Britzman, "If the Story Cannot End: Deferred Action, Ambivalence, and Difficult Knowledge," in *Between Hope and Despair: Pedagogy and the Remembrance of Historical Trauma*, eds. Roger I. Simon, Sharon Rosenberg, and Claudia Eppert (New York, NY: Rowman & Littlefield, 2000), 27–58; Deborah Britzman, *Lost Subjects, Contested Objects* (Albany, NY: State University of New York Press, 1998).

35. Ayala Fridman, Marian Bakermans-Kranenburg, Abraham Sagi-Schwartz, and Marinus Van IJzendoorn, "Coping in Old Age with Extreme Childhood Trauma: Aging Holocaust Survivors and their Offspring Facing New Challenges," *Aging and Mental Health* 15, no. 2 (2011): 232–42; Dov Shmotkin, Amit Shrira, Shira Goldberg, and Yuval Palgi, "Resilience and Vulnerability among Aging Holocaust Survivors and their Families: An Intergenerational Overview," *Journal of Intergenerational Relationships* 9, no. 1 (2011): 7–21; Jochanan Stressman, Aaron Cohen, Robert Hammerman-Rozenberg, Michael Bursztyn, Daniel Azoulay, Yoram Maarivi, and Jeremy Jacobs, "Holocaust Survivors in Old Age: The Jerusalem Longitudinal Study," *Journal of the American Geriatrics Society* 56, no. 3 (2008): 47–477.

36. Jonathan Jansen, *Knowledge in the Blood: Confronting Race and the Apartheid Past* (Stanford, CA: Stanford University Press, 2009).

Bibliography

Aarons, Victoria, ed. *Third Generation Holocaust Narratives: Memory in Memoir and Fiction*. Lanham, MD: Lexington Books, 2016.
———, and Alan Berger. *Third Generation Holocaust Representation: Trauma, History, and Memory*. Evanston, IL: Northwestern University Press, 2017.
Ahearn, Frederick, Jr., and Jean Athey, eds. *Refugee Children: Theory, Research, Services*. Baltimore, MD: Johns Hopkins University Press, 1991.
Ahmed, Sara. *The Cultural Politics of Emotion*. Edinburgh: Edinburgh University Press, 2004.
Akhtar, Salman, and Maria Teresa Savio Hooke, eds. *The Geography of Meaning: Psychoanalytic Perspectives on Place, Space, Land, and Dislocation*. New York, NY: Routledge, 2007.
———. *Immigration and Identity: Turmoil, Treatment, and Transformation*. London: Jason Aronson, 1999.
———, ed. *The Mother and Her Child: Clinical Aspects of Attachment, Separation, and Loss*. Lanham, MD: Jason Aronson, 2012.
Alexander, Jeffrey. *Remembering the Holocaust: A Debate*. Oxford: Oxford University Press, 2009.
———. *Trauma: A Social Theory*. Malden, MA: Polity, 2012.
Alexander, Jeffrey, Ron Eyerman, Bernhard Giesen, Neil Smelser, and Piotr Sztompka. *Cultural Trauma and Collective Identity*. Berkeley, CA: University of California Press, 2004.
Associated Press. "Pope Calls Abortion 'White Glove' Equivalent of Nazi Crimes." *The New York Times*, June 16, 2018.
Auerhahn, Nanette, and Dori Laub. "Discussion." In *Cinematic Reflections on the Legacy of the Holocaust: Psychoanalytic Perspectives*, edited by Diana Diamond and Bruce Sklarew, 226–246. New York, NY: Routledge, 2019.
Baer, Elizabeth, ed., and Myrna Goldenberg. *Experience and Expression: Women, the Nazis, and the Holocaust*. Detroit, MI: Wayne State Press, 2003.

Bar-On, Dan. *Fear and Hope: Three Generations of the Holocaust.* Cambridge, MA: Harvard University Press, 1988.

———, Jeanette Eland, Rolf Kleber, Robert Krell, Yael Moore, Abraham Sagi, Erin Soriano, Peter Suedfeld, Peter van der Velden, and Marinus van Ijzendoorn. "Multigenerational Perspectives on Coping with the Holocaust Experience: An Attachment Perspective for Understanding the Developmental Sequelae of Trauma across Generations." *International Journal of Behavioral Development* 22, no. 2 (1988): 315–338.

Bartov, Omer, Doris Bergen, Andrea Orzoff, Timothy Snyder, Anike Walke, et al. "An Open Letter to the Director of the US Holocaust Museum." *New York Review of Books Daily*, July 1, 2019. https://www.nybooks.com/daily/2019/07/01/an-open-letter-to-the-director-of-the-holocaust-memorial-museum/.

Bass-Wichelhaus, Helen. "Resilience in Child Survivors: History and Application of Coding of the International Study of Organized Persecution of Children." In *Children in the Holocaust and its Aftermath: Historical and Psychological Studies of the Kestenberg Archive*, edited by Sharon Kangisser-Cohen, Eva Fogelman, and Dalia Ofer, 170–186. New York, NY: Berghahn, 2017.

Bekerman, Zvi. *Teaching Contested Narratives: Identity, Memory, and Reconciliation in Peace Education and Beyond.* Cambridge: Cambridge University Press, 2012.

———, and Michalinos Zembylas. *Psychologized Language in Education: Denaturalizing a Regime of Truth.* London: Palgrave Macmillan, 2018.

BenEzer, Gadi. "Trauma Signals in Life Stories." In *Trauma—Life Stories of Survivors*, edited by Kim Lacy Rogers and Selma Leyedesdorff, 29–44. New Brunswick, NJ: Transaction Publishers, 2004.

Berbrier, Mitch. "The Victim Ideology of White Supremacists and White Separatists in the United States." *Sociological Focus* 33, no. 2 (May 2000): 175–191.

Berger, Alan, and Naomi Berger. *Second Generation Voices: Reflections by Children of Holocaust Survivors and Perpetrators.* Syracuse, NY: Syracuse University Press, 2001.

Bergmann, Martin, and Milton Jucovy, eds. *Generations of the Holocaust.* New York, NY: Basic Books, 1982.

Bernard-Donals, Michael. *An Introduction to Holocaust Studies.* New York, NY: Routledge, 2005.

———. *Figures of Memory: The Rhetoric of Displacement at the United States Holocaust Memorial Museum.* Albany: SUNY Press, 2016.

———. *Forgetful Memory: Remembrance and Representation in the Wake of the Holocaust.* Albany, NY: SUNY Press, 2008.

Betancourt, Theresa, and Kashif Khan. "The Mental Health of Children Affected by Armed Conflict: Protective Processes and Pathways to Resilience." *International Review of Psychiatry* 20, no. 3 (June 2008): 317–328.

Bloch, Alice, Nando Sigona, and Roger Zetter. *Sans Papiers: The Social and Economic Lives of Undocumented Migrants.* Chicago, IL: Pluto Press, 2014.

Bonanno, George, Sara Romero, and Sarah Klein. "The Temporal Elements of Psychological Resilience: An Integrative Framework for the Study of Individuals, Families, and Communities." *Psychological Inquiry* 26 (2015): 139–169.

Bonovitz, Jennifer. "When Mother Isn't There: Finding Alternate Pathways to Development." In *The Mother and Her Child: Clinical Aspects of Attachment, Separation, and Loss*, edited by Salman Akhtar, 121–133. Lanham, MD: Jason Aronson, 2012.

Bowlby, John. *Attachment and Loss, Vol. 1: Attachment.* New York, NY: Basic Books, 1969.

———. *Attachment and Loss, Vol. 2: Separation: Anxiety and Anger.* New York, NY: Basic Books, 1973.

Brenner, Ira. *The Handbook of Psychoanalytic Holocaust Studies: International Perspectives.* New York, NY: Routledge, 2019.

Bretherton, Inge, and Kristine Mulholland. "Internal Working Models in Attachment Relationships: Elaborating a Central Construct in Attachment Theory." In *Handbook of Attachment Theory, Research, and Clinical Application*, edited by Jude Cassidy and Phillip R. Shaver, 102–127. New York, NY: Guilford Press, 2008.

Britzman, Deborah. *Lost Subjects, Contested Objects.* New York, NY: SUNY Press, 1998.

———. "If the Story Cannot End: Deferred Action, Ambivalence, and Difficult Knowledge." In *Between Hope and Despair: Pedagogy and the Remembrance of Historical Trauma*, edited by Sharon Rosenberg, 27–58. Lanham, MD: Rowman & Littlefield, 2000.

Bronfenbrenner, Urie. *The Ecology of Human Development: Experiments by Nature and Design.* Cambridge, MA: Harvard University Press, 1979.

Brown, Wendy. *States of Injury: Power and Freedom in Late Modernity.* Princeton, NJ: Princeton University Press, 1995.

Caruth, Cathy, ed. *Trauma: Explorations in Memory.* Baltimore, MD: Johns Hopkins University Press, 1995.

Castles, Stephen, Hein de Haas, and Mark Miller. *The Age of Migration.* New York, NY: Palgrave Macmillan, 2013.

Charny, Israel, ed. *Holding on to Humanity: The Message of Holocaust Survivors: The Shamai Davidson Papers.* New York, NY: New York University Press, 1992.

Cicchetti, Dante, ed. *Developmental Psychopathology*, 3rd Edition. New York, NY: Wiley, 2016.

———. "Resilience under Conditions of Extreme Stress: A Multimethod Perspective." *World Psychiatry* 9, no. 1 (2010): 145–154.

Cole, Alyson. *The Cult of True Victimhood: From the War on Welfare to the War on Terror.* Stanford, CA: Stanford University Press, 2006.

Cosse, Eva. "The Alarming Rise of Anti-Semitism in Europe." *Human Rights Watch Dispatch*, June 4, 2019.

Danieli, Yael, ed. *International Handbook of Multigenerational Legacies of Trauma.* New York, NY: Springer, 1998.

———, Fran Norris, and Brian Engdahl. "Multigenerational Legacies of Trauma: Modeling the What and How of Transmission." *American Journal of Orthopsychiatry* 86, no. 6 (2016): 639–651.

Dean, Carolyn. *Aversion and Erasure: The Fate of the Victim after the Holocaust.* Ithaca, NY: Cornell University Press, 2010.

Delbo, Charlotte. *Auschwitz and After*. New Haven, CT: Yale University Press, 1995.
Durst, Nathan. "Child-Survivors of the Holocaust: Age-Specific Traumatization and the Consequences for Therapy." *American Journal of Psychotherapy* 57, no. 4 (October 2003): 499–518.
Epstein, Helen. *Children of the Holocaust: Conversations with Sons and Daughters of Survivors*. New York, NY: Putnam and Sons, 1979.
Erikson, Erik. *Identity and the Life Cycle*. New York, NY: Norton, 1980.
———. *Identity: Youth and Crisis*. New York, NY: Norton, 1968.
———. *Childhood and Society*. New York, NY: Norton, 1950.
Fazel, Mina, Ruth Reed, Catherine Panter-Brick, and Alan Stein. "Mental Health of Displaced and Refugee Children Resettled in High-Income Countries: Risk and Protective Factors." *Lancet* 379 (January 2012): 266–282.
Felman, Shoshana, and Dori Laub, eds. *Testimony: Crises of Witnessing in Literature, Psychoanalysis, and History*. New York, NY: Routledge, 1992.
Feldman, Daniel. "Children's Play in the Shadow of War." *American Journal of Play* 11, no. 3 (Spring 2019): 288–307.
Feldman, Jackie. *Above the Death Pits, Beneath the Flag: Youth Voyages to Poland and the Performance of Israeli National Identity*. New York, NY: Berghahn, 2010.
Fishbane, Matthew. "Soon There Will be No More Survivors." *Tablet Magazine*, January 27, 2014. https://www.tabletmag.com/jewish-arts-and-culture/160324/soon-there-will-be-no-more-survivors.
Flanzbaum, Hilene, ed. *The Americanization of the Holocaust*. Baltimore, MD: Johns Hopkins University Press, 1999.
Freud, Anna, and Sophia Dann. "An Experiment in Group Upbringing." *The Psychoanalytic Study of the Child* 6, no. 1 (1951): 127–168.
Freud, Sigmund. *Beyond the Pleasure Principle*. New York, NY: W.W. Norton, 1961.
Fridman, Ayala, Marian Bakermans-Kranenburg, Abraham Sagi-Schwartz, and Marinus Van IJzendoorn. "Coping in Old Age with Extreme Childhood Trauma: Aging Holocaust Survivors and their Offspring Facing New Challenges." *Aging and Mental Health* 15, no. 2 (2011): 232–242.
Gampel, Yolanda. "Reflections on the Prevalence of the Uncanny in Social Violence." In *Cultures under Siege: Collective Violence and Trauma*, edited by Antonius C. G. M. Robben, 48–69. Cambridge: Cambridge University Press, 2000.
Garbarino, James. "An Ecological Perspective on the Effects of Violence on Children." *Journal of Community Psychology* 29, no. 3 (2001): 361–378.
———, and Kathleen Kostelny. "What Do We Need to Know to Understand Children in War and Community Violence." In *Minefields in their Hearts: The Mental Health of Children in War and Community Violence*, edited by Roberta Apfel and Bennett Simon, 33–51. New Haven, CT: Yale University Press, 1996.
———, Nancy Dubrow, Kathleen Kostelny, and Carolyn Pardo, eds. *Children in Danger: Coping with the Consequences of Community Violence*. San Francisco, CA: Jossey Bass, 1992.
Garrett, Paul Michael. "Questioning Tales of 'Ordinary Magic': 'Resilience' and Neo-Liberal Reasoning." *British Journal of Social Work* 46 (2015): 1909–1925.

Gatrell, Peter. *The Making of the Modern Refugee*. Oxford: Oxford University Press, 2015.

Giladi, Lotem, and Terece Bell. "Protective Factors for Intergenerational Transmission of Trauma among Second and Third Generational Holocaust Survivors." *Psychological Trauma: Theory, Research, Practice, and Policy* 5 (2013): 384–391.

Gilbert, Shirli, and Avril Alba, eds. *Holocaust Memory and Racism in the Post War World*. Detroit, MI: Wayne State University Press, 2019.

Gonzales, Roberto, and Nando Sigona, eds. *Within and Beyond Citizenship: Borders, Membership, and Belonging*. New York, NY: Routledge, 2018.

———, Nando Sigona, Martha Franco, and Anna Papoutsi. *Undocumented Migration*. New York, NY: Polity, 2019.

Graver, Lawrence. *An Obsession with Anne Frank*. Berkeley, CA: University of California Press, 1995.

Green, David B. "This Day in Jewish History – 1948: The Altalena Arms Ship Reaches Israel, and Is Attacked with Friendly Fire." *Haaretz*, June 22, 2015. https://www.haaretz.com/jewish/.premium-1948-altalena-arms-ship-sunk-by-friendy-fire-1.5373581.

Greenblatt, Jonathan. "It's Time to Call Out Anti-Semitism by Both the Left and the Right." *Washington Post*, October 26, 2018.

Grunwald-Spier, Agnes. *Women's Experiences in the Holocaust: In their Own Words*. Gloucestershire, UK: Amberley, 2019.

Hass, Aaron. *In the Shadow of the Holocaust: The Second Generation*. Cambridge, UK: Cambridge University Press, 1990.

Hilberg, Raul. "Developments in the Historiography of the Holocaust." In *Comprehending the Holocaust: Historical and Literary Research*, edited by Asher Cohen, Yoav Gelber, and Charlotte Wardi, 28–29. New York, NY: Peter Lang, 1988.

Hirsch, Marian. "Surviving Images: Holocaust Memories and the Works of Post-Memory." *Yale Journal of Criticism* 14, no. 1 (2001): 5–37.

———, and Leo Spitzer. "The Witness in the Archive." *Holocaust Studies/Memory Studies* 2, no. 2 (2009): 151–170.

Hobfoll, Stevan. "Resource Caravans and Resource Caravan Passageways: A New Paradigm for Trauma Responding." *Intervention: Journal of Mental Health and Psychosocial Support in Conflict Affected Areas* 12, no. 4 (2014): 21–332.

———, and Jeremiah Schumm. "Conservation of Resources Theory: Application to Public Health Promotion." In *Emerging Themes in Health Promotion Practice and Research: Strategies for Improving Public Health*, edited by Ralph DiClemente, Richard Crosby, and Michele Kegler, 285–312. San Francisco, CA: Jossey-Bass, Inc., 2002.

———, Natalie Stevens, and Alyson Zalta. "Expanding the Science of Resilience: Conserving Resources in the Act of Adaptation." *Psychological Inquiry* 26, no. 2 (2015): 174–180.

———, Vanessa Tirone, Lucie Holmgreen, and James Gerhart. "Conservation of Resources Theory Applied to Major Stress." In *Stress: Concepts, Cognition,*

Emotion, and Behavior: Handbook of Stress, Vol. 1, edited by George Fink, 65–71. New York, NY: Academic Press, 2016.

Hoffman, Eva. *After Such Knowledge: Memory, History and the Legacy of the Holocaust*. New York, NY: Public Affairs, 2004.

"Holocaust and the History of Gender and Sexuality." *German History* 36, no. 1 (March 2018): 78–100.

Horvath, Rita, and Katalin Zana. "Both Valuable and Difficult: A Meeting Point between Historical and Psychological Interviews." In *Children in the Holocaust and its Aftermath: Historical and Psychological Studies of the Kestenberg Archive*, edited by Sharon Kangisser Cohen, Eva Fogelman, and Dalia Ofer, 81–98. New York, NY: Berghan, 2017.

Hou, Wai Kai, Brian Hall, and Stevan Hobfoll. "Drive to Thrive: A Theory of Resilience Following Loss." In *Mental Health of Refugees and Conflict-Affected Populations: Theory, Research, and Clinical Practice*, edited by Nexhmedin Morina and Angela Nickerson, 111–134. Cham, Switzerland: Springer Nature, 2018.

Jansen, Jonathan. *Knowledge in the Blood: Confronting Race and the Apartheid Past*. Stanford, CA: Stanford University Press, 2009.

Jilovsky, Esther. "Holocaust Generations of the Past and Future." *Journal of Modern Jewish Studies* 9, no. 2 (2010): 275–278.

———. *Remembering the Holocaust: Generations, Witnessing, and Place*. London: Bloomsbury, 2017.

———, Jordan Silverstein, and David Slucksi, eds. *In the Shadow of Memory: The Holocaust and the Third Generation*. London: Vallentine Mitchell, 2016.

Josselson, Ruthellen, Amia Lieblich, and Dan McAdams, eds. *The Meaning of Others: Narrative Studies of Relationships*. Washington, DC: American Psychological Association, 2007.

JTA and TOI Staff. "Rafi Peretz Says Intermarriage among US Jews is 'Second Holocaust'." *Jerusalem Post*, July 10, 2019.

Juang, Linda, Jeffry Simpson, Richard Lee, Alexander Rothman, Peter Titzmann, Maja Schachner, Lars Korn, Dorothee Heinmeier, and Cornelia Betsch. "Using Attachment and Related Perspectives to Understand Adaptation and Resilience among Immigrant and Refugee Youth." *American Psychologist* 73, no. 6 (2018): 797–811.

Jucovy, Milton. "The Holocaust." In *The Reconstruction of Trauma: Its Significance in Clinical Work*, edited by Arnold Rothstein, 153–170. Madison, CT: International Universities Press, 1986.

Kahn, Charlotte. "Interviewing: The Crossroad between Research and Therapy." In *Children during the Nazi Reign: Psychological Perspective on the Interview Process*, edited by Judith S. Kestenberg and Eva Fogelman, 91–108. Westport, CT: Praeger, 1994.

Kangisser-Cohen, Sharon, Eva Fogelman, and Dalia Ofer, eds. *Children in the Holocaust and its Aftermath: Historical and Psychological Studies of the Kestenberg Archive*. New York, NY: Berghahn, 2017.

Kaplan, Suzanne. *Children in Genocide: Extreme Trauma and Affect Regulation*. New York, NY: Routledge, 2018.

———. "Children in Genocide: Extreme Traumatization and the 'Affect Propeller'." *International Journal of Psychoanalysis* 887 (2006): 725–746.

———, and Andreas Hamburger. "The Developmental Psychology of Social Trauma and Violence: The Case of the Rwandan Genocide." In *Psychoanalysis and Holocaust Testimony: Unwanted Memories of Social Trauma*, edited by Dori Laub and Andreas Hamburger, 104–124. New York, NY: Routledge, 2017.

Keller, Heidi. "Attachment and Culture." *Journal of Cross-Cultural Psychology* 44 (2013): 175–196.

Kellerman, Natan. "Transmitted Holocaust Trauma: Curse or Legacy? The Aggravating and Mitigating Factors of Holocaust Transmission." *Israel Journal of Psychiatry and Related Sciences* 45, no. 4 (February 2008): 263–270.

———. *Holocaust Trauma: Psychological Effects and Treatment*. Bloomington, IN: iUniverse, 2009.

———. "Transmission of Holocaust Trauma: An Integrative View." *Psychiatry* 64, no. 3 (2001): 256–267.

Kestenberg, Judith, and Charlotte Kahn, eds. *Children Surviving Persecution: An International Study of Trauma and Healing*. London: Praeger, 1998.

Kestenberg, Judith, and Eva Fogelman, eds. *Children during the Nazi Reign: Psychological Perspectives on the Interview Process*. Westport, CT: Praeger, 1994.

Kestenberg, Judith, and Ira Brenner. *The Last Witness: The Child Survivor of the Holocaust*. Washington, DC: American Psychiatric Publishing, 1996.

Kharakh, Ben, and Dan Primack. "Donald Trump's Social Media Ties to White Supremacists." *Fortune*, March 22, 2016.

Krajewski, Stanislaw. *Poland and the Jews: Reflections of a Polish Polish Jews*. Warsaw: Wydrawnictwo Austeria, 2005.

Krell, Robert. "Resilience." In *The Handbook of Psychoanalytic Holocaust Studies: International Perspectives*, edited by Ira Brenner, 41–50. New York, NY: Routledge, 2019.

———, and Marc Sherman, eds. *Medical and Psychological Effects of Concentration Camps on Holocaust Survivors*. New Brunswick, NJ: Transaction Publishers, 1997.

Krystal, Henry, ed. *Massive Psychic Trauma*. New York, NY: International Universities Press, 1968.

Kushner, Tony. "Finding Refugee Voices." *Yearbook of the Research Center for German and Austrian Exile Studies* 12 (2011): 121–139.

———. *Remembering Refugees: Then and Now*. Manchester, UK: Manchester University Press, 2006.

LaCapra, Dominick. *Representing the Holocaust*. Ithaca, NY: Cornell University Press, 1996.

———. *Writing History, Writing Trauma*. Baltimore, MD: Johns Hopkins University Press, 2000.

Landsberg, Alison. *Prosthetic Memory: The Transformation of American Remembrance in the Age of Mass Culture*. New York, NY: Columbia University Press, 2004.

Langer, Lawrence. *Holocaust Testimonies: Ruins of Memory*. New Haven, CT: Yale University Press, 1991.

———. *Using and Abusing the Holocaust*. Bloomington, IN: Indiana University Press, 2006.
Laub, Dori. "Bearing Witness, or the Vicissitudes of Listening." In *Testimony: Crises of Witnessing*, edited by Shoshana Felman and Dori Laub, 57–74. New York, NY: Routledge, 1992.
———. "An Event without a Witness: Truth, Testimony, and Survival." In *Testimony: Crises of Witnessing*, edited by Shoshana Felman and Dori Laub, 75–92. New York, NY: Routledge, 1992.
Lemberger, John, ed. *A Global Perspective on Working with Holocaust Survivors and the Second Generation*. Jerusalem: Brookdale Institute of Gerontology and Human Development and National Israeli Center for Psychosocial Support of Survivors of the Holocaust and the Second Generation, 1995.
Lehrer, Erica. *Jewish Poland Revisited: Heritage Tourism in Unquiet Places*. Bloomington, IN: Indiana University Press, 2013.
Levi, Neil, and Michael Rothberg. *The Holocaust: Theoretical Readings*. New Brunswick, NJ: Rutgers University Press, 2003.
Levine, Hillel. *In Search of Sugihara: The Elusive Japanese Diplomat Who Risked his Life to Rescue 10,000 Jews from the Holocaust*. New York, NY: Free Press, 1996.
Levy, Daniel, and Natan Sznaider. *The Holocaust and Memory in the Global Age*. Philadelphia, PA: Temple University Press, 2006.
Lindert, Jutta, and Itzhak Levav, eds. *Violence and Mental Health: Its Manifold Faces*. New York, NY: Springer, 2015.
Lizarazu, Maria Roca. "Remembering the Holocaust: Generations, Witnessing, and Place." *Holocaust Studies* 24, no. 1 (2018): 128–130.
———. "Third Generation Holocaust Narratives: Memory in Memoir and Fiction." *Holocaust Studies* 24, no. 1 (2018): 124–128.
Lothe, Jacob, Susan Rubin Suleiman, and James Phelan, eds. *After Testimony: The Ethics and Aesthetics of Holocaust Narrative for the Future*. Columbus, OH: Ohio State University Press, 2012.
Marcus, Paul, and Alan Rosenberg. *Healing their Wounds: Psychotherapy with Holocaust Survivors and their Families*. New York, NY: Praeger, 1989.
Masten, Ann. "Global Perspectives on Resilience in Children and Youth." *Child Development* 85 (2014): 6–20.
———. "Pathways to Integrated Resilience Science." *Psychological Inquiry* 26 (2015): 187–196.
———. "Resilience Theory and Research on Children and Families: Past, Present, and Promise." *Journal of Family Theory and Review* 10 (March 2018): 12–31.
———, Angela Narayan, Wendy Silverman, and Joy Osofsky. "Children in War and Disaster." In *Handbook of Child Psychology and Developmental Science*, 1–42. Hoboken, NJ: Wiley, 2015.
———, and Angela Narayan. "Child Development in the Context of Disaster, War, and Terrorism: Pathways of Risk and Resilience." *Annual Review of Psychology* 63 (2013): 227–257.

———, and Dante Cicchetti. "Resilience in Development: Progress and Transformation." In *Developmental Psychopathology*, 3rd Edition, Vol. 4, edited by Dante Cicchetti, 271–333. New York, NY: Wiley, 2016.

Matthaus, Jurgen, and Emil Kerenji. *Jewish Responses to Persecution, 1933–1946: A Source Reader*. New York, NY: Rowman & Littlefield, 2017.

McAdams, Dan, Ruthellen Josselson, and Amia Lieblich, eds. *Turns in the Road: Narrative Studies of Lives in Transition*. Washington, DC: American Psychological Association, 2001.

McGlothlin, Erin. *Second Generation Holocaust Literature: Legacies of Survival and Perpetration*. Rochester, NY: Camden House, 2006.

Mendelsohn, Daniel. *The Lost: A Search for Six in Six Million*. London: Harper Perennial, 2008.

Michaels, Walter Benn. "You Who Were Never There: Slavery and the New Historicism – Deconstruction and the Holocaust." In *The Americanization of the Holocaust*, edited by Hilene Flanzbaum, 181–197. Baltimore, MD: Johns Hopkins University Press, 1999.

Michnik, Adam. "Poles and the Jews: How Deep is the Guilt?" *New York Times*, March 17, 2001.

Miller, Kenneth, and Lisa Rasco, eds. *The Mental Health of Refugees: Ecological Approaches to Healing and Adaptation*. New York, NY: Routledge, 2004.

Mintz, Alan. *Popular Culture and the Shaping of Holocaust Memory*. Seattle, WA: University of Washington Press, 2015.

Mishra, Pankaj. *Age of Anger: A History of the Present*. New York, NY: Farrar Straus and Giroux, 2017.

Mollica, Richard. "Caring for Refugees and other Highly Traumatized Persons and Communities: The New H5 Model." In *Harvard Program in Refugee Trauma*. Boston, MA: Massachusetts General Hospital, Harvard Medical School, 2014.

———, Robert Brooks, Solvig Ekblad, and Laura McDonald. "The New H5 Model of Refugee Trauma and Recovery." In *Violence and Mental Health: Its Manifold Faces*, edited by Jutta Lindert and Itzhak Levav, 341–378. New York, NY: Springer, 2015.

Morina, Nexhmedin, and Angela Nickerson, eds. *Mental Health of Refugee and Conflict-Affected Populations: Theory, Research, and Clinical Practice*. Cham, Switzerland: Springer Nature, 2018.

Moritz-Rabson, Daniel. "Gun Rights Group Criticized for Using Holocaust Pictures to Attack Rabbi Backing Gun Control Legislation." *Newsweek*, October 30, 2018.

Moscovici, Claudia. *Holocaust Memories: A Survey of Holocaust Memoirs, History, Novels, and Films*. New York, NY: Hamilton Books, 2019.

Muller, Beate. "Trauma, Historiography, and Polyphony: Adult Voices in the CJHC's Early Postwar Child Holocaust Testimonies." *History and Memory Studies* 24, no. 2 (2012): 157–195.

Novick, Peter. *The Holocaust in American Life*. New York, NY: Mariner Books, 2000.

Nickerson, Angela. "Pathways to Recovery: Psychological Mechanisms Underlying Refugee Mental Health." In *Mental Health of Refugee and Conflict-Affected Populations: Theory, Research, and Clinical Practice*, edited by Nexhmedin Morina and Angela Nickerson, 91–109. Cham, Switzerland: Springer Nature, 2018.

Ornstein, Anna. "Childhood Losses, Adult Memories." In *The Mother and her Children: Clinical Aspects of Attachment, Separation, and Loss*, edited by Salman Akhtar, 107–120. Lanham, MD: Jason Aronson, 2012.

———. "Trauma, Memory, and Psychic Continuity." *Progress in Self Psychology* 10 (1994): 131–146.

———. "The Holocaust: Reconstruction and the Establishment of Psychic Continuity." In *The Reconstruction of Trauma: Its Significance in Clinical Work*, edited by Arnold Rothstein, 171–194. Madison, CT: International Universities Press, 1986.

———. "Survival and Recovery: Psychoanalytic Reflections." *Harvard Review of Psychiatry* 9, no. 1 (January–February 2001): 13–22.

Panter-Brick, Catherine, and James Leckman. "Editorial Commentary: Resilience in Child Development: Interconnected Pathways to Well-Being." *Journal of Child Psychology and Psychiatry* 54 (April 2013): 333–336.

Peto, Andrea, Louise Hecht, and Karolina Krasuska, eds. *Women and the Holocaust: New Perspectives and Challenges*. Warsaw: Central European University Press, 2015.

Polonsky, Antony. *The Jews in Poland and Russia: A Short History*. London: Littman Library of Jewish Civilization, 2013.

———, and Joanna Michlic, eds. *The Neighbors Respond: The Controversy over the Jedwabne Massacre in Poland*. Princeton, NJ: Princeton University Press, 2004.

Prince, Robert. *The Legacy of the Holocaust: Psychohistorical Themes in the Second Generation*. Ann Arbor, MI: University of Michigan Research Press, 1985.

Robben, Antonious, and Marcelo Suarez-Orozco, eds. *Cultures Under Siege: Collective Violence and Trauma*. Cambridge, UK: Cambridge University Press, 2000.

Rosen, Alan, ed. *Literature of the Holocaust*. Cambridge, UK: Cambridge University Press, 2013.

Rosenfeld, Alvin. *The End of the Holocaust*. Bloomington, IN: Indiana University Press, 2013.

Rosenfeld, Gavriel. *Hi Hitler: How the Nazi Past is Being Normalized in Contemporary Culture*. Cambridge, UK: Cambridge University Press, 2015.

Roskies, David, and Naomi Diamant, eds. *Holocaust Literature: A History and Guide*. Waltham, MA: Brandeis University Press, 2012.

Rothberg, Michael. *Multidirectional Memory: Remembering the Holocaust in the Age of Decolonization*. Stanford, CA: Stanford University Press, 2009.

Rustin, Margaret. "Finding Out Where and Who One Is: The Special Complexity of Migration for Adolescents." In *Enduring Migration through the Life Cycle*, edited by Arturo Varchevker and Eileen McGinley, 39–60. London: Karnac, 2013.

Rutter, Michael. "Annual Research Review: Resilience: Clinical Implications." *Journal of Child Psychiatry and Psychology* 54 (April 2013): 474–487.

———. "Protective Factors in Children's Response to Stress and Disadvantage." In *Primary Prevention of Psychopathology, Vol. 3: Social Competence in Children*, edited by Martha Whalen Kent and Jon E. Rolf, 49–74. Hanover, NH: University Press of New England, 1979.

———. "Psychosocial Resilience and Protective Mechanisms." *American Journal of Orthopsychiatry* 57 (1987): 316–331.

Ruttenberg, Danya. "Never Again' Means Nothing if Holocaust Analogies are Always Off-Limits." *Washington Post*, June 19, 2019.

Sagi-Schwartz, Abraham, Marian Bakermans-Kranenburg, Shai Linn, and Marinus Van Ijzendoorn. "Against All Odds: Genocidal Trauma is Association with Longer Life-Expectancy of the Survivor." *PLoS One* 8, no. 7 (2013): e69179.

Sandler-Saban, Gila, Mark Sossin, and Anastasia Yaski. "Age, Circumstance, and Outcome in Child Survivors of the Holocaust: Considerations of the Literature and a Report of a Student Using Narrative Content Analysis." In *Children in the Holocaust and its Aftermath: Historical and Psychological Studies of the Kestenberg Archive*, edited by Sharon Kangisser Cohen, Eva Fogelman, and Dalia Ofer, 15–42. New York, NY: Berghan, 2017.

Schafer, Roy. *Retelling a Life: Narration and Dialogue in Psychoanalysis.* New York, NY: Basic Books, 1994.

Scharf, Miri, and Ofra Mayseless. "Disorganizing Experiences in Second and Third Generation Holocaust Survivors." *Qualitative Health Research* 21 (2011): 1539–1553.

Schweitzer, Petra. *Gendered Testimonies of the Holocaust: Writing Life.* New York, NY: Lexington Books, 2016.

Shandler, Jeffrey. *While America Watches: Televising the Holocaust.* New York, NY: Oxford University Press, 1998.

Shenker, Noah. *Reframing Holocaust Testimony.* Bloomington, IN: Indiana University Press, 2015.

Shmotkin, Dov. "Vulnerability and Resilience Intertwined: A Review of Research on Holocaust Survivors." In *Between Stress and Hope: From an Disease Centered to a Health Centered Perspective*, edited by Rebecca Jacoby and Giora Kelnan, 213–234. Westport, CT: Praeger, 2003.

———, Amit Shrira, Shira Goldberg, and Yuval Palgi. "Resilience and Vulnerability among Aging Holocaust Survivors and their Families: An Intergenerational Overview." *Journal of Intergenerational Relationships* 9, no. 1 (2011): 7–21.

Silove, Derrick, Peter Bentevogel, and Susan Rees. "The Contemporary Refugee Crisis: An Overview of Mental Health Challenges." *World Psychiatry* 16 (2017): 130–139.

Simon, Bennett, and Roberta Apfel, eds. *Minefields in their Hearts: The Mental Health of Children in War and Communal Violence.* New Haven, CT: Yale University Press, 1996.

Simon, Roger. "The Paradoxical Practice of Zakhor: Memories of 'What has Never Been My Fault or Deed'." In *Between Hope and Despair: Pedagogy and the Remembrance of Historical Trauma*, edited by Sharon Rosenberg, Roger Simon, and Claudia Eppert, 9–26. Lanham, MD: Rowman & Littlefield, 2000.

———. *The Touch of the Past: Remembrance, Learning, and Ethics.* New York, NY: Palgrave Macmillan, 2005.

———, Sharon Rosenberg, and Claudia Eppert, eds. *Between Hope and Despair: Pedagogy and the Remembrance of Historical Trauma.* Lanham, MD: Rowman & Littlefield, 2000.

Sinnreich, Helene. "Anti-Vaxxers are Comparing Themselves to Holocaust Victims – Who Relied on Vaccines to Survive." *Washington Post*, April 10, 2019.

Slucki, David. *Sing This at My Funeral: A Memoir of Fathers and Sons.* Detroit, MI: Wayne State University Press, 2019.

Snyder, Timothy. *Black Earth: The Holocaust as History and Warning.* New York, NY: Tim Dugan Books, 2015.

———. "It Can Happen Here." *Slate*, July 12, 2019.

Southwick, Steven, George Bonanno, Ann Masten, Catherine Panter-Brick, and Rachel Yehuda. "Resilience Definitions, Theory and Challenges: Interdisciplinary Perspectives." *Journal of Psychotraumatology* 5 (October 2014): 1–14.

Spence, Donald. *Narrative Truth and Historic Truth: Meaning and Interpretation in Psychoanalysis.* New York, NY: W.W. Norton, 1982.

Sternberg, Robert. *Beyond IQ: A Triarchic Theory of Human Intelligence.* Cambridge, UK: Cambridge University Press, 1984.

Stier-Livny, Liat. *Remaking Holocaust Memory: Documentary Cinema by Third Generation Survivors in Israel.* Syracuse, NY: Syracuse University Press, 2019.

Stressman, Jochanan, Aaron Cohen, Robert Hammerman-Rozenberg, Michael Bursztyn, Daniel Azoulay, Yoram Maarivi, and Jeremy Jacobs. "Holocaust Survivors in Old Age: The Jerusalem Longitudinal Study." *Journal of the American Geriatrics Society* 56, no. 3 (2008): 47–477.

Stroufe, L. Alan. "The Place of Attachment in Development." In *Handbook of Attachment: Theory, Research, and Clinical Applications*, edited by Jude Cassidy and Phillip Shaver, 997–1011. New York, NY: Guilford Press, 2016.

Suleiman, Susan R. *Crises of Memory and the Second World War.* Cambridge, MA: Harvard University Press, 2012.

Sztybel, David. "Can the Treatment of Animals be Compared to the Holocaust?" *Ethics and the Environment* 11, no. 1 (2006): 97–132.

Thomas, Lawrence Mordekhai. "Suffering as a Moral Beacon: Blacks and Jews." In *The Americanization of the Holocaust*, edited by Hilene Flanzbaum, 198–210. Baltimore, MD: Johns Hopkins University Press, 1999.

Thompson, A. C., Lucas Waldron, and Christopher Mathias. "Despite Crackdown, White Supremacist and Neo Nazi Videos Take Stubborn Root on You Tube." *ProPublica*, March 15, 2019.

Thompson, Ginger. "Listen to Children Who've Just Been Separated from Their Parents at the Border." *ProPublica*, June 18, 2018.

Trezise, Thomas. *Witnessing Witnessing: On the Reception of Holocaust Survivor Testimony.* New York, NY: Fordham University Press, 2013.

Ungar, Michael. "Systemic Resilience: Principles and Processes for a Science of Change in Contexts of Adversity." *Ecology and Society* 23, no. 4 (2018): 219–235.

United Nations Children's Fund. *For Every Child, Every Right: The Convention on the Rights of the Child at a Crossroads.* New York, NY: UNICEF, 2019.
"United Nations High Commission on Refugees." *Population Statistics Database,* 2019. http://www.popstats.unhcr.org/en/overview.
United States Holocaust Memorial Museum. *Encyclopedia of Camps and Ghettos, 1933–1945.* https://www.ushmm.org/research/publications/encyclopedia-camps-ghettos.
van der Kolk, Bessel. *The Body Keeps the Score: Brain, Mind, and Body in the Healing of Trauma.* New York, NY: Penguin Books, 2014.
Varchevker, Arturo, and Eileen McGinley, eds. *Enduring Migration through the Life Cycle.* New York, NY: Routledge, 2013.
Volkan, Vamik. *Immigrants and Refugees: Trauma, Perennial Mourning, Prejudice, and Border Psychology.* London: Routledge, 2018.
———. "The Linking Objects of Pathological Mourners." *Archives of General Psychiatry* 27, no. 2 (1972): 215–221.
———. "Transgenerational Transmission and Chosen Traumas: An Aspect of Large-Group Identity." *Group Analysis* 34, no. 1 (March 2001): 79–97.
———, Gabriele Ast, and Willian F. Greer, Jr. *The Third Reich in the Unconscious.* New York, NY: Brunner-Routledge, 2002.
Wardi, Dina. *Memorial Candles: Children of the Holocaust.* New York, NY: Routledge, 1992.
Waxman, Zoe. "Unheard Testimony, Untold Stories: The Representation of Women's Holocaust Experiences." *Women's History Review* 12, no. 4 (2003): 661–677.
Weine, Stevan, Norma Ware, Leonce Hazikimana, Toni Tugenberg, Madeleine Currie, Gonwo Dahnweih, Maureen Wagner, Chloe Polutnik, and Jacqueline Wulu. "Fostering Resilience: Protective Agents, Resources, and Mechanisms for Adolescent Refugees' Psychosocial Well-Being." *Adolescent Psychiatry* 4, no. 4 (2014): 164–176.
Weissman, Gary. *Fantasies of Witnessing: Postwar Efforts to Experience the Holocaust.* Ithaca, NY: Cornell University Press, 2004.
Wiseman, Hadas, and Jacques Barber. *Echoes of Trauma: Relational Themes and Emotions in Children of Holocaust Survivors.* Cambridge, UK: Cambridge University Press, 2008.
———. "The Core Conflictual Relationship Theme Approach to Relational Narratives: Interpersonal Themes in the Context of Intergenerational Communication of Trauma." In *Healing Plots: The Narrative Basis of Psychotherapy,* edited by Amia Lieblich, Ruthellen Josselson, and Dan P. McAdams, 151–170. Washington, DC: American Psychological Association, 2004.
Wiseman, Hadas, Einat Metzl, and Jacques Barber. "Anger, Guilt, and Intergenerational Communication of Trauma in the Interpersonal Narrative of Second Generation Holocaust Survivors." *American Journal of Orthopsychiatry* 76, no. 2 (May 2006): 17–184.
Winnicott, Donald W. *Home is Where We Start From: Essays by a Psychoanalyst.* New York, NY: Norton & Co., 1990.

———. "Transitional Objects and Transitional Phenomena: A Study of the First Not-Me Possession." *The International Journal of Psychoanalysis* 34 (1953): 89–97.

Wolf, Diane. "Postmemories of Joy? Children of Holocaust Survivors and Alternative Family Memories." *Memory Studies* 12, no. 1 (February 2019): 74–87.

Yehuda, Rachel, Amy Lehrmer, and Linda Bierer. "The Public Reception of Putative Epigenetic Mechanisms in the Transgenerational Effects of Trauma." *Environmental Epigenetics* 4, no. 2 (2018): 1–7.

Young, James. *The Texture of Memory: Holocaust Memorials and Meaning.* New Haven, CT: Yale University Press.

———. *Writing and Rewriting the Holocaust: Narrative and the Consequences of Interpretation.* Bloomington, IN: Indiana University Press, 1988.

Zauzmer, Julie. "Holocaust Study: Two Thirds of Millennials Don't Know What Auschwitz Is." *Washington Post*, April 12, 2018.

Zembylas, Michalinos. *Emotion and Traumatic Conflict: Reclaiming Healing in Education.* Oxford, UK: Oxford University Press, 2015.

———. *The Politics of Trauma in Education.* London: Palgrave Macmillan, 2008.

Index

accumulation of risk, theory of, 13
adolescents: moralism in, 144; unique vulnerability of refugee, 43
agency, active sense of in children, 6, 44, 128, 146
Akhtar, Salman, 12, 42, 110, 143
Alexander, Jeffrey, 165
Altalena, 156
Americanization of the holocaust, 164
American Jewish Joint Distribution Committee, 155
anti-Semitism, 4, 159, 163–64; Peronist, 155
apartheid, South African, 157
Apfel, Roberta, ix, 6, 59
attachment, 13, 45, 79, 149; non-monotropic forms of, 45
awareness control. *See* dissociation, as response to trauma

Barber, Jacques, 14, 150
Bar-On, Dan, 152
Bekerman, Zvi, 165
belonging, sense of, 89, 168, 169
Bernard-Donals, Michael, 165
body, challenges to integrity of, 88, 128
British resettlement program in Africa, 73
Bronfenbrenner, Urie, 12

cemetery. *See* Okopowa Street Cemetery
"chosen trauma," 165
Ciano, Count, 53
cognitive intactness, factors sustaining, 141, 169–70
compartmentalization, as coping strategy, 79, 145
containment, seeking feeling of, 143
convent. *See* nuns, Catholic

Davidson, Shamai, 45, 140
Dean, Carolyn, 166
defiance, as self-affirmation and hope, 88, 128, 136, 141, 144–45
Delbo, Charlotte, 10
development: alternative avenues for, 137–38; theorized stages in, 13
"difficult knowledge," 167
displaced persons, 154. *See also* refugees
Displaced Persons Act, 157
dissociation, as response to trauma, 45, 140
diversity, of war experiences, 138, 145–46, 168

early adulthood, paradoxes of, 78
Epstein, Helen, 159

Erikson, Erik, 13, 59, 140, 144

family: formation of alternative forms, among refugees, 156; role in child development, 8–9; support for intactness of, 139
"fantasies of witnessing," 165
Final Solution, 109–11, 123–24
Fogelman, Eva, ix, 12
Freud, Anna, studies of Terezin children, 137

Garbarino, James, 13, 22
Gatrell, Peter, 5
gender: role in holocaust experiences, 110, 122, 134, 146, 158; in strategic deployment of cultural tropes, 129
genocide: contemporary, 109, 163; potential for trivialization of, 14, 165
geography, as psychic landscape, 110
gossip, as strategy, 109, 142
grief, 143, 159
guilt. *See* survivor guilt

Hirsch, Marianne, 11
Hobfoll, Stevan, 13, 43
Hoffman, Eva, 159
holocaust: representations of, in popular culture, 79, 164–65; survivors of, living in poverty, 164. *See also* Americanization of the holocaust
home: non-place-based configuration of, 138–39; rituals as attempt to recreate sense of, 78; theories of role in child development of, 42–43
hope, 129, 143–45, 170
Hou, Wai Kai, 13, 43

identity: politics of, 165–66; refugee, 79; theories of, 3. *See also* nationalism, nationalist movements
identity development: interplay of internal and external factors in, 9; socio-ecological models of, 12–13; stages in, 13
imaginative capacity, as resource, 59, 142
immigrants/immigration: displaced persons and, 5; detention of Central Americans and, 3, 164; separation of refugee families in, 4–5
intellectual curiosity, as strategy, 140
internalized images of lost family members, role of, 141

Jansen, Jonathan, 171
Japan, 66–68, 123–24, 134
Japanese consul, 50, 55, 58, 65, 66, 68. *See also* Sugihara, Chiune

Kangisser-Cohen, Sharon, 12
Kaplan, Suzanne, 109
Kaunas, 52, 55, 57, 65, 138
Kestenberg, Judith, 12
Kostelny, Kathleen, 22
Krakow, 36, 49, 58, 65

LaCapra, Dominick, 165
Langer, Lawrence, 9
Laub, Dori, 10–11
Lehrer, Erica, 79
Licee Francais de Varsovie, 25
"linking objects," 46

Mauthausen, 8, 131–32, 136, 155; liberation of, 136
memoir, use as evidence, 9–10. *See also* testimony, literary and psychological theories of
memory: crisis of, 164; displacement of, 165; politics of remembrance and, 4–5, 14, 163; post-, 160; prosthetic, 164; surfeit of, accusations regarding, 166; traumatic, as ritual object, 165–66
mourning, 11, 46, 152, 153

narrative: methods, use in studies of the holocaust, 12; polyphony in,

10; presentation of self in, 10–11; "tombstones," 11
nationalism, nationalist movements, 4; collective trauma as weaponized element in, 165–66; global resurgence of, 164–66; in Israeli holocaust narratives, 164–65
Northern Rhodesia, 7, 75–77
nuns, Catholic, 67, 122, 129, 157–58

Ofer, Dalia, 12
Okopowa Street Cemetery, 21, 135, 159
Ornstein, Anna, ix, 6, 138

Palestine, 50, 54, 60, 72–73; land ownership and visa applications, 60
parenting, effects on children in crisis, 138–39
Pawiak Prison, 8, 118–19; underground activities in, 118
Pearl Harbor, 68, 77
peer group, children's access to, 139
Plaszow, 81, 87, 113–14, 127, 131, 156
Poland: complexity of Jewish-Polish interactions in, 58, 158–60; Jewish images of, 158; Jewish population and culture in, 137, 153–54; Jewish property repatriation claims in, 159; re-opening following collapse of Soviet Union, 158
Polish Government in Exile, 73
Polish resistance movement, 8, 78, 82–83, 116–17, 144; activities inside prison, 20; activities involving Jews as members or recipients of aid, 83, 107, 116, 126; attitudes towards Jews in, 64, 144; Home Army, 64

racism, 4
realism, in children's awareness of risk and opportunity, 43, 129, 144, 146, 169
reciprocity, expressions of, 138, 143, 169

reconstitution, refugee strategies in, 42–45, 59, 87, 170
refugees: family separation of, 22; generalization about, 4–6, 169–70; growth in numbers of, 63; identity of, as context-bound, 79; policy related to, 170; role of family and peer group in outcomes for, 139; theories of child development in research on, 11. *See also* displaced persons
rejection, experience of, 59, 78, 138, 140, 169
remembrance. *See* memory
resilience: as emergent property, 138, 146, 168; in research on refugee and migrant children, 2, 13
resource: caravans, 59; conservation of, 13; reservoirs, 43
rituals, family, 143
"rooted cosmopolitanism," 167
Rothberg, Michael, 14, 165–66
Rwanda, 109, 163

sabotage. *See* defiance, as self-affirmation and hope
sarcasm, 44, 59, 145, 170
Schafer, Roy, 10
selection, for death, 105–6, 123, 131–32
self-care, as defiance, 88
Shanghai, Jewish community in, 133
Shoah Foundation. *See* USC Shoah Foundation
Simon, Bennett, ix, 6, 59
Simon, Roger, 163
slave labor, 8, 65, 78–79, 110, 113–16, 141
social maps, as children's representations of the world, 22–23
Soviet Union: betrayal of Polish resistance movement, 158; collapse of, 158; propaganda narrative about the war, 159; suspicion of Jewish collaboration with, 64

"space-creating" processes, 109, 128, 143
Spence, Donald, 79
Stalingrad, 83, 116, 128, 132
Sugihara, Chiune, ix, 65–66, 78, 138, 157
Suleiman, Susan, 4, 164
survivor guilt, 129, 152, 169
symbolism, as language, 141–42

tattoo, 115, 128, 142
teachers, role in supporting children, 109, 138, 143
testimony, literary and psychological theories of, 9–11
transformation of passive into active, 88
transitional phenomena, 88
Trans-Siberian Railway, 66
trauma: clinical research about, 149–50; experience of psychic fragmentation in, 109; generalizations about, 2–3, 5–6, 146; grandchildren role in healing from, 152; intergenerational transmission, models of, 14, 150; politics of, 165–67; psychopathology resulting from, 150; somatic experience in, 127–28
Trezise, Thomas, 10, 166–67

United Nations Convention of Rights of the Child, 5

United States, attempt to enter, 57, 59, 67, 157
United States Holocaust Memorial Museum, 163
USC Shoah Foundation, ix

Volkan, Vamik, 46, 110, 165

Warsaw: Chamber of Commerce, 21, 25; construction of ghetto in, 35; Jews in pre-war, 21; uprising in, 133, 158
Warsaw ghetto, 91–111; education in, 93–110, 142–43; Jewish resistance in, 119, 123
Weigl Method, 83–84
Weissman, Gary, 165
Wieliczka, 36–37, 49–50, 58
Wilno, 40, 54–57, 65–68, 138
Winnicott, Donald, 42, 88
Wiseman, Hadas, 14, 150

Yad Vashem, ix
YIVO Institute: archive of, 153; Wilno school, 41–42, 53, 151
Young, James, 11

Zambia. *See* Northern Rhodesia
Zembylas, Michalinos, 165

About the Author

Shira Birnbaum is a medical writer at Children's Hospital of Philadelphia and an educator specializing in learning theory and research ethics. She is also a registered psychiatric nurse and the author of several previous books about education, child development, and mental health. This book was written in connection with membership in the Affiliate Scholar program of the Boston Psychoanalytic Society and Institute.

www.ingramcontent.com/pod-product-compliance
Lightning Source LLC
Chambersburg PA
CBHW050906300426
44111CB00010B/1402